Acclaim for Madhur

CLIMBING THE

"A lyrical writer."   *ie Boston Globe*

"A superb example of the happy ne_____ of food memoirs."
—*Newsweek*

"There is some rough history here . . . but also secret ancestral recipes and luscious tales of picnics in the Himalayas. . . . With such earthly pleasures, heaven can wait."
— *O, The Oprah Magazine*

"Her memoirs are an honest and clear account of a significant time in Indian history, seen though the eyes of a normal—and hungry—Indian teenager."   —*The New York Sun*

"A vivid and compelling look at [Jaffrey's] childhood in 1930s and 1940s India."   —*Concord Monitor* (New Hampshire)

Madhur Jaffrey

Climbing the Mango Trees

Madhur Jaffrey is the author of many previous cookbooks, including the classic *An Invitation to Indian Cooking* and *Madhur Jaffrey's Taste of the Far East*, which was voted Best International Cookbook and Book of the Year for 1993 by the James Beard Foundation. She is also an award-winning actress with numerous major motion pictures to her credit. She lives in New York City.

Climbing the Mango Trees

CLIMBING
THE
MANGO TREES

*A Memoir of a
Childhood in India*

Madhur Jaffrey

Vintage Books
A Division of Random House, Inc.
New York

FIRST VINTAGE BOOKS EDITION, OCTOBER 2007

The Library of Congress has cataloged the Knopf edition as follows:
Jaffrey, Madhur.
Climbing the mango trees : a memoir of a childhood in India / by Madhur Jaffrey.
—1st American ed.
p. cm.
1. Jaffrey, Madhur—Childhood and youth. 2. Cooks—India—Biography.
3. Cooks—United States—Biography. 4. Women cooks—India—Biography.
5. Cookery, Indic. 6. India—History—British occupation, 1765–1947. I. Title.
TX649.J34.A3 2006
641.5092—dc22
[B]   2006045255

Vintage ISBN: 978-1-4000-7820-2

Book design by Anthea Lingeman

www.vintagebooks.com

Printed in the United States of America
10 9 8 7 6 5 4 3 2 1

This book is dedicated to
Bari Bauwa and Babaji,
my grandparents,
for
helping make their grandchildren who we all are,
and
to my daughters,
Zia, Meera, and Sakina,
and their cousins,
as well as
to my grandchildren,
Robi, Cassius, and Jamila,
for
carrying on the line of the inkpot-and-quill set
so bravely
and innocently

Contents

Contents

Contents

Contents

My Family Tree

✳

Raja Raghunath Bahadur,
Finance Minister to Emperor Aurangzeb (1590–1665)

Munshi Girdhari Lal

Rai Jeewan Lal Bahadur (aka Rai Bahadur Jeewan Lal),
my grandfather's grandfather (1806–84)

Raj Narain (Babaji), my grandfather (1864–1950)
m. Bari Bauwa

1 Chand Narain (Taoji)	2 Bhuaji	3 Shibbudada	4 Shammo Bhua	5 Prem Bhua	6 Dadaji (my father)	7 Saran Bhua	8 Kiran Bhua
m. Bari Taiji	*m.* Phupaji	*m.* Taiji	*widowed*	*m.* Wazir	*m.* Kashmiran Rani	*m.* Prakash	*m.* Jeesh Phupaji
				Chand Phupaji	(Bauwa)	Narain Phupaji	
Prakashdada	Anup Jija	Raghudada *m.* Thelma					
Kailashdada	Kripaldada	Sheila		Harish Bhaisa'ab	Brijdada	Ravi (Lovy)	Mahesh
Jagdishdada	Prema	Rajesh		Toshijiji	Bhaiyyadada	Shashi	Brijesh
Kanti	Krishna			Suresh	Lalit	Vijay	Yogesh
					Kamal		Naresh
					Madhur		
					Veena		

Climbing the Mango Trees

PROLOGUE

I was born in my grandparents' sprawling house by the Yamuna River in Delhi. Grandmother welcomed me into this world by writing *Om*, which means "I am" in Sanskrit, on my tongue with a little finger dipped in honey.

Perhaps that moment was reinforced in my tiny head a month or so later, when the family priest came to draw up my horoscope. He scribbled astrological symbols on a long scroll, and declared that my name should be "Indrani," or "Goddess of the Heavens." My father, who never paid religious functionaries the slightest bit of attention, firmly named me "Madhur," which means "Sweet as Honey," an adjective from the Sanskrit noun *madhu*, or "honey." My grandfather, apparently, teased my father, saying that he should have named me "Manbhari," or "I am sated," instead, as I was already the fifth child. But my father continued to procreate, and I was left with honey on my palate and in my deepest soul.

My sweet tooth remained firmly in control until the age of four, when, emulating the passions of grown-ups, I began to explore the hot and the sour. My grandfather had built his house in what was once a thriving orchard of jujubes, mulberries, tamarinds, and mangoes. His numerous grandchildren, like hungry flocks of birds, attacked the mangoes while they were still green and sour. As grown-ups snored through the hot afternoons in rooms cooled with wetted, sweet-smelling vetiver curtains, the unsupervised children were on every branch of every mango tree, armed with a ground mixture of salt, pepper, red chilies, and roasted cumin. The older children, on the higher branches, peeled and sliced the mangoes with penknives and passed the slices down to the smaller fry on the lower branches. We would dip the slices into our spice mixture and eat, our tingling mouths telling us that we had ceased to be babies.

Winters were another matter. That was when the vegetable garden came into its own. Around eleven each morning, between breakfast and lunch, we would be served fresh tomato juice made from our own tomatoes. At about the same time, the gardener would offer the ladies sunning themselves on the veranda a basket full of fresh peas, small kohlrabies, white radishes, and feathery chickpea shoots. Some of these we ate raw, and the rest were sent off to the kitchen after a studied appraisal ("Radishes sweeter than last year, no?"). As this was also the season when the men went hunting, the kitchen was deluged with mallards, geese, quail, partridge, and venison as well.

Dinners were fairly generous affairs, with about forty or more members of the extended family sitting down to venison kebabs laden with cardamom, tiny quail with hints of cinnamon, chickpea shoots stir-fried with green chilies and ginger, and tiny new potatoes browned with flecks of cumin and mango powder.

Winter was also the season of weddings. My father was always in charge of the caterers, and I was his permanent sidekick. In those days caterers had to cook at their clients' homes, and, certainly in our home, they had to cook under family supervision. So a gang of about a dozen caterers would arrive a few days before the actual wedding and set up their tent under the tamarind tree.

First my father would examine all the raw ingredients. Were the spices "wormy"? Were there broken grains in the Basmati rice? Were the cauliflower heads taut and young?

The outward suspicion from one side and obsequious reassurances from the other were a game that each side dutifully played. In reality, we loved these caterers, who were known for the magic in their hands. They could conjure up the lamb meatballs of our erstwhile Moghul emperors and the tamarind chutneys of the street with equal ease. One of the few dishes that they alone cooked was cauliflower stems. For one meal they would cook the cauliflower heads. Then they were left with hundreds of coarse central stems. They cleverly slit the stems into quarters and stir-fried them in giant woklike *karhai*s with sprinklings of cumin, coriander, chilies, ginger, and lots of sour mango powder. All I had to do was place a stem in my mouth, clamp down with my teeth, and pull. Just as with artichoke leaves, all the spicy flesh would remain on my tongue as the coarse skin was drawn away and discarded.

Decades later, in New York City, when the culinary guru and my friend and neighbor, James Beard, was very ill, I helped him teach some of his last classes. One of them was on taste. The students were made to taste nine different types of caviar and a variety of olive oils, and do a blind identification of meats with all their fat removed. Somewhere towards the end of the class, the big, frail man, confined to a high director's chair, asked, "Do you think there is such a thing as taste memory?"

This set me thinking. Once, several of us who had known each other for decades were sitting by a fireplace in France, talking and reading. My American husband, a violinist, was studying the score of Bach's chaconne. "Can you hear the music as you read it?" a friend asked.

It was the same question in another form. When I left India to study in England, I could not cook at all, but my palate had already recorded millions of flavors. From cumin to ginger, they were all in my head, waiting to be called into service. Rather like my husband, I could even hear the honey on my tongue.

ONE

The orchard site had housed our family homestead only since the early decades of the twentieth century. My family actually came from the walled city, often called Old Delhi, just to the south, built by the Moghul emperor Shah Jahan in the seventeenth century. My family referred to it simply as Shahar, or the City.

There are many Delhis, as we were to study in school, all built either alongside each other or wholly or partly on top of each other, often reusing building materials knocked down in bloody efforts at domination. Our own original family home was in Chailpuri, in the narrow lanes of the Old City. It had as its carefully chosen foundation sturdy stones "borrowed" from the walls of Ferozshah Kotla, the fourteenth-century fortress and palace of a fourteenth-century emperor in a fourteenth-century Delhi.

Starting with the ancient Vedic city of Indraprastha, which flourished in the fifteenth century B.C., a succession of Delhis was built, first by generations of Hindu rajas, only to be followed in A.D. 1193 by a roll call of Muslim dynasties: Ghori, Ghaznavi,

Qutubshahi, Khilji, Tughlak, Lodhi, and Moghul. They seemed to trust the dubious comfort of walled cities, and their leaders chose to name Delhi, again and again, after themselves. This ended, at least from the point of view of my childhood, with the British version, sans walls, New Delhi, designed by Sir Edwin Lutyens and built in the ruin-filled wilderness south of the Old City walls.

The Moghul capital, Shahjahanabad, or the Old City or the City, or Shahar, was where the written history of my family began. We were only blessed with our paternal side of it. My mother's side either kept few records or humbly kept its accomplishments under wraps. This written history, bound in red, was kept in my grandfather's home office.

When my grandfather—Babaji, as we called him—decided to move out of the City to the orchard estate, he was already a very successful barrister. His new house, the one in which I was born, was a brick-and-plaster version of a multi-roomed, high-ceilinged Moghul tent with bits of British fortress and Greco-Roman classicism thrown in to hint vaguely at grandeur. The road it was built on was named after my grandfather, Raj Narain Road (with the patriotic Hindification of names that followed Independence, it is now Raj Narain Marg), and had the number 7 on its front gate. From the time I can remember, we always referred to that house as Number 7, as in "I'm going to Number 7," or "You know that big tamarind tree in Number 7. . . ."

Not wishing to waste money, and full of the brio of someone recently "England-returned" (he had been studying law in London), he designed it all himself. As the family story goes, it was at this time that the British had decided to move their capital from Calcutta to Delhi, and Lutyens was in the process of building the new capital, to be named New Delhi. Lutyens asked my grandfather to pick any piece of land in New Delhi and build on it—Lutyens might have designed the house himself had my grandfather asked—but my grandfather dismissed the whole idea, saying, "Who wants to live in that jungle?" Properties in "that jungle" are now worth as much as those in central London and midtown Manhattan.

Years later, having proceeded beyond my three score and ten years, I was awarded an honorary CBE (Commander of the British Empire) by Queen Elizabeth II in Washington, D.C., a city very similar in design to Lutyens's New Delhi, in a house designed by Lutyens himself, the British ambassador's residence. As I stared at my reflection there in a pair of dark Lutyens mirrors, dotted with glass rosettes, I couldn't help thinking that my life might have come full circle. I could have been born in a Lutyens house and received a grand recognition of my life in a Lutyens house. But I was not destined for such easy symmetry, for easy anything.

Babaji's whitewashed house consisted of a central "gallery"—a hall, really—leading to five very large rooms with fireplaces. One of these was the drawing room, and the others served as bedrooms, one to a family. Running along the front and back of the house were two long verandas lined with semi-classical, semi–Greco-Roman pillars. The back, east-facing veranda looked out on the Yamuna River, or, as we called it with great familiarity, the Jumna River. It was here that so many of us, as infants, were rubbed with oil and left to absorb the morning sun. Because the land must have sloped down to the water, this veranda was one floor up, built over a very large, partially underground, damp, always cool cellar, or *taikhana*. My grandfather used to make wine here from grapes he imported from Afghanistan, but that must have been before I was born.

Number 7, Delhi, so nearly designed by Lutyens. In front of the house stands our beri *(jujube) tree, in which we loved to sit as children. All the young of my generation had our favorite reserved spots among the branches.*

The front, west veranda faced the gardens, which had incorporated the remnants of the old orchard and now included a winding drive to the front gate. The front and back verandas ended in rooms at each corner of the house, the front ones being shaped somewhat like turrets. The functions of these corner rooms changed over the years, but one of them at the back, facing east and south, always remained my grandmother's—and the family's—chapel-like Pooja ka Kamra, or Prayer Room. On top of the house were two levels of flat roofs, the one in the center being higher, and both edged with a battlement-like balustrade.

But the main house was not large enough to fit the only army Babaji was to see, a growing army of spirited grandchildren produced by his eight children. Some of these progeny lived at Number 7 all the time, and some came and went. Babaji firmly believed in the joint-family system, with himself presiding as the head of his brood, a system that had been followed by his father and grandfather and, indeed, by all his ancestors.

So, in addition to the main house and gardens, across two vast brick courtyards to the north and south of the main house were two long, trainlike, one-room-wide annexes. Made of unpainted brick, they had a more casual, country feel. The one to the north started at the river end with the dining room and then went on to pantries, storage rooms, and the kitchen. Beyond it, across another bit of courtyard on the same north side, was the Boiler, industrial in size and used for making extra hot water for our winter baths, and an annex of bathrooms. The annex to the south, known simply as the Rooms (Kamras), also started at the river end. It contained my middle uncle's bedroom and offices, then my grandfather's offices, and then extra rooms for guests. Besides all this there was a shed for cows and horses, a servants' annex, and two sets of large garages.

It was in my grandfather's southern-annex office that I one day discovered, by complete chance, a book bound in red that was the family's history. (I must have been thirteen at the time.)

There were actually two types of family history. There was the documented version that sat properly in my grandfather's office. But there was also the undocumented version, consisting of fables, family customs, and hearsay passed along by my grandmother Bari Bauwa and the other women of the house. This version had begun seeping into us since birth, very subtly, with the honey on our tongues. And, to start with, it was the only one I knew.

Every autumn, at the religious festival of Dussehra, Bari Bauwa would demand that we bring all our writing implements to the Prayer Room. The men would be asked to bring their guns as well.

She would arrange these in the altarlike temple she had set up—Parker pens, bottles of blue-black Quink, pencils, hunting rifles—all mixed in with gods, sacred threads, and marigolds. The women and children would gather inside the Prayer Room, with the men always hovering, unconvinced, by the doors. We would begin praying and sprinkling these rather ordinary implements with yellow turmeric powder, red *roli* powder, grains of rice, holy water, and flower petals. I thought then that all of India was doing what we were doing: asking blessings for pens and pencils and guns.

What I did not realize was that on that day most Hindus were asking God to bless the implements they worked with: farmers wanted blessings for their bulls and plows, and traders for their weights, measures, and coins.

But who were we, and why was my bottle of Quink in the Prayer Room? According to the women's oral history—and this was never taught to us, just deduced slowly over time—we were a subcaste of Hindus known as Kayasthas: Mathur Kayasthas, to get the sub-subcaste right. Even as a child, I saw it so clearly in my imagination. . . . Roll the film: Ancient India. Day. A vast meeting of notables is being held on a mountainside to finalize the caste system. At the top of the heap, it is announced, are to be the self-satisfied priests, the Brahmins, who will be the only ones allowed the privilege of reading, writing, and making laws. There is much cheering from their quarter. Below them are to be the warriors, Kshatriyas, who will fight and rule kingdoms. This lot seems overjoyed, too. Lower on the totem pole will be the traders and farmers, Vaishyas, whose eyes glint at the thought of making money, and even further down, the menial workers or Shudras, who stand glum and silent.

The camera shifts. Next day. Night. A small hall lit with oil lamps. A smaller meeting of agitated intellectuals. They are overwrought because they are viscerally against all these categories. In any case, they do not fit neatly into any of them. Reading, writing, and making laws is what gives them the most satisfaction, but religious orthodoxy scares them, and they want none of it. They have no fear at all of ruling any part of the world, but they will not give up their precious books. They lack both the sort of entrepreneurial spirit that makes successful traders (in fact, hush, they look down on traders), and the physical strength and desperation that sustain farmers. So they vote rather boldly to form a union of their own, a separate subcaste of freethinking writer-warriors to be known as Kayasthas. The End.

That is my version of events. There is actually a real legend, if legends can be real, that goes something like this: Just after Brahma, the God of the Universe, had created the caste system with, in descending order, the Brahmins, Kshatriyas, Vaishyas, and Shudras, a worried Yama, God and Chief Justice of the Underworld, approached him, saying, "I need an assistant who has the ability to record the deeds of man, both good and evil, and to administer justice." Brahma went into a trance. When he opened his eyes, he saw before him a glorious figure of a man holding a pen in one hand, an inkpot in the other, and with a sword tied around his waist. Brahma spoke: "Thou hast been created from my body [*kaya*], therefore thy progeny shall be known as Kayasthas. Thy work will be to dispense justice and punish those that violate Divine laws." Brahma gave him the special caste of Dwij-Kshatriya, twice-born warrior.

Another such "history" lesson came directly from my grandmother. I will never forget the day.

It was one of those sunny but crisp, cold winter Sundays that Delhi loves. Winter lasted only two months a year, and our family turned quite British for this season. At least in our clothing. All the tweed coats and jackets (British fabrics, Indian tailors) and cardigans (British wool and patterns, family-women knitters) came out of mothballed trunks. They were spread out on the lawn and sunned repeatedly for days, in a desperate effort to rid them of their naphthalene odor, after which they were hung or folded up and put into cupboards. The women wore hand-knitted cardigans on top of their sarees and then bundled themselves further in Kashmiri shawls.

I was ten and looking smart as smart can be in my pale blue herringbone-patterned woolen overcoat, made to measure at Lokenath's in Connaught Place, New Delhi. (My two older sisters had exactly the same coats.) It was January, and so cold that we had to wear overcoats both inside and outside the house. I smelled of mothballs.

About twenty of us had barely collected in the dining-room annex for breakfast when the Lady in White arrived. Of the same age as my grandmother, she was habitually enshrouded in a long white skirt or *lahanga*, a white bodice, and a white covering over her head. Her skin color matched her clothing. I used to think that my mother was the whitest Indian I knew until I met the Lady in White. My mother was the color of cream. The Lady in White was the color of milk. What mattered most to us, though, was not her milky color but the milky ambrosia that she carried on her head.

Yes, balanced there, on a round brass tray, were dozens of *mutkaina*s, terra-cotta cups, filled with *daulat ki chaat*, which could be translated as "a snack of wealth." Some cynic who assumed that all wealth was ephemeral must have named it. It was, indeed, the most ephemeral of fairy dishes, a frothy evanescence that disappeared as soon it touched the tongue, a winter specialty requiring dew as an ingredient. Whenever I asked the Lady in White how it was made, she would sigh a mysterious sigh and say, "Oh, child, I am one of the few women left in the whole city of Delhi who can make this. I am so old, and it is such hard work. What shall I tell you? I only go to all this trouble because I have served your grandmother from the time she lived in the Old City. First I take rich milk and add dried seafoam to it. Then I pour the mixture into nicely washed terra-cotta cups that I get directly from the potter. I have to climb up the stairs to the roof and leave the cups in the chill night air. Now, the most important element is the dew. If there is no dew, the froth will not form. If there is too much dew, that is also bad. The dew you have to leave to the gods. In the early morning, if the froth is good, I sprinkle the cups with a little sugar, a little *khurchan* [milk boiled down into thin, sweet, flaky sheets], and fine shavings of pistachios. That, I suppose, is it."

Those cups were the first things placed before us at breakfast that day. Our spoons, provided by the Lady in White, were the traditional flat pieces of bamboo. Heavenly froth, tasting a bit of the bamboo, a bit of the terra-cotta, a bit sweet and a bit nutty—surely this was the food of angels.

But it was finished too fast. After every bit had been licked up, we were still hungry. So orders went out to the kitchen: "*karara* [crisp on the edges] fried eggs," "rumble-tumble [scrambled] eggs with tomato, onions, and green chili," "rumble-tumble with tomato, no onion, green chili, and cilantro," "*masala* [spiced] omelette with bacon."

All the eggs were served with toast. That day, my cousin Rajesh, the youngest son of my middle uncle, downed his breakfast at breakneck speed and dashed outside. I, his devoted follower, still had most of my toast left to finish; I just grabbed it in one hand and ran after him.

We were both racing through the northern brick courtyard, headed towards the gardens. Just above the northwestern turret room was a tall electric pole where a kite had made its perch. That moment, the kite saw fit to swoop down and take my toast away from me, leaving, thank God, my eye whole, but a deep, bleeding gash just under it. Then it swooped back up to its perch. I screamed, and my cousin, startled out of his wits and feeling deeply responsible, rushed inside for his .22 Daisy air rifle, which he aimed and fired. His pellets missed. But the noise and commotion brought the whole family out into the courtyard. He was lectured by his mother, I by my mother, and both of us by our grandmother. What my grandmother Bari Bauwa had to say was much more than a simple admonition. My cousin, she said, had almost killed the savior and patron of our *kul*, our clan.

Then she told us this story: In ancient times, when much of North India was divided into small principalities, our ancestors were the rulers of a kingdom called Kukraj, somewhere near Jaipur, in Rajasthan. There was a devastating war with a neighboring raja, and our entire clan was massacred, all save an infant boy whose mother had fled with him to a nearby town called Narnaul. The only reason he lived was that a big kite flew down, landed on the ground, and spread her wings over him, shielding him from view—and harm. The family priests immediately decided that if the boy lived they would declare the kite *kuldevata*, tutelary goddess of his family. The boy did survive, and his descendants took to treating all kites with the deepest reverence.

It was in the early summer three years later that I discovered the red leather-bound book, the real history of our family, in my grandfather's office.

TWO

Summer Lunch • *The Red Book* •
The Story of My Ancestors • *Muslim Influence*

W e were still in Delhi and had not yet left for our annual
holidays in the hills. My grandfather's short, gnarled
manservant, Ishri, always in his old-fashioned dhoti and with
most of his teeth missing, had announced lunch. The family had,
as usual, crossed the northern courtyard in small groups, and
trooped into the dining-room annex. This day we lunched on
fresh *phulka*s (fluffed whole-wheat flatbreads), *alan ka saag* (a
kind of *dal* made with chickpea flour, *moong dal*, and spinach)
eaten with fresh squeezes of lime juice, small bitter gourds stuffed
with fennel and browned onions, homemade yogurt, and pencil-
thin, long, curling-at-the-end summer cucumbers, *kakri*s, eaten
raw with their delicate pale green skins still on them. These were
hawked in the streets of Delhi with this enticement, "*Laila ki
unglian hain, Majnu ki pasliyan*" ("These are the fingers of Juliet,
the ribs of Romeo"). We had ended the summer meal with
bunches of fresh litchees from Dehradun, and tiny, sweet-sweet
melons that my father's younger sister, Saran Bhua, had parceled
to us from Lucknow. We were all so full. The elders had ambled

17

off to their bedrooms, their heads already leaning towards their pillows.

Most afternoons in the summer, the children were free of all adult supervision. This day, even my cousins must have fallen prey to lethargy, as I distinctly remember being alone.

As a child, I was very happy being alone. We were so surrounded by love, concern, family tensions, cousinly competition, and the general goings-on of a large joint family, that it was almost a relief to paint all that out. I would instinctively shift gears and, within seconds, reach a zone I kept for myself where I was welcomed by a silent and blank canvas. I was free to fill this with new, shifting dreams.

It was in such a state of half-wakefulness that I had walked across the front of the house, unlatched the door to my grandfather's office, and entered.

I often went there when I was alone. Babaji himself hardly ever used the place anymore. Ishri, his manservant, had given up his regular dustings, so a thin layer of sand from the Rajasthani desert had crept under the door and spread its gritty self on the big desk in the room's center, the brass duplicating-machine on top of the desk, and all the bookshelves that lined it.

The dust did not bother me. I made the duplicating machine go up and down a few times, I opened and shut the desk drawers, and I rummaged through my grandfather's papers. Then I went to my accustomed spot near the farthest bookshelf and sat down on the floor.

Most of the cases held legal tomes. But in one of the lower shelves, filling its entire length, was a series of large books called *The Books of Knowledge*. I had already read them all from cover to cover many times over. I had read about Marconi and Madame

Curie, about Laplanders and pharaohs and every Greek myth the books could supply. I was planning on reading about Adonis again when my eye fell on a red cover nearby. I reached over and pulled out that book.

I loved history in school. India was still a colony, so we were taught British history, of course, but Indian history as well. What I was holding in my hand was a history all my own, with familiar family names, a book in which the two histories I was studying in school seemed to merge.

The cover indicated that the book was a *Short Account of the Life and Works of Rai Jeevan Lal Bahadur, Late Honorary Magistrate, Delhi, with Extracts from His Diary Relating to the Time of Mutiny, 1857.*

Rai Jeewan Lal Bahadur, also known as Rai Bahadur Jeewan Lal, was my grandfather's grandfather, born on April 2, 1806. Luckily for us, the book contained relevant details of recorded family history that preceded Jeewan Lal at one end, and at the other went beyond the death of Jeewan Lal to the time when my own grandfather, his grandson, turned twenty-one. It covered almost a century.

I read it over several afternoons, returning it to its place each time. After my grandfather's death in 1950, an aunt sold off the entire contents of the office to the *kabaaria*, or rubbish man. Books by the yard. Pages from our history were probably used as plates to sell snacks in the City. Spicy potato- and pea-filled samosas oozing their grease on ". . . By command of his Excellency the Viceroy and Governor-general, this certificate is presented in the name of her Most Gracious Majesty Victoria, Empress of India, To Rai Jeewan Lal. . . ." Or perhaps some family member had quietly walked off with it before it could suffer such an ignominious fate. At any rate, it disappeared from my life. Another fifty years would elapse before I would see it again. Not the original, but a reprint.

The book—clear, precise, and filled with copies of letters and documents to substantiate all claims—was put together by one of Jeewan Lal's sons. It began, strangely enough, in mythology, retelling my grandmother's story about the kingdom of Kukraj, the infant boy, and the kite in a slightly different version. But then it tried to imbue the myth with a modicum of weight by adding that in Jeewan Lal's time an ancient piece of wood, tied with an equally ancient piece of thread, known always as the throne (Kukraj ki Patri) as well as the family protectress, the kite, was included in all domestic prayers.

Whatever the truth of these old beliefs, the family's real story began in the seventeenth century, when our ancestor Raja Raghunath Bahadur left his hometown, Narnaul, north of Jaipur, and came to the glittering Delhi court of the Moghul emperor of India, Shah Jahan. The city—Shahjahanabad then—was completely walled. The emperor, a direct descendant of Genghis Khan and Tamerlane (tenth in descent from Tamerlane), lived and worked in the Red Fort, behind another sometimes double, sometimes triple set of walls, and ruled from his famed peacock throne, which boasted six solid gold feet and encrustations of rubies, emeralds, and diamonds, including the Kohinoor diamond, now broken up and in Queen Elizabeth II's crown.

Raghunath Bahadur would not have been allowed just to walk into the court of the "Grand Moghul," one of the world's richest and most powerful emperors. This was a time when the emperor could be approached only with eyes lowered to the ground and full cognizance of the Persian couplet, "Should the King say that it is night at noon / Be sure to cry, Behold the moon." There were already other, lesser members of our Kayastha community toiling in the court: "The Hindus [read Kayasthas] took so zealously to Persian education that, before another century had elapsed, they had fully come up to the Muhammadans [Muslims] in point of literary acquirements," doing much of the collecting of revenue, keeping of accounts, and conducting of official court correspondence.

My ancestor's way into the Moghul court was eased by the sponsorship and patronage of the finance minister, Asadullah Khan, who soon appointed him his deputy. As Shah Jahan aged and the bloody wars of succession between his sons began, Raghunath Bahadur was shrewd enough to align himself with the eventual victor, Aurangzeb. For his sagacity, Aurangzeb, when emperor, amply rewarded my ancestor with titles, money, an army of twenty-five hundred horsemen, and, on Asadullah Khan's death, the post of finance minister.

Aurangzeb was the last of the Grand Moghuls. Europeans—the English, French, and Dutch—desirous of enriching themselves in the spice trade, had begun encroaching as early as the fifteenth century. By now, they were on a roll and had set up well-fortified colonies in major port cities and moved inland. They were warring with local chieftains and with each other. The Moghul Empire was falling apart. All the major movers and shakers in the Moghul court were leaving to set up their own kingdoms. One branch of my family took off with the general who would form the southern princely state of Hyderabad and run the nizam's revenue department. My own ancestors went on to work in another Muslim court nearby, that of the Nawab of Kunjpura (in Haryana today).

Hindu India was under the domination of Muslim rulers from the late twelfth century until the nineteenth century. What struck me as I sat reading on the floor of Babaji's office was that my family, without being told to do so, never ceased fulfilling its destiny as scribes. Were we choosing freely? Or was Brahma, with the image of the man with the quill and inkpot firmly before him, tugging at strings attached to the left side of our brains—or is it the right side—generation after generation?

At a time when most Hindu families kept their distance from Muslim families, ours not only went to work for Muslim rulers but mastered their court language, Persian, with such zeal that we were relied upon to write history, keep records, and manage taxes and accounts.

This Muslim influence did not just "stay at the office." It went to the core of the men's being, affecting their etiquette and manners, even their style of courtship. When they came home, they changed into Muslim-style clothes—white-on-white kurtas embroidered in Lucknow on top of loose white pajamas—and amused themselves with recitations of Persian poetry, some of which they composed themselves, and the pursuit of art and literature. Indeed, when my grandfather's grandfather Rai Bahadur Jeewan Lal died, the *Statesman*, dated May 3, 1884, declared his collection of old and rare Persian books, architectural plans, and miniature paintings to be most valuable and unique, and stated that "in him we have lost perhaps the best informed student of Indian history in North India."

I remember once, just before the Partition of India in 1947, when Hindu-Muslim angers were running deep, a Hindu school friend chastised me for being too "broad-minded," as if it were a sin, and then dismissed me, saying, "Well, you Mathur Kayasthas are half Muslim anyway!"

There was indeed a strong overlay of Muslim culture in our house, and a genuine spirit of tolerance towards all faiths, leading

My eldest aunt, Bhuaji, thirteen years old, with the groom on her wedding day.
She wears fashionable iẓars (culottes) in rich damask and is laden with jewelry,
including a gold jhumar *(head ornament) in Muslim style, a large gold*
nose-ring, and six pairs of anklets.

to a strange split between the highly educated men and the less educated women. If the men spoke Persian and Urdu, the women kept up their Hindi and read the holy *Ramayana* from front to back each year. If the men drank and ate kebabs, the women served them willingly enough but went back into the kitchen to prepare meals that included *kadhi* (a thick chickpea-flour soup with dumplings), potatoes with ginger, and summer squashes with tomato and cumin.

The women's clothing was a mixture of Muslim and Hindu.

My mother and all my aunts were raised wearing the izars and *kurti*s of the Muslim world, culottelike loose pants either embroidered for special occasions or made of chintz, and small thigh-length shirts. Once they married, they moved on to *lahanga*s, traditional Hindu long skirts. They did not wear the more modern saree until the 1920s, when my grandfather bought identically designed sarees by the dozen and doled them out to all the women of the house.

In spite of the Islamic influence, neither the men nor the women ever veered from being completely Hindu. Jeewan Lal may have been a great Persian scholar, but he was also a master of Sanskrit. If the men greeted their friends by raising a hand to the forehead in a very Muslim salaam or *aadaab*, they greeted the family with joined palms and a solid "*Jai Ramji Ki*" ("Praise be to Lord Rama").

Yet another influence was to enter our family's life: that of the British. Were we going to turn half British, too?

THREE

When British rule was extended to Delhi in the early part of the nineteenth century, the court of a "resident" (best compared to a governor) was established there. The British capital remained, for the time being, in Calcutta. Many of the Indian rulers, struggling for influence with the newest power, sent their emissaries to this court. The Nawab of Kunjpura sent a trusted lawyer, Girdhari Lal, who was the father of the main character in our family history book, Jeewan Lal. The resident, Sir David Ochterlony, took to him to such an extent that he tried to steal him away with the offer of a job as his *munshi*, or record-keeper. Feeling he would be disloyal to the nawab at a critical time in the nation's history, he refused, but cleverly suggested his son for the job, saying that by taking his son the resident would get two for the price of one, as he himself would, naturally, give his son all necessary assistance. And so Jeewan Lal came to be employed by the British, first under Lord Ochterlony and then under Sir T. T. Metcalfe, rising to the rank of *mir munshi*, chief record-keeper and honorary magistrate. The men of our family who once knew

Persian now had also learned English. The British side of our family saga had begun.

We now reach the period of the 1857 Mutiny. The British declared it a mutiny as it did start with a rebellion by Indian foot soldiers, Hindus and Muslims alike, angry at being forced to use cow and pig grease on their bullets. It soon grew into a nation-wide, protracted, and very bloody insurrection against the British, an endless series of battles that were joined on the Indian side by provincial chiefs, nawabs, rajas, masses of Indian soldiers and common folk. The Moghul emperor dithered at first, but in the end joined the rebellion. Many decades later, the first Indian prime minister, Jawaharlal Nehru, was to call this the First Indian War of Independence.

Eventually, the colonial rulers prevailed, though not without the help of reliable "loyalists" like Jeewan Lal. For this and his general services, Jeewan Lal was given the title of "Rai Bahadur" by the viceroy and governor-general of India, Lord Lytton. (The Moghul emperor was banished to Burma. Nearly all the citizens of Delhi were expelled.) Jeewan Lal was also offered a substantial reward, but he turned it down, saying that he had more than enough for his needs.

This refusal was to haunt the family later, when it fell on hard times. As a "loyalist," Rai Bahadur Jeewan Lal had suffered irreparable losses during the Mutiny. Here I quote from his diary:

> May 11, 1857 . . . Sohan [a servant] also stated that he heard the city *badmash*es [miscreants], who were pointing out to the rebels the abode of the nobles of the town, utter my name also, and say that they should repair to the house of the Mir Munshi of the Agent and Commissioner and plunder it. "I tell you for the sake of loyalty," said Sohan, "that you close the gates of your house and put heavy locks on them so that no *badmash* may enter

the house and create disturbance." Accordingly, the writer forth-with made the necessary arrangements. Although the house I lived in was very spacious and strong like a fort and had very large stones from the Kotla [Fortress] of Ferozshah put in its foundation . . . I found it advisable to lock both the gates and put heavy locks on them. I hid myself in the dark *taikhana* [cellar] built of the same stones and above it stationed my servants as guards to keep watch and give me information if any persons came here . . . and, considering for what a long time I have been eating the salt of the Government [deriving my bread and butter from the Government], and was its well-wisher, and that this was a time to repay it all and try with my heart and soul for my masters, I appointed the same Sohan to go to Sir John Metcalfe . . . , tender my respects to them, and ask them to give me orders for whatever service they might wish me to perform.

May 12: Two Mooglee Telungas [rebel soldiers] came to my house and made a disturbance. [We] paid them four rupees and made them go away.

May 13: Two other rebel soldiers entered my house, and took away my goods—viz., carpet, door, pillows, books, and one box containing cash and jewels and shawls, etc., value 2000 rupees.

May 19: [Miscreants] reached my house by climbing from roof to roof of adjacent houses, and plundered it, taking away women's jewels, carpets, etc., value 2500 rupees.

May 23: Rebel soldiers, hearing that I was sending news to the British officers, and being exasperated at their fruitless search after me, demolished all the buildings in my garden, and plucked off fruit from trees, inflicting a loss of 3000 rupees.

July 1: Bahadur, gardener, came and reported that the rebels had gone to my garden . . . cut down the trees, and carried them away.

July 19: . . . came to me wearing the King's [Moghul emperor's] livery and threatened me saying, "The King's [Moghul emperor's] rule is now established, not a trace of the

English is left, your *kamra* [city room or office] in Chandni Chowk [the main street in the Old City] is in my possession, bring out the title deed, etc., and deliver them to me. . . ." So I gave him the title deeds and wrote the lease, upon which he became the owner of my premises, worth 5000 rupees.

August 1: The [Moghul] King's officials . . . demand that I present myself with Rs. 50,000. I recite the following verse in my mind: God rescue me from this trouble / No one [but thee] knows what is passing in my mind.

August 4: Nazir Ali, Thanedar [Jail Superintendent] of the Emperor, came to arrest me . . . accompanied by one hundred rebel soldiers with unsheathed swords in their hands. . . . The females of my family were sitting by Maharaja Lal [his second son], who was suffering dreadfully in those days, the stone having been recently extracted from his bladder, and ran pell-mell to the upper story at the sight of the rebels. The rebels took away the *paandan* [betel box] containing jewels left by the females. The writer was arrested and, placed in a palanquin, carried under the escort of the rebels, holding naked swords in hand, to the *kotwali* [police station]. [Here] an old *subedar* [sergeant] . . . ran up to stab me with his drawn dagger, shouting, "This is the man who sends news to the English." [Jeewan Lal was rescued by a Moghul friend.]

It was the custom then for one man, the head of a household that included children and grandchildren, to be responsible, financially and otherwise, for all of them. That was the joint-family system. The family coffers had been emptied during the Mutiny. Rai Bahadur Jeewan Lal's death in 1884 was soon followed by that of his eldest son. His next son, Maharaja Lal, unable to work because of severe deafness, appealed to the British government for the reward that the family had once refused. He asked that the younger generation, which included

My grandparents, circa 1926, some of the clan, and the two Number 7 family dogs. The sarees were ordered in bulk by my grandfather and are here worn in the old-fashioned way with a pin at the shoulder. Back row: Prakashdada, Saran Bhua, Shibbudada, Taoji, my father, Kiran Bhua. Middle row: Bhuaji, Taiji (Shibbudada's wife), Bari Taiji (Chand Narain's wife), Babaji, Bari Bauwa, my mother, Shammo Bhua. Front row: Anup Jija, Raghudada, Kripaldada, Prem Bhua, Harish Bhaisa'ab, Kailashdada, Brijdada.

my grandfather, be given a chance at sitting for entrance examinations at London law schools.

My grandfather, Raj Narain, was barely twenty-one and already a student at St. Stephen's College in Delhi. Even his college submitted a petition for him. In the end, my grandfather did go to London, and the reward, consisting of land and villages outside Delhi, did come through. Some of this was sold, the money used both for education and to purchase the orchard estate, a huge piece of land that was procured by the joint family and then divided up among them. My grandfather ended up with a choice among curving plot overlooking the Yamuna River, Number 7. His younger brother lived next door, in Number 16; his elder brother's family was down the road, in Number 8; his cousins in Number 4, and so on. The numbers were picked haphazardly, according to personal preferences. Our entire neighborhood consisted of family, several generations in each large house.

fOUR

The Freedom of Kanpur • My Mother and Father •
A Fairy-Tale Marriage • A Desire to Excel

I was born on August 13, 1933, on the night of Janmashtmi, the
dark eighth day of the waning moon, the feast day of Lord
Krishna's birth, in my grandfather's orchard house. I was delivered by Dr. Keany, a British missionary lady-doctor, while my
sister Kamal banged at the door and cried because she was not
allowed in. In the India of that time, you were what your family
was (I borrow shamelessly from Brillat-Savarin), and my family
was a hybrid: it was Hindu by origin but heavily veneered with
Muslim culture and English education; it considered itself very
liberal but lived by the ancient rules of the joint-family system,
whereby men dominated, only men made it to history books, and
all marriages were with other Kayasthas—more inkpot and quill.
I may have been born with honey on my tongue, but I was also
born squirming against the status quo.

When I was about two, my father took a job as the manager of
a ghee (clarified butter) factory. This was not real ghee but the
hydrogenated cooking-oil variety, a kind of shortening known in

India as *vanaspati*. The factory, Ganesh Flour Mills, was owned by my father's cousins, in fact the cousins who lived at Number 4, so it was all in the family. Except that the factory was not in Delhi but in Kanpur (Cawnpore in those days), an overnight journey by train.

All through my grown-up life I have written many times about Kanpur, but I have rarely identified it—I have always merged it with Delhi. They were really quite distinct. But in my childhood memory we would leave the house in Kanpur, get into our car, drive along the gardens, go through the high, gated walls, fall asleep in a train, and pass through a less severe, white-painted gate and down another drive, and there, in front of us, would be the Delhi house, Number 7. Both houses were our homes, and they were seamlessly adjacent.

At this stage, my parents, whom we called Dadaji and Bauwa, had five children: my two older brothers, Brij and Bhaiyya; my sisters, Lalit and Kamal; and me. Brijdada and Bhaiyyadada (the "dada" being a term added out of respect for older men, especially brothers) were twelve and ten years old, and already going through the rigors of Delhi's Modern School. Pulling them out was considered a very bad idea, so they were left under the general supervision of the joint family, with my middle uncle, Shibbudada, keeping a special eye on them. I was just two. My schooling had not even begun. Lalit at seven, and Kamal at five, were at Queen Mary's School, but so bright that a move for them at that age was not considered a problem at all.

Our years in Kanpur were such a happy time for my parents. My father was freed from orbiting around as second fiddle in the rarefied spheres of his autocratic father and his highly popular, music-loving, entrepreneurial middle brother, Shibbudada. My mother did not have to be a dutiful daughter-in-law or sister-in-

*My father, Kamal, Lalit, my mother, and
me on holiday in the hills in about 1936.*

law or aunt. She could just be a mother and wife. Kanpur was the
only place my parents thrived.

Even though they were in Kanpur for eight years, Delhi
remained their official home. My grandfather would not have it
otherwise: he loosened the strings only so far. Thus every holi-

day we returned to Delhi, to the same room where I was born, the room that balanced out my grandfather's large room at the back of the house. When my father wanted to buy a separate house in New Delhi for himself, my grandfather said no and my father fell silent. That is how the joint-family system, the respect-for-elders routine, worked.

My father, Dadaji, was one of the best-looking men I knew. He was tall—well, tallish by Western standards, about five foot eleven—straight-backed, and even-featured, with fine dark hair that he parted on the side and then brushed backwards with his English brushes. His clothes were British, all arranged very neatly on hangers by my mother, tweeds for the winter and khakis for the summer. For formal occasions he had Muslim-style *achkan*s (like Nehru jackets but knee-length) in different weights of wools and cottons, which he wore with tight *churidar* pajamas (tight poplin "leggings" with extra folds at the bottom). He dressed, smoked, and drove his ever-changing British and American cars with the style of a man about town.

My mother, Bauwa, was just as short as my father was tall: on a good day she might have reached five feet. So she always wore heels to compensate. When she was born, she was so startlingly light-skinned that her family bestowed upon her the name Kashmiran Rani (Queen of Kashmir), which signified the height of beauty. Her face, as sweet and open as her nature, could be classified as softly pretty, but in the India of that time her color and smooth skin were enough to lift her into a special class of the "highly desirable."

She, too, dressed with uncommon flair, but, although her taste was impeccable, perhaps because of her size and rounded frame, she lacked my father's flamboyance. She wore only sarees: cottons in the day; printed silks for simple shopping excursions; chif-

*My parents, stylish in their summer whites, in the
mango orchard of Number 7.*

fons, georgettes, and heavy Benaresi or South Indian silks for
evening parties. Her cupboards were as neat as my father's—
naturally, as she was everybody's cupboard-keeper. The cottons,
nicely starched by the *dhobi* (laundryman), were stacked one on
top of another on shelves, the everyday silks were on hangers, but
a very special treatment was reserved for the dressier sarees.

My meticulous mother would first get rectangles of heavy

cardboard, all cut to the same size, about sixteen inches by thirteen inches. She covered each with sturdy brown paper. She would then take a saree and fold it into a very long rectangle the same width as the cardboard, place the cardboard in the center of this rectangle, and fold the saree over it in thirds. That was not all. Muslin, bought by the bolt, had been cut into large squares. Each folded saree was then enfolded again in the muslin, like putting a letter in a freshly made envelope.

Bauwa had hundreds of heavy, dressy sarees. Some that she wore regularly were in her cupboard, and others, not in use, were stashed in trunks and stowed away. When she needed to wear one, it was unwrapped. It came out of the muslin and off the cardboard and was then draped on her body as she stood in front of her long dressing-table mirror. When she returned home, she undraped the saree, folded it up, put it on the cardboard, and wrapped it again in muslin. The girls, generally in identical dresses, stood in a row and watched. We, her daughters, have most of her sarees now. They are all in perfect condition.

Sometimes in Kanpur, when my mother would be sitting on a *takht* (divan), her legs folded to one side, doing her mending on a small Singer sewing machine, I would ask her for the umpteenth time to tell me how she got to marry my father. She was still filled with the wonder of it all, and for me the story was more moving than anything in *Grimm's Fairy Tales*.

It was an arranged marriage, of course. Everything took place in the Old City.

In the Old City of Delhi, there were two large families living just a few narrow lanes apart. One was rich and powerful. The other was humble but good. Their paths rarely crossed, as the rich family was always busy with important government people and important university people and important industrialists.

One day, when the handsome youngest son of the rich family had just finished college, his father approached him, saying, "Son, it is time for you to marry. As is the tradition among us, we have asked the barber to nose around and find a girl who is worthy of you." "I am perfectly willing to marry," the handsome son said, "but I want a girl who is beautiful, sweet-natured, bright, and talented. Is this at all possible?" "We can only try," said his father.

The barber-matchmaker was dispatched. He went to Agra and did not find anyone. He went to Jaipur and did not find anyone. He went to Lucknow and Allahabad and saw no one who fit the handsome son's desires. The barber returned to the Old City and reported to the father, "I am sorry to bring bad news, but such a girl does not exist."

Just then, the handsome boy's sister spoke up: "But I know such a girl. She is my friend. She went to school with me. The barber should look there. It is just a few minutes' walk from here."

The barber looked, talked to the girl's parents, and asked for her horoscope.

The barber returned to the rich family's home and handed the horoscope to the handsome boy's parents. "Now, I have done my work. If the girl's horoscope matches with that of your son, we are in business."

The horoscopes matched perfectly. A wedding was arranged. But the girl had never even set eyes on the boy.

One day the handsome son's sister went to play with her friend at the humble family's home. They were eating some squiggly *jalebi*s [pretzel-like sweets filled with syrup] when the sister looked out of the window and saw her handsome brother walking by. "Look, look, look," she said to her humble friend,

"there, outside the window, is the man you are about to marry."
The humble girl looked out and was astounded. "Why, he is a
prince," she exclaimed.

On the wedding day, as the sound of the *shehnai* [oboelike
instrument] that led the wedding procession got closer and
closer, the humble girl's heart beat faster and faster. Her prince
was approaching on a big white horse and he would take her
away.

That was my mother's version of the story, as told to a little
girl. But the truth was that she never stopped thinking of my
father as the prince who had, by some miracle, taken her to his
heart. She trod lightly through life, feeling no urge to leave an
imprint. My princelike father, on the other hand, was totally
dependent on her quiet strength. In our large joint family with
many strange marriages, my parents' union seemed the most
comfortable and joyous.

They were, in many respects, quite different from each other.
My father had a B.A. degree from St. Stephen's College and
spoke English fluently. He liked to read biographies and histories
and study maps. He smoked. He listened to the BBC news in the
evenings as he drank his whiskey and soda. He played bridge and
tennis at the club. He loved to hunt and fish with his friends. He
loved good food, especially the meats, pullaos, and breads that
came with our Islamic veneer.

My mother was "eighth-class-pass," which meant that she had
not even gone to high school. She spoke no English. Whenever
the rest of her family went on for too long in English, she would
say in Hindi, "*Arey Ram* [Oh God], so much git-pit, git-pit, git-
pit." That is what English sounded like to her: git-pit, git-pit, git-
pit. But, rather like an American mother whose children can

manage to natter away in French, she also looked pleased. Pleased to have lucked out with this git-pitting group.

My mother made up for her lack of schooling with her uncommon intelligence. After she died, we found in her neat cupboard, still laid out with pride, several silver medals that she had won in school for top scholastic honors. In those days, it was not thought necessary for girls to study too long. After all, their only purpose was to be married off. Whatever my mother did do, she did to perfection. She cooked the foods my father loved to eat plus all the traditional Hindu festival foods, *papri*s (chickpea-flour poppadums) for Holi, the Spring Festival of Colors; glazed lotus seeds for Janmashtmi, the birthday of Lord Krishna; and *pua*s (sweet whole-wheat dumplings) for Karvachauth, the day women prayed for their husbands. She sewed, she knitted, she embroidered with silk and gold thread, not just ordinary things but extraordinary creations. One of them, a set of finely wrought gold-thread-and-sequin crowns she made for herself and her firstborn to wear at a horoscope naming ceremony, I have had framed, and they sit in my New York living room.

I feel I inherited my mother's desire to excel. But whereas she quietly accepted the limitations of her times, I was given the luxury of rebellion by very loving and indulgent parents. I was already the fifth child, and a girl. I was way beyond the heir and the spare. They could take a chance with me as they could not with their older ones.

FIVE

My memory begins in earnest at about the age of four. We were in Kanpur. Dadaji, determined to get his daughters as educated as his sons, had explored Kanpur schools and had come up with two very different options: there was the Mahila Vidyalay, an all-girl school where every subject was taught in Hindi and the emphasis was on Hinduism and Indian traditions; and there was St. Mary's Convent, a coeducational school, at least until the middle grades, where most of the teachers were German and Irish nuns, the medium of instruction was English, and the education was basically Western. And, of course, Christian.

I remember my father driving us slowly past the Mahila Vidyalay again and again, as if by just looking at the school and the girls who came rushing out he would be able to divine its suitability for his daughters. I think that a part of him, the part that was fighting for Indian independence as a member of the Indian Congress Party, would have liked us to go there. But the girls at the Vidyalay seemed to lack the all-round sophistication he thought we should have, and in the end he put my two older sisters in the convent. He trusted us to withstand tsunamis of Westernization and Christianity that might follow, and to hold on to our Indianness as he and his father before him had managed to do. His approach contained inherent contradictions, but that was how we seemed to live our lives.

Bauwa woke us up early each morning, only to rush us to the sink in our bathroom to brush our teeth and do our "milk cleansing." My mother was the simplest of women, who wore minimal East-West makeup. There was her *bindi,* the dot of red powder (*sindhoor*) she put between her brows; the kohl she made herself by burning camphor under an upturned terra-cotta bowl, collecting the soot and adding oils to it, which she used to line her eyes (and ours); and there was the Hazeline Vanishing Cream, which she put on her face. When she went out, she dabbed on her neck a few drops of Evening in Paris perfume from a small blue bottle.

I have no idea where she picked up the milk "beauty secret" or why she set so much store by it. Perhaps my father offhandedly mentioned to her that Cleopatra had bathed in ass's milk. Perhaps she was made to do it as a little girl and it really was some ancient family beauty secret going back to well before 4000 B.C., when Aryans with their cows came from the Ural Mountains in great waves to set up dominion in North India. She never explained, we never asked, and in India you never know. She did have a convincing air of authority about her, and who could question a walking advertisement for perfect skin?

There would be a bowl of fresh raw cow's milk waiting at the sink. It came from our cows, which had been milked at dawn, delivered by the *gwala,* or cowherd. It was rich and creamy. First we splashed this onto our faces. It clung to our lashes, big white blobs of it. Then we had to rub the milk in with our fingers, back and forth, back and forth, until it dried and came off in little dirty threads. We could now wash our faces with warm water—and was our skin soft and smooth!

After our baths, my mother went off to pray in the little section of the storeroom she had decorated with her *pooja* (worship) paraphernalia. She would water the *tulsi* (holy basil) plant just outside the storeroom and then help her husband and daughters get ready for work and school.

For breakfast the girls and Bauwa always had tall glasses of milk. My mother never developed a taste for tea or coffee, though she served them at all proper occasions in the prettiest of English porcelain. We had hot milk in the winter and cold in the summer. Those who wished could add Ovaltine to it. I never wished such a thing. The milk, of course, came from the same cows that had provided our beauty treatment. India is a milky nation: milk with sugar; milk with saffron and nuts; tea with milk or cream; yogurt with fruit, nuts, vegetables, dumplings, and rice; steamed yogurt; hung-up yogurt; fresh milk cheese (*paneer*); fresh-milk-cheese sweets from *rasagulla*s to *chum chum*s; milky rice puddings (*kheer* and *phirni*); and milk ices and ice creams. Without milk, India, this highly lactosed country, would just wither away.

My father had tea, two fried eggs, and toast for breakfast, day after day. He ate the whites of the eggs first. Round and round he'd go with his fork and knife, the whites slowly disappearing, until all that was left were two glistening yellow orbs, shaking like Jell-O on his white plate. He would pick up one whole yolk on his fork and slip it into his mouth. He would chew it slowly, the blue vein at his temple throbbing in rhythm. Then he would pick up the second yolk. All activity stopped as we gazed in wonderment.

With our milk we sometimes had bread and cheese, sometimes just fruit, and sometimes eggs sprinkled with my mother's special salt, which was always kept in small cut-glass containers on the table. We now considered this the "house salt," and the recipe, apparently my grandmother's, consisted of salt, pepper, and ground roasted cumin seeds. Breakfast was, except on special weekends, Western, with jams in proper silver-lidded cut-glass jam jars, toast in silver toast-racks, Kraft cheese straight out of a tin—tins were considered modern and exotic—Marmite housed in its traditional dark brown bottle, and, every now and then, ham or bacon or sausages bought from Valerio's, a specialty bakery and meat shop owned by a Goan couple, Mr. and Mrs. Noronha.

One car with a driver then took my sisters to school. My father either drove himself to his office or walked: the office was right inside the walled compound that included the ghee factory and the homes of other, lesser officers of the company.

My day was then all my own, and I spent it mostly in the garden. Perhaps I should say "gardens," as there were several of them, including vast lawns, a badminton court, a tennis court, a rose garden, mixed flower borders edged with sweet peas, and several gardens devoted just to flowers and vegetables. We grew not only almost every kind of flower that might flourish in our subtropical climate, from cannas to lupines, but all our own vegetables—potatoes, onions, carrots, okra, eggplant, cauliflower, cabbage, kohlrabi, peas, and tomatoes. There was a head *mali* (gardener) with assistants to do the hard labor, but all the designing, choosing of trees, ordering of seeds, and planting was micromanaged by my father, whose chief passion in life, other than his family, was his garden.

The farthest garden area, at one end of the compound, was the cowshed, which I visited several times a day. A very long, narrow path formed by the high brick compound wall, hedges and trees on one side, and an endless trellis of green beans on the other, led up to it. I would skip along the path, or tricycle along it, breaking off beans and nibbling them as I went. Dadaji had created such a complete universe for us. For a dreamy little girl growing up, it lacked absolutely nothing. There was the reality of the specially ordered "black" roses, which were really a deep purple, or the snapdragons, which could be made to "bark" by pinching the flowers in the middle, or the marigolds, whose centers we called "coconuts" and devoured. But there were also little corners of the garden where I could escape, lean my head against a tree, and vanish into a kaleidoscopic world of English knights and princesses, Indian gods with multiple arms, Bombay movie heroes, Indian detectives from my mother's nightly readings-aloud of Hindi detective stories, and characters from British and American comic books.

At the cowshed the tethered cows would be engrossed in licking hunks of rock salt suspended before them with wire. Like determined sculptors, they would lick them and lick them with their coarse tongues, smoothing out all rough edges until creations worthy of Henry Moore would magically appear. Every day the sculptures changed slightly, getting smaller and smaller and more full of holes. Every day I would note the changes and marvel at their ravishing forms.

I would then rush to observe the daily churning of butter. It was done just outside the pantry, on the covered brick pathway leading to the kitchen. We ate only white homemade butter. I did not know any other kind existed. White homemade butter smeared thickly on our toast. Sometimes with salt and pepper on it. The milk was poured into a round earthenware pot to which the wooden churner was attached. As ropes pulled the churner this way and that, this way and that, little bits of white butter flew out onto the ground. Crows would collect to eat this. One day, as I watched, I decided to shoo the crows away. Most looked angrily at me and left, but one stayed. I took a step forward to shoo it. The crow took two steps forward in defiance. I ran away in fear.

All morning I wandered around with the *mali*, dogging his footsteps. I carried salt and pepper with me so I could season and then bite into a red-ripe tomato still smelling of its green sepals. I helped dig up tiny potatoes while mud still clung to them. I broke off the sweetest green peas, shelling and eating half of them, throwing the rest into the *mali*'s basket. And I helped pick the prickly okra, which, when cooked and combined with the equally glutinous split pea called *urad dal*, sent me into paroxysms of ecstasy. (Perhaps that accounts for my partiality to Japanese glutinous foods, like mountain yam and fermented beans, *natto*.) When the *mali* went to the massive pit that held the manure and organic leafy matter, there I was, watching him turn the compost around. I could not leave the *mali* alone even when he ate his lunch.

He always settled down to eat near the shady water tank. I followed him there. First he would wash his hands and feet and dry them off. Then he would sit down with a deep sigh, throwing all the weight of the world off his shoulders, and open up a small cloth bundle to reveal two thick whole-wheat *roti*s (flatbreads), some sliced raw onion, and some green chilies. I would sit down with him, leaning against the same brick wall he was. Bauwa had warned me not to take the *mali*'s food, but the *mali* was too generous and I was too greedy. I never took too much—just a bite. All I know is that nothing tasted more heavenly than that simple combination: grainy whole-wheat *roti*, raw onion, and green chili. Years later, as I traveled the world, I would compare this to the pasta with olive oil, garlic, and red chili I had in Italy, or the

plain rice with chili *sambal* I had in an Indonesian village . . . the
wonder of very basic national starches enhanced only with the
most basic of local seasonings.

In our Kanpur home, my mother, Bauwa, had the daily task of
keeping household accounts. In the morning she would give the
cook a list of what was needed and the money to buy it. Generally, it was just meat and spices, as we produced all dairy and vegetables ourselves and buying fruit was my father's responsibility.
The cook would then go off on his bicycle. On his return he
would have to recite what he had bought and what it cost while
my mother, sitting on her bed with her knees pulled up, wrote it
all down in the endless registers she filled up in Hindi. The smallest item, with its price, was noted down. Even salt. She may not
have had much education, but she did not have ancestral ink
flowing through her veins for nothing. Her job, our job, was to
keep records.

When my father returned from work, we all gathered around
him as he had his tea. The girls were subjected to their second
glass of milk for the day. If it was summer, I sat out on the back
lawn watching my parents and sisters try their hand at badminton
while I listened to the crickets. Or my father taught the girls how
to ride a bicycle. As we built up a sweat, we were allowed cooling
fresh lemonade (*neebu ka sharbat*), fruit squash (fruit syrup
diluted with ice water), and that newfangled drink Vimto as well.
If it was winter, my father stayed indoors listening to the news on
his Phillips radio. War was on the horizon, and my father did not
like what he was hearing.

SIX

My youngest sister was born when I was five, just before the first salvos of World War II, during our summer holiday in Dalhousie, a "hill station," built on three Himalayan peaks at about seven thousand feet above sea level and named after a British governor-general in India, the tenth Earl of Dalhousie.

The large house we had rented that year was, rather grandly, named Teera Hall. As usual, the entire extended family was present, with a few dozen, including my mother, sleeping in a large dormitory-like room on the second floor. As my sister was expected, a hill palanquin (*daandee*) was kept at the ready to take my mother to the hospital if needed. But my sister was born suddenly, during the night. At first we were all asked to cover our heads with our quilts, and then my mother was rushed to my grandmother's room, which was adjacent to ours. I could hear my mother moaning gently. Every now and again her door would fly open and an aunt would rush out for hot water or towels, shutting the door behind her. I was frightened out of my wits. Then I heard an infant crying. The door opened. A weary aunt stepped out and whispered to a cousin, who ran down the room yelling, "She's been born, he's been born" ("*Ho gai, ho gya*"). He'd been told of a birth but not the sex of the child.

I started school the same year as my sister Veena was born, and my father had begun to worry seriously about the war. What happened to me was what probably happened to my sisters as well. At the age of five, I was thrown into an English-speaking class of Indians, Anglo-Indians, and Britons, speaking not a word of English myself. Until then, I had spoken to my mother and the servants in Hindustani. My father and sisters also switched languages when speaking to me or to my mother, so, even though I had heard English spoken all around me, I could not speak a word of it myself.

But I learned fast. Rather like learning to swim by being dropped in the deep end of a pool, I kicked my hands and feet and within a month surfaced speaking the language of our colonial masters. I could git-pit with the rest of them.

My school years in Kanpur were, like everything else in our lives, sometimes severely compartmentalized and sometimes a zany mix and match of cultures. In the morning we got into our white blouses, navy blue tunics, socks, and tightly laced shoes, which my mother double-knotted. We were *never* going to lose these shoes! We could not even get out of them. Our coconut-oiled hair was parted in the middle, braided tightly into two pigtails, and secured firmly at the bottom ends with black ribbons. Our pigtails were not going to come loose, either.

My mother handed us our khaki solar topees (hard, brimmed

*My sisters Lalit (to my left) and Kamal and me (aged
about four), wearing my favorite red dress, in the back
garden of the house in Kanpur.*

hats) and our hard leather schoolbags, filled with textbooks she
had covered with brown paper, and then escorted us to the car,
her lightly starched cotton voile saree crackling as she walked.

Once we got out of our front gate, it was we who were in
charge. We instructed the driver to go "faster, faster." The whole
aim of this was to be at top speed as we reached a small arched
bridge over a narrow tributary of the Ganges River. At that

speed, the car went up the bridge and then flew. Our stomachs lurched, and we held our breaths until we landed with a bit of a thud. Not very good for the car, but it made our morning and prepared us for the nuns!

Our convent school, quite naturally, recognized only one religion: Catholicism. If you were not a Catholic, you could not go to the chapel for mass in the morning. This was a bit of a disappointment, as the chapel always looked and smelled so, well, holy. Instead, all non-Catholics, the few Hindus and Parsis—and many Anglo-Indian Protestants—had to attend Bible-history class, which was held in our everyday classrooms. I enjoyed reading the King James Bible. Even more, I enjoyed the free exchange of holy pictures afterwards. I liked to collect the slightly raised ones printed on hard, smooth cardboard, outlined with gilt.

At school we recited "Half a pound of tuppenny rice, half a pound of treacle" and "four and twenty blackbirds, baked in a pie" as if to the manor born, even though we had never eaten a pie in our lives and had no real sense of what treacle was. At morning break, we were allowed to use the small daily allowance given by our mother, about two annas each (an anna was a sixteenth of a rupee), on goods offered by the toffee man. This was the highlight of the school day.

The toffee man was Indian but had been vetted by the nuns. He sat cross-legged on the stone floor of a back veranda, his homemade wares taken out of a tin trunk, spread on a cloth in front of him, and sold to us on squares of paper. And what wares: half pink, half white coconut toffees, cut in diamond shapes that melted in the mouth; chocolate toffees that were part fudge and part caramel, cut in thin squares; and the barley sugar . . . fat twists and roughly shaped, dimpled balls of candy in yellow and orange and red, opaque on the outside, translucent inside, not too brittle, but hard to bite off and, once in the mouth, teeth-sticking and chewy. These were treats only the toffee man had. They disappeared from our lives once we left St. Mary's Convent.

Not entirely. Years later, in the 1980s, I was in Calcutta's covered New Market researching a cookbook and preparing to act in Merchant Ivory's *Heat and Dust* to be shot in Hyderabad a week later, after a stop in Delhi. I looked at the fish shops selling Bengal's famed *rahu* (a kind of carp) and *hilsa* (a shadlike mackerel), and the men who shopped for them in the early hours of the morning. I went to the spice shops to examine Bengal's Five-Spice Mixture, which once included the now disappearing spice *radhuni*. All of a sudden, something made me turn my head, and there, across a narrow market lane, was a shop that announced "Barley Sugar." It just could not be true. Barley-sugar labels had deceived my sisters and me many times before. It always turned out to be some brittle, machine-made rubbish that lacked the chewy texture and the very slightly caramelized taste of the real thing. Barley sugar was now a mirage, surely.

I crossed the narrow lane anyway. Lord, it looked like the real thing: fat, twisted sticks; misshapen, dimpled balls. I tasted a piece. This was it. This was it. The Anglo-Indian (mixed-race, with Indo-British ancestry) owners had been making and selling it for decades. I could have kissed them. I bought several pounds of it, carrying it on the plane to Delhi to offer to my sister Kamal. She was skeptical at first, having been deceived many times before, but one bite convinced her. Kanpur came rolling back, and the two of us went out of our minds. Even though we admonished each other with "Are you crazy? It's pure sugar!" we behaved like children and managed to finish every last bit of the barley sugar in less than a week. I personally put on six pounds, which I had to get rid of with a month-long diet of just tandoori chicken and salad at my Hyderabad hotel.

The toffee man was followed by arithmetic, which I loathed; English—reading or essay writing or dictation—which I loved; and nature study, which allowed me both to draw and to write, so it was a great favorite. By then it was lunchtime. My sisters and I would meet up again; our food was freshly made and came in a four-tiered tiffin-carrier from home. Our turbaned bearer brought it. In the car. It was the second trip for the car.

One of the side verandas of the school was lined with benches and tables for all the children whose food came from home. The bearers' job—our bearer and other people's bearers—was to spread out tablecloths and set the crockery, cutlery, and napkins before the end of the last class. As my sisters and I came flying out, our bearer would open up the tiffin-carrier and spread out the containers, putting a serving spoon in each of them. The food was still warm. There might be *kofta*s with cinnamon and cardamom in one, rice with peas or chapatis in another, cauliflower with potatoes in a third, and perhaps homemade yogurt or a salad in a fourth. Afterwards there were some easy-to-eat fruits such as bananas or the Indian orange, which is really like a large, loose-skinned tangerine.

I was very curious to see what those around me were being served. Some children had sandwiches. Tomato-and-cheese was popular, as was the spiced-egg sandwich. Some children had left-over roast from the night before. One Anglo-Indian girl with thin brown hair, who sat at the bench next to me, always startled me with her unusual combinations. I remember looking over once and seeing on her plate the following: at nine o'clock there were cornflakes; at twelve o'clock there was plain rice; at three o'clock there was cooked *masoor dal* flowing slightly into the rice; and at six o'clock there was an English sausage. She ate all this with a fork and spoon.

After lunch there was drill (up, two, three, four; down, two, three, four; feet astride, two, three, four), singing (hated it) or needlework (loved it but hated needle-nosed Sister Alberta, who taught it—"WHAT did you say? WHAT DID YOU SAY? Get up, young lady. You will NOT say 'thanks.' The expression is 'thank you.' Say, 'Thank you, Sister.' Stand up and put your needlework down. Now. Put your needlework down NOW"), then history or geography (loved both) and library, where I took out just as many books as was possible, the whole world of English classics.

After school, the car would bring us back home. I would tear off my uniform, my shoes and socks, fling down my hat and bag, put on *chappal*s (backless sandals) and a cotton frock of my mother's design, and, with my sisters, make a dash through the dining room into the pantry. Whoever got there first got the end of the bread loaf.

I do not know who started this, but suspect it was my sister Lalit. My mother now had our baby sister, Veena, to look after, so she often rested in the afternoon. All the servants were off taking a break as well. Knowing how hungry we would be when we came home from school, my mother would leave food in the cast-iron warming oven, whatever she and my father had eaten for lunch, generally a meat—my father rarely ate a meal without meat—some goat-and-potato curry, and some chapatis. At first we used to roll the meat up in a chapati and eat it in a form that my mother called a *batta*. Then my sisters began improving on the chapati roll. They ignored the chapati completely. Instead, they cut the thickest end slice from a loaf of bread and hollowed it out, removing most but not all of the soft portion. Into this crusty "container" they first put a layer of meat, then of potatoes, then of mango or lime or chili pickle. As they could run much faster than I, the two of them generally ended up with both crusty ends of the loaf; I was left with the softer middle. But often they were known to share.

That was the trouble with my two older sisters: they were models of decorum and decency—thoughtful, fair, polite, pretty, demure, soft-spoken, and considerate. If I was hurt and angry, I bawled and beat my fists; they cried softly into their pillows. If I rode first our tricycle and then our "lady's" bike like a fiend, they wafted along on them like dainty clouds. If I complained about the behavior of an uncle or a cousin, they pointed out his good side. If I was the somewhat unruly Elizabeth Bennet, they were decidedly versions of Jane Bennet. If I was Jo in *Little Women*, they were just as clearly an amalgam of Meg and Beth. I was doomed by comparison. (Yet you see how I reserve the role of heroine for myself?)

I sometimes think that I was a creation of my father's imagination. Everything he could not allow himself to be, he let me be. When I came along, he already had his perfect family, two good-looking boys followed by two good-looking girls, all bright and healthy. I was odd-looking anyway. Huge, honest, I-see-everything, you-can't-fool-me eyes, and angry, flaring nostrils. With me, he let go. He let me be outspoken and independent.

SEVEN

When we came home from our convent school, we put our holy pictures aside and reverted to being a simple Hindu family. If it was Karvachauth, the fourth day of the waning moon in autumn, we knew my mother would be fasting for the health and longevity of my father and would not eat until the moon showed its face in the dark sky. She did this every year, as did all the married women we knew—though why my mother was obliged to pray for my father and my father never felt the need to pray for her remained perplexing. The ritual was writ in stone and never varied.

At night we all slept in a row on the veranda that faced the rose-and-jasmine garden. Even though our beds were next to each other, we were really quite isolated, as each bed was enshrouded by a large white mosquito net held up by four bamboo poles. My father slept at one end, with my mother next to him, then my baby sister, then me and my two older sisters.

Since married women were supposed to begin their Karvachauth fast at sunrise, my mother would set the alarm for four o'clock in the morning. This would allow her to get a quick bite to eat before the official fast began. The alarm would disturb my father, who would twist and turn and pull the quilt over his head.

My mother would emerge from her mosquito net, awaken any of her daughters who had so requested (Lalit, Kamal, and me), and begin to brush her teeth vigorously with a twig from a neem tree. We would then all tiptoe to the pantry. Here my mother would take out *labdharay aloo* and *poori*s (sauced spicy potatoes and deep-fried puffed breads) from the warming oven and begin to eat. We sisters sat and watched. Every now and then, Bauwa would pop a bit of food from her plate into our mouths. Perhaps at that witching hour, when it was neither night nor day, my mother was quietly passing on an ancient tradition from her generation to ours.

Eventually, we dressed and went to school, and never said a word about what was happening at home. Even though I felt like shouting out, "My mother is fasting for my father today so he won't die," I said nothing. It was understood that what happened at home and what happened at school were unconnected. I had no school friends. I did play with and talk to many of the children, including Nash Engineer, a Parsi boy who was sweet and clever at arithmetic, but I never saw him or any other student outside the school. Our only real friends were our cousins in Delhi.

That evening my mother and the girls would go into the storeroom, where, in the prayer section, mats had been laid down, oil lamps burned, fresh flowers poked out of brass vases, and the "holy food," *pua*s (sweet whole-wheat dumplings, rather like Italian zeppoles), were heaped on the lids of spouted terra-cotta *karva* pots. We sat down cross-legged on the mats and began praying for my father. My father meanwhile smoked, read the paper, and listened to the BBC.

Dadaji was much less distant at Diwali, the Festival of Lights, which also happened to be the Indian New Year. He did not participate much in the prayer part—he left that to my mother—but the lighting, the beautification of the house, and the parties were just up his alley. Here was a Hindu festival that demanded—not suggested but demanded—that the house be cleaned and painted, that it be lit up, and that its owners open the doors wide, party, and gamble so that the bright lights, gaiety, and clinking of money might entice Lakshmi, the Goddess of Wealth, to visit and perhaps stay.

The scraping of old paint would start a good six weeks before, but my father's planning would start much before that. Each and every one of his friends had dressy Diwali dinners, preceded and followed by gambling. No one gambled the rest of the year. But Diwali was, well, Diwali. As the dinners went on for a whole month and were held every day except Diwali Day, when celebrations were family affairs, dates had to be cross-checked, invitations handwritten, envelopes licked shut and posted to friendly addresses all around Kanpur.

My father's lighting designs for his house were like no one else's. Our neighbors might believe in tiny and large electric lights running around their doors and bushes, but this would be too common for my father. He believed only in oil lamps and candles: candles in the verandas, and oil lamps outside, where a few drips would not make a mess. Not only did oil lamps line the roof and every parapet, but my father had railings of rough wooden branches built around the gardens, onto which dollops of wet clay were put at four-inch intervals. Small terra-cotta oil lamps were pressed into the clay and allowed to dry in place. On Diwali Day, oil was poured into the lamps from long-spouted jugs, and wicks that we had all helped make out of cotton wool were dropped in the center of each lamp.

Prayers began at dusk, and as soon as they were over, the first oil lamps were lit in the prayer room. We would rush out with these and use them to start lighting all the candles and lamps. Soon the whole house would be glowing. My father would set off rockets, and the children would be handed sparklers. Round and round I would spin with my sparkler, until the house and I felt like one big ball of glitter.

Just before Veena was born, Dadaji decided that he would not just paint the house but enlarge it to almost double its size. He would add an inner courtyard, two bathrooms, a new bedroom, a dressing room for his wife, a study for his girls, a dining room, a pantry, a storeroom, and a long back veranda that aped the one at Number 7 in Delhi.

He consulted my eldest sister, Lalit, about the study. What color would she want it? After poring over color charts, she came up with mauve. For the molding, she suggested gold. And why not? We probably had the only mauve and gold study in India, with a desk and chair made to my father's specifications.

Dadaji got even bolder with the dining room. He was a grand designer at heart, saddled in this life with a ghee factory. The dining room was large and rectangular, about thirty feet in length. First he had the walls covered with thick plaster. Then, while the plaster was still wet, he had the workmen go in with stiff, round brushes, stick them into the thick plaster, and twist them slightly to form rosettes. Once the plaster dried, he had the walls painted a bright salmon pink. While his friends held back their dismay, he fearlessly went further and had the painters spray the rosettes whimsically with uneven showers of gold. Every day, when we had returned from school, we were glued to the daily developments in the dining room, unable to tear ourselves away. There was a fireplace in the dining room as well, and all the lighting fixtures were European Art Deco. We were so proud.

My father ran all manner of contests here in that room to teach us table manners. One of them was aimed at keeping our starched white damask napkins as clean as possible. The *dhobi* (laundryman) came once a week, and the napkins had to last us for seven days. As our breakfasts were generally Western, the napkins fared pretty well except for the occasional bit of egg yolk. Lunches were Indian, and on weekdays we ate them in school. Dinners were often a mixture of what we called "English" food and Indian food. We might start off with soup—a tomato soup made with our overabundant produce and served with slices of bread, nicely crisped in the oven—then go on to an Indian course, *rogan josh* (goat with cardamom), beet curry, okra with onions, and whole-wheat chapatis, and end with a freshly made jam tart which our cook prepared to perfection.

There were many places to slip up here. The napkins could pick up dabs of tomato from the soup. With the Indian course we were in really dangerous territory. We ate this course with our hands, naturally. My father would put his meat, with its sauce, in a *katori* (small metal bowl), which sat on his plate. First he would eat the pieces of meat with his chapati. Then—and he really loved this combined flavor—he would ask for the bowl of beets, add some of the sauce from the beets to the meat sauce, and scoop it all up with more chapati.

Naturally, I wanted to do what my father did. But there were some slip-ups, and traces of beet sauce with the dreaded yellow turmeric would find their way to the napkin. My father and mother both lectured us, "Only use the tips of your fingers to eat. . . . You must not dirty more than the first digit. . . ." We were offered finger bowls after the Indian course, but we dunked once and then used our napkins. So my father started checking our napkins, and whoever had the cleanest napkin at the end of the week was declared the winner. Always anxious to win, I stopped using my napkin altogether. In emergencies, I used my frock. My father soon put a stop to that, but with another such vice he was a bit more encouraging.

This had to do with bones. It started one cold winter day when we had just eaten a chicken curry for dinner.

The chickens were always bought live, usually by my father. I remember going with him to the poultry market, where the birds were kept in rope cages. While the poultry man held on to the squawking chicken, my father's long fingers with their beautifully shaped nails would advance towards the bird, go through the feathers, and begin probing and prodding. He said he needed to feel their breasts to see if there was any meat on the bones. The chosen bird would ride back in the car with us, still squawking away. The slaughtering was done at home, near the grapevines— it was thought that the blood would make the grapes redder. Then the chicken was plucked and taken to the kitchen, which was at the end of a long, covered walkway. My mother would go there in the early evening to "start off" the cooking. Standing there perspiring, her cotton saree tucked between her legs, she would take some of the seasonings already chopped or ground by the *masalchi* (human spice-grinder) and throw them into the hot oil in the *pateela* (cooking pot). Cardamom, cinnamon, bay leaf, cloves would go in, then some sliced red onions, then a ground mixture of onions, garlic, and ginger. This would be stirred around with a sprinkling of water until it was all golden. Some freshly ground cumin, coriander, and turmeric would follow. Not too much chili powder, as my father could not stomach very hot food. Now the chicken pieces, all cut and skinned, would be added and stirred and stirred. My mother always said that the secret of a good curry lay in browning the spices and meat to just the right degree. Then she would add water and salt and leave. Her job was done. She could bathe and get dressed for the evening. The finishing of the chicken curry was left to the cook.

Needless to say, such lovingly made food tasted good to the last bone. I enjoyed all of the chicken, but I loved the bones and would suck them and chew them until there was almost nothing left. This particular day, I was still chewing on a bone when everyone got up from the table to listen to the radio. I followed, bone in hand, still chewing. My mother gave me an angry look, commented on my bad manners, and asked me to return to the dining room and leave the bone on my plate. I was considering complying when my father came in with "Let her chew on the bone. She probably needs it." And from that day on, I was allowed to chew on bones until they were reduced, in the case of chicken at least, to smithereens.

Marrow bones from a goat curry were another matter. All flavored with cumin and coriander and onions and ginger, with the dark marrow popping out, they were glorious, and we all wanted them. My parents had bought two sleek silver marrow spoons to take the marrow out, but the problem was, there were never enough of the marrow bones themselves to go around. We just had to take turns: "You had the marrow bone yesterday, so it's MY turn today."

All of us sisters liked to read. We could be caught all over the house in the weirdest positions: legs flung over the back of a wicker chair, book on chest; lying flat on the *takht* (divan) on our stomachs, book on floor; head down on the desk, book an inch from eyes. Sometimes we read in the garden. As it got darker, my mother would ask us to come in. Lalit and Kamal listened. I went on reading until Bauwa yelled, "If you go on reading in the dark, you will end up with glasses."

Eventually, my eyes were checked. Sure enough, I needed glasses. Another woe! I would never be a pretty girl. Meanwhile, my sisters, already teenagers and already dainty and lovely, pranced around in their new multicolored wedge-heel shoes!

Around this time, my parents became very friendly with a doctor. She was always referred to as a "lady-doctor" and was the only respectable female I knew who worked. I immediately resolved to be a doctor. I followed Dr. Chandrakanta around whenever she visited, admiring her firm manner, her large watch, her sanitized smell, and her simple handloomed sarees. She was not married, as all the women around me were, and had a clear sense of mission. I so desperately wanted to be her.

EIGHT

*My Caring, Reticent Sister • The Useful
Club • The Death of a Cousin*

A s the girls got older, the responsibility for our general welfare fell more and more on Lalit. It probably started with homework and then crept up from there. My mother could hardly help us with schoolwork, as it was all in English. Lalit had already gone over what Kamal and I were studying, so we naturally turned to her. And, of course, it was her own nature to help us out. She began to choose the patterns for our dresses and coats, she remembered our birthdays, and at Easter she made sure I got a prettily decorated Easter egg from the Goan bakers at Valerio's, which she knew would make me giddy with joy.

Once, when we were all playing on a high pile of rolled-up winter quilts, my youngest sister, Veena, tumbled down and broke her arm. It was Lalit who held her and telephoned my parents, who were away at a dinner party.

Perhaps because of this responsibility for her sisters' wellbeing, and because she was a teenager in a walled-up compound, she began disappearing into herself, into some inner recesses where I could not always follow her. When she spoke, if the subject was anything other than intellectual or of a household nature, I felt that more was left unsaid than was said. I was so used to unburdening myself of every last emotion that, as I got older, I began noticing her reticence more and more. I remember, years later, asking her in some desperation, "But what are you feeling? What are you FEELING?" She had learned to keep her feelings to herself. She never stopped being a very caring, loving older sister to me, listening to every last outburst of mine through the years, calming and soothing me, but her own heart remained private.

And then a cousin died. This was the first death in our joint family, and it left me desolate. I was about seven years old.

As we moved seamlessly from Kanpur to Delhi, we would take up with the cousins who were of similar ages to us as soon as we got there. The cousin who was closest in age to me was Brijesh, the second son of my father's youngest sister, Kiran Bhua. We would climb trees together, eat *chaat* (spicy snacks) together, and go for walks to the Yamuna River, hand in hand. I even started dressing like him, in boy's shorts. Best of all, we had started a club together.

A few years before, when we had both been sitting under the stairs that led to the roof of Number 7, we decided to cement our friendship by forming a very private club with just two members, him and me.

"What would the club do?" I wondered.

"Well, it could collect something," Brijesh ventured. He had a fine nose, thin well-shaped lips, and thick dark hair.

What might we collect that mattered deeply to us? The answer was clear. It would have to be stationery. We both loved stationery. Special stationery. And so began the collection of The Useful Club (which I have to this day)—pens that could write in six colors, matching sets of silver pads and pencils for keeping bridge scores (all the cousins played bridge, starting around the age of six), pencils with tassels, boxed gold pencils, sleek wooden rulers, erasers that looked like toffee. . . . It was decided that I would be in charge of this collection and that it would be housed in the large bottom drawer of a cupboard my mother kept in our Kanpur bedroom. Of course, whenever I visited Delhi for the holidays, I would bring the collection with me so we could examine it and add to it.

Lalit went on a trip to Delhi, I think with my father. The rest of us stayed behind in Kanpur. This is the story she told on her return, and it is permanently etched in my head: It was the afternoon of a very hot day, and most of the household in Delhi were napping. She was sitting alone on the long front veranda when she noticed a stray dog with a strange gait meandering down the front drive. The next thing she remembers is hearing screaming and sounds of a struggle. She ran through the opening in the henna hedge into the south courtyard. There, in front of the bedroom of my middle uncle, Shibbudada, was the dog, growling, frothing at the mouth, and clutching Brijesh's hand. She tried to shake the hand free, but the dog's teeth were firmly embedded around Brijesh's thumb, so it took a while. In the meantime, she yelled for help, but not before getting a lot of blood on herself as well. Family and servants came running, and the dog was ultimately captured for examination in case it had rabies.

Lalit and my father left for Kanpur. It was in Kanpur that we got the call from Delhi saying that the dog did have rabies, that Brijesh was getting his rabies injections, and that Lalit should get them, too.

Lalit got her shots at the hospital on the way to school. I would go in with her. She would have to lie down and expose her stom-

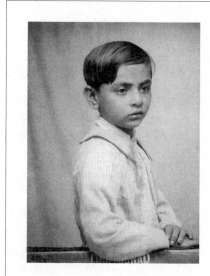

My cousin Brijesh, aged about four.

ach. The biggest, thickest needle would be poked slowly right into her soft belly. The medicine went in slowly, too. Her face expressed her agony, but she did not make a sound. I wanted to cry for her but did not dare. It seemed to take forever. I would think of Brijesh, too. He was so much younger. The same would be happening to him.

Some months later, we learned that Brijesh had rabies and that he was in a hospital. The injections had not worked for him. It happened sometimes, they said. We got daily reports from Delhi. It was an agonizing death, they said, complete with hydrophobia and all the havoc that rabies wreaks. He cried for water but could not swallow a single drop.

NINE

*Divided Loyalties • Preparing for War • Film
Buffs • The Nazi Connection • Wolfie and the
Gray Horse • The End of the Kanpur Idyll*

World War II was in full swing, and it was testing loyalties. My father's undefined ambivalences were seeping into all of us. We trusted our father enough to want to think like him, but what was he thinking?

First of all, there was the British Army in Europe, fighting the Nazis. Thousands of Indians were fighting along with them and were dying daily, just as they had done in World War I. We would get the reports: so-and-so's son was killed in Italy; so-and-so's brother was killed in Turkey. This was not in the British press; we just heard it. Indians were dying for the British while we, as a nation, were fighting the British in India for our independence. We were fighting nonviolently, under the guidance of Mahatma Gandhi, but we were fighting nonetheless. Although we wanted the British to win in Europe, we wanted to be free of them in India.

The British Army was also in the jungles of Burma, skirmishing with the Japanese, who were advancing towards India. Fighting along with them were seven hundred thousand Indians, many of them Gurkhas, who were dying daily, too. Now, in the same Burmese jungles, fighting *with* the Japanese and *against* the British, were Indians of the INA, the Indian National Army, whose leaders were such heartthrobs that, when they were captured by the British and tried in Delhi's Red Fort, all teenage Indian girls cried their hearts out. The INA hoped to march into India with the Japanese and free the country.

Meanwhile, much of North India, and this included us, was preparing for war, with air-raid drills and blackouts. We did not know who was going to bomb us, but we were ready. By the early 1940s, our windows and skylights had black shades on them. My father had trenches dug all along one side of the house, and we were fully prepared to dive in at the slightest hint of warfare from any quarter.

Life continued, however, and as a family we went to the movies almost every week, partly to take our minds off the war. The name "Bollywood" had yet to be invented, but Bombay Talkies was a major Bombay studio of the time, and we managed to see every film it made, even its "war-effort" films, which studios around the world were producing en masse then, each from its own national point of view. Bombay Talkies films were decidedly pro-British. We saw "war-effort" British films, "war-effort" American films, and "war-effort" Indian films, or whatever was showing at the picture house. We were film buffs. My father once declared, "Joan Crawford is a very handsome woman." I did not know until then that a woman could be called handsome.

In those days, each movie concluded with a recording of the national anthem, then "God Save the King." Everyone was supposed to stand up as soon as the Union Jack waved on the screen. Well, after he had seen the pro-British "war-effort" film, and enjoyed it, my father's form of protest against British rule was to walk out as soon as the flag appeared. His wife followed him, and the girls, like little ducklings, waddled behind them in support. Here, at least, we had devised a clear procedure to follow.

A much more serious issue was my father's cousin and dear friend, Guru Chacha. Guru Chacha had gone to Germany to study. There he had fallen in love with and married a German girl, Toni Aunty. As the drumroll for the war began, Guru Chacha took to the German airwaves, on the Nazi side.

My poor father was appalled. He glued himself to his large Phillips radio, hand on dial. There would be electronic whining and static, and then my uncle's voice would come forth, as clear and sharp as ever. "Guru is on. Guru is on," my father would cry hysterically. We would all come running. My mother would make sure that my father had a cup of tea or a whiskey in hand to calm him down. We listened to Guru Chacha and then to the BBC, talking of the same war.

I remember Guru Chacha and Toni Aunty returning to India after the war, after Indian independence. Guru Chacha had put all his savings into buying a large machine that he was convinced would make him a fortune in the new India. It was a doughnut machine.

Poor, lost Guru Chacha. Post-independence India, however sweet-toothed, did not take kindly to doughnuts, and his venture proved quite ruinous. The last I heard of them, he and Toni Aunty had turned to some Indian religious group for solace and peace.

During the war years, we had also acquired some unusual protection in the shape of a dog. My mother had, until then, clung to the old Hindu school of thought that all animals were dirty, germ-carrying creatures that should be kept outside the house. She was not prepared for Wolfie. Wolfie was a German shepherd, and he was not, strictly, ours. His original German master, Karl Schneider, had come to work in my father's factory as a chemist, but once the war started, he was interned, and I never saw him again. Before he was carted off, he begged my father to take care of Wolfie. My father begged my mother, and she ultimately relented. And so we got our first dog.

The war also brought us a horse, a dappled gray-and-white beauty that I loved. We could no longer go to school in our car, as there was a shortage of petrol and it was strictly rationed. My father hired a tonga, a very simple horse carriage, to take us back and forth. That particular horse, attached to that particular carriage, had the inexplicable tendency to fall down, just give up and lie prone on the road, at the oddest moments, leaving the carriage part high in the air with three girls in pigtails, identical blue tunics, and white blouses screaming their heads off. My father had enough of this arrangement and ultimately bought his own horse and a very fancy high-off-the-ground red tonga painted on the sides, with an equally fancy get-out-of-the-way, tinkle-tinkle bell in front that the turbaned coachman could depress with his foot. The stables, where my adored gray horse could rest on straw, were near my father's office, so this gave me another destination to walk to every day as I did the rounds of the gardens. After every tonga ride, the horse needed to be walked. I would walk along with him, admiring my father all the more for being the most stylish man in the world.

Our cocooned idyll in Kanpur, such as it was, came to an abrupt end in 1944, when my father decided to leave his job and return to Delhi.

The pull of Delhi, with my grandfather tugging at the strings, had been constant, and now Babaji was getting really old. My father's guilt was mounting. There were probably other triggers, but I never really understood them. All I know is that the announcement seemed sudden and my mother was heartbroken. She cried almost constantly for a month. We would go to visit my parents' friends for farewell parties, and my mother would end up in a flood of tears. My father seemed distracted, as if his eyes were confronting a hundred ghosts. Both my parents seemed to know that perhaps the best part, the most independent part, of their lives was coming to an end. Henceforth, they would be mere cogs in a joint-family machine controlled by other, more domineering figures.

Schooling, that constant problem, was a consideration again. While my parents and I and my baby sister would be joining my brothers after nine years of on-again, off-again companionship, we would be leaving my two older sisters behind. They were to start off in a school in Kanpur and then, after two years, transfer to a boarding school, a sister convent, in the Himalayan hill-station-beside-a-lake, Nainital.

There was one concession that my father did wrest from my grandfather: we would have our own house. No, not in New Delhi, a respectable distance away, as my father had wanted, but just across the street from my grandfather, on the inner corner of that same road named after my grandfather, a much smaller, rough-and-ready house, one of two my grandfather had built as rental properties, Number 5. We could live there, but we would still have to eat all our main meals in Number 7.

TEN

Spellbinding Shibbudada • *Two Tragic Marriages* • *Sadness and a Conspiracy of Silence*

O ur lives in Delhi, during the eight years when we were also in Kanpur, had continued apace but had an entirely different flavor.

If there was one man around whom the sun and the moon rose and set in our joint family, it was Shibbudada, my father's middle brother, who lived at Number 7. If he smiled upon you, you swelled with confidence and security. If he ignored you or looked down on you, you withered on the vine. If his gaze and generosity flowed in your direction, you thawed immediately. If it did not, you would have to depend upon your own inner resources. Some invariably fared better than others. We all felt only as good as the benediction he bestowed on us.

As an infant, he had suffered a strange accident. My grandmother Bari Bauwa was transporting him from one town to another in a bullock cart and had fallen asleep, holding him in her arms. As her grip loosened slightly, one of the baby's feet, which had been dangling outside, began scraping against a wheel. Over the course of the journey, most of his arch got rubbed away. He healed, but was saddled with one oddly shaped foot.

He was not as tall or as good-looking as my father or his eldest brother, Chand—the tallest of them all, who was an engineer by profession, and usually away in the Eastern states of Orissa and Bihar. What endeared Shibbudada to most of our world was his vivacity and ebullience, which he could turn on and off.

He had grown up to be his mother's darling—indeed, the darling of his brothers and sisters and the whole town. He wooed those he favored with overly generous gestures and a determined intensity, charming them with his deep and genuine passion for Indian classical music, Persian and Urdu poetry, and his well-honed raconteurial skills. He could hold you spellbound.

As a young man he had come across a beautiful, delicately framed Kayastha girl and fallen passionately in love with her. I never met her or saw any photographs of her, but could well imagine what she might have looked like, as this same uncle, tidal force that he was, continually made plans to bind her family to ours with irrevocable ties by arranging marriages between her relatives and members of our family. Her youngest sister would marry a cousin, and her niece is now married to my eldest brother, both marriages arranged courtesy of Shibbudada.

He was determined to marry his love, but there was the slight matter of the horoscopes. They did not match. Though priests were cajoled, they would not budge. They predicted not the usual vague "seven years of bad luck," but a disastrous marriage ending in the quick death of the bride.

Shibbudada was too deeply in love and unstoppable. The marriage took place, and six months later the bride died of typhoid. Shibbudada was still a young man, and after the few years allowed for bereavement, his family began suggesting that he marry again. He kept saying no. They kept asking until they wore him out, and he told them to go ahead and arrange it.

In those days marriages were nearly always arranged, and it was the bride's side that sent offers to the families of eligible young men. Shibbudada was highly eligible—he was a very successful lawyer then—and marriage offers were pouring in. One offer from a family in Agra looked promising, and my aunts, my father's sisters, were sent on the delicate mission of checking out the young lady in question. They so wanted to get it right and make their adored brother happy again.

The story gets a bit hazy here. This is the version provided by an eyewitness, my aunt Saran Bhua (my father's second-youngest sister): She and some of her sisters were asked to go to a house in the Old City of Agra and to climb the stairs to the roof. The possible bride-to-be would be on an adjacent roof, or on a roof just across a narrow lane (there is some confusion here), and available for viewing. The possible bride-to-be appeared and was dazzling. According to my aunt, dusk was approaching, the sun was just setting behind the possible bride-to-be, and perhaps they missaw. Or were they deliberately deceived by the old bait-and-switch trick? No one dared assign any blame, as it could have fallen anywhere.

Throughout the wedding ceremony, the bride had her face covered by her *ghoonghat* (veil), as was customary. When the *ghoonghat* was lifted, it revealed a decidedly plain, slow-gaited, heavy woman. It did not reveal the wit and intelligence the woman possessed in plenty, but, whatever he saw, it was enough to make my poetry-spouting, beauty-loving middle uncle hate her for life.

He hated her enough to shift to his own separate quarters. As far back as I can remember, his wife, Taiji, was left to find solace in the middle room, between our northeast room in Number 7 and that of my grandfather's southeast room. My middle uncle, meanwhile, lived in the annex across the south courtyard. He hated her but he still had four children with her, one of them a harelipped baby that neither one of them could stomach. My dear, softhearted mother breastfed this baby until he died.

Shibbudada's children, who seemed initially to take after their mother, did not appeal to him. He ignored them. It was as if they did not exist. In a joint family, this was hard to do and easy to do. As he was the self-designated Pied Piper for the family's young hordes, he could, in general terms, be arranging fun and games for all of them while actually showering his loving glance on just a chosen few. Like a magician drawing a rabbit out of a hat, he did magical deeds for all the children, eliciting from them whoops of delight.

Nothing excited me more than an announcement by Shibbudada that he had asked the *khomcha-wallah* over for our Saturday tea. That was akin to telling a Western child that he could have a whole candy shop for the entire afternoon.

A *khomcha-wallah*, as it happened, had nothing sweet to offer. His normal habitat was the street, usually busy thoroughfares. Here he would wander eternally, or so it seemed to me, a basket balanced on his sturdy head, a cane stool tucked into the crook of his free arm. Whenever the crowd seemed promising, he set his stool down, lowered his basket to rest on it, and then began hawking his wares.

The basket was a mini-shop, containing a category of food

unknown in the West—hot sour-and-savory snacks known through much of North India as *chaat*. The food was half prepared, and many permutations—of ingredients, seasonings, sauces, and dressings—were possible. If one asked, say, for *dahi baras*, the *khomcha-wallah* would take split-pea patties (they had already been fried and soaked in warm water, which also got rid of their oiliness) and put them on a "plate" of semi-dried leaves. Then he took some plain yogurt beaten to a creamy consistency, and spread it over the top. Over the yogurt went the salt and one or more of the yellow, red, or black spice mixtures that sat in wide bowls. Those who wanted a mild cumin–black pepper–dried mango flavor got only the black mixture. Those who said gleefully, as I did, "Make it *very* hot," also got the yellow and red mixtures, filled with several varieties of chilies. If we had an extra craving for a sweet-and-sour taste, we would ask for a tamarind chutney. A wooden spoon would disappear into the depths of a brown sauce as thick as melted chocolate. It would emerge only to drop a dark, satiny swirl over our *dahi baras*. As we ate them, the *dahi baras* would melt in our mouths with the minimum of resistance, the hot spices would bring tears to our eyes, the yogurt would cool us down, and the tamarind would perk up our taste buds as nothing else could. This to us was heaven.

It was a taste of heaven with many emotional ifs and buts. We would watch our three cousins, Shibbudada's two sons and daughter, jumping around in general glee with the rest of us, but every now and then they would throw a quick glance at their father, their large dark eyes begging for another kind of crumb. Perhaps a hug, a touch of the hand. They never got it. The worst part was that we were all Shibbudada's unwitting accomplices. Because he made himself indispensable, we all wanted a piece of the Pied Piper. The children joined what the elders, perhaps bur-

*Pied Piper–like, Shibbudada gathers together his own children and many of us
cousins in the lovingly cultivated garden of Number 7. I am hiding behind the
chrysanthemums, busily chatting.*

dened with the responsibility of having arranged the match at all,
had already established, a conspiracy of silence on the subject of
Shibbudada's behavior towards his family. The *chaat* was heavenly for sure, but the aftertaste was slightly bitter.

Every now and then Taiji, Shibbudada's wife, would send one
of her children to their father to wish him good day or ask for
something they needed. It was, at times, just her desperate way of

trying to reach him. She seemed to love him and want him to the end. The child would stand uncomfortably, like a stranger, at his annex door. Sometimes the child would be asked in, and sometimes there would be a summary dismissal.

From a very young age, I lived with this constant possibility of emotional havoc. After every such destabilizing incident, I would need to bury my head in my mother's starchy saree or my father's tweedy coat. Most of the time, my father was not there. He would travel with us on the train to drop us off in Delhi, say salaam to all, and return to his work in Kanpur. Besides, Shibbudada was his worshipped, godlike older brother. Dadaji never, *ever*, questioned him. My mother's position on the joint-family totem pole was lowly. She was the youngest daughter-in-law in a household where the only women who were expansively comfortable were my all-powerful grandmother and her visiting daughters. This was not my unassertive mother's turf. She merely watched and felt a lot, but was too restrained to speak. I could not say anything, either. I had to learn to live as if this mayhem were not happening at all.

ELEVEN

*My Gang • Fishing, Shooting, and
Swimming • The Watermelon Fields •
Ear-Piercing Antiseptic*

My cousin Rajesh, the one who rushed for his air gun after my toast was snatched away by the kite, was Shibbu-dada's youngest child. He was just a little bit older than me, and as he always lived in Delhi, I spent nearly all my time with him whenever I was there, especially after Brijesh's death. I also played with other visiting cousins my age, who all happened to be boys. Mahesh was the eldest in our gang. He had soft greenish brown eyes, was the son of my father's youngest sister, Kiran Bhua, and was to grow up to be a very prominent nuclear scientist. Then there was Lovy (Ravi, actually), my aunt Saran Bhua's oldest, who was to become a geologist, and his younger brother Shashi, who seemed to resemble my strapping grandfather, according to old photographs that I had seen. There was Suresh, the youngest son of my third aunt, Prem Bhua, and, of course, Rajesh. This was my gang.

It was Rajesh who taught me how to fish and shoot and swim. These were, supposedly, boys' activities, but as I hung around only with boy cousins—the girl cousins and my sisters being

A family group gathers for a formal portrait, complete with couch, on a picnic in about 1940. My grandparents sit in the center. I am in the front row with my "gang" (left to right): Suresh, Lovy, me, Rajesh, Mahesh, and Shashi. A turbaned bearer stands top right, waiting on us all.

much older—I seemed destined for the periphery. I could watch the boys play cricket and sometimes, as an indulgence, be allowed to bowl underhanded or even bat. But when the boys had their matches, I could only watch.

While I was still little, fishing, too, was out of my reach. It seemed to be an exotic male ritual in which I could play no part. Oh yes, I could stand around as the boys went under the *beri* (jujube tree) to dig for their earthworms. I was not allowed to dig them up myself. I could watch them attach lead weights to their fishing lines to make them sink, and pieces of cane to make them float. But when I said, "I can do that," no one listened.

The year I turned five, all this changed, thanks to Rajesh. "May I come with you this time, please?" I had asked him.

"No," was his initial reply.

The Yamuna River was just across the street below us, and our little world was considered quite safe for children to wander about in, as long as we did not actually go into the water. The boys would pack their gear, and off they would go whenever the sun relented.

"Why?" I had persisted.

"Because you are a girl."

I hated being unfairly limited. "But I can do everything you can."

"No, you can't. Why did you scream so much yesterday when we were digging up earthworms?"

"Because you cut an earthworm in half with your spade and both halves were wriggling."

"The boys didn't scream."

"I'll get used to it. Please let me come fishing with you."

In the end he relented, and I donned my boy's shorts. Rajesh even threaded a worm on my hook for me, and when I caught my first fish, a freshwater eel so snakelike that I dropped my rod and ran in fear, he put his arm around me and calmed me down. It would be easier the next time, he said.

It was Rajesh who taught me to shoot as well: since I could fish, perhaps I could shoot, too. "Hold the gun up. Higher, higher. Now close one eye. No, not that eye, silly, the other one. *Arey* . . . that . . . wasn't . . . bad." It turned out that I was "not a bad" shot.

We approached swimming quite another way. When winter winds blowing down from the northern Himalayas gave way to hot desert blasts from the south, we had three months to go into the river before the monsoon rains would make its waters rage and rise. Morning, before breakfast, was the best time. We would roll our bathing suits into our towels and start walking.

In the early years, when we were still small and threatening to go into the water, not just fish on its edges, the women came along. Sometimes it was Shibbudada who took us. Later, an older cousin was considered adequate.

We were all so familiar with the two miles or so of the Yamuna River that meandered just beyond our house. After all, we had grown up there and developed a proprietary passion for this stretch of sand, scrub, and water. We had charted every detail of its topography, felt it with our feet. *Our* patch of the river started to the north with the Bund, a stone embankment that tried, quite fruitlessly, to prevent the river from flooding in our direction during the monsoon season, and ended, south of our house, with a small temple that had steps leading down to the water. Between the Bund and the temple were stretches of sand and rock we felt we owned.

It seemed to be the tradition in Delhi that, although the men and boys could swim in the river, the women and girls could only bathe and "dip." When the women came with us, they wore their sarees, soft summer greens and pinks and yellows. They would take off their *chappal*s as soon as they hit the sand and then walk into the river fully clothed. Here they would sit down in the water, their heads disappearing beneath the gentle waves. All that could be seen were their sarees, greens and yellows and pinks, billowing and puffing up around them. This was a "dip" and about as far as the women went. They would take one or two or three dips. If the day was really hot, they might sit around in the water for a while and then just walk out, their sarees now clinging to their plump, voluptuous bodies. All this time the boys swam and the girls splashed about.

There was no formal place for ladies to undress, and it was not expected. Centuries of custom had taught the women to improvise individual tents around themselves with their fresh, dry sarees. Inside this handheld enclosure, they could slip out of their wet clothes, their modesty fully guarded. Moving arms, elbows, legs, and knees kept the outlines of the tents in constant motion. Heads would emerge, followed by arms and clad torsos. Soon the dry sarees, having performed their changing-room functions, would be wound around the body—once, twice, and, with a flick of the hand, the heavily embroidered ends would be flung over their left shoulders.

The wet hair would be unwound. The ladies would then bend their bodies forward so their hair would fall over their faces and almost touch the ground. With towels stretched between two hands, the wetness would be beaten out and the hair flung back again. Then the call would come, "Out of the water. Time to go home." After a brief stop at the temple to have cooling sandalwood paste smeared on our foreheads, the group would amble back.

I knew that I would never be content with "dips," so I turned again to my cousin Rajesh. He had studied swimming at Modern School, the same school where my brothers had gone. He streaked through the water like a torpedo, and I wanted to do the same.

We started with the watermelon.

Across the river from the Bund, up beyond a sand embankment, were the watermelon fields. Most summer mornings, we would lie together in our beds and talk to each other through the mosquito netting. As indoor ceiling fans barely made a dent in the relentless heat, we were all driven out of our rooms to sleep at night on the front lawn. Twenty or so beds would be lined up between the jujube tree and the hedge near the tamarind tree in two or three rows, gauzy rectangular containers, each holding a prone body. The first rays of the sun and the incessant chattering of birds would bring the prone bodies to life. We would begin making plans for the day. "Let's go and get a watermelon," a cousin would suggest. Someone's mother, overhearing us from another row of beds, would add, "Take Jai Singh with you. He will help you carry it back."

Jai Singh was Shibbudada's personal manservant, whose accrued special status resulted directly from the special status of his master. Because Shibbudada's say carried weight, so did Jai Singh's. Like most of our servants, he was from "the hills." "The hills," a British euphemism for the Himalayas, the highest mountains in the world, had, scattered across them, thousands of small, picturesque, but impoverished villages where farmers' children walked barefoot in the snow and families kept warm in winter by huddling on the floor just above their animals. Some family members stayed behind to tend the fields, but most of the young men came down in droves looking for work on "the plains."

Many of them worked for us and were housed in a long row of servants' quarters that ran west from the tamarind tree. Jai Singh was one of them. A fine-looking man with a chiseled nose and small piercing eyes that saw everything, he could have been, had he been educated, a leader of men. In his present situation, he was shrewd and calculating and a possessor of many family secrets.

Once, when he was escorting us to the river and I had jumped off a rock onto a jagged piece of glass, he had run all the way home with me in his arms. As I bled and cried, he tried to amuse me by imitating my lisp. I cannot actually remember that I lisped. And I do not even know why I remember this incident at all, as I must have been about three at the time. But I do have a clear image of Jai Singh's face, smelling of the *bidi*s (small cheroots) he smoked, bending down over me, laughing at me as he ran up the steep road that curved around to the front of Number 7, and teasing me with, "Say *khirki* [window] again. You can't say it now, can you? O.K., say it your way, *khilki*. Who says *khilki*, huh?"

With Jai Singh as escort, we had gone down to the river for a watermelon that day, when I was about five. He stayed on the near shore with our clothes while we donned our bathing suits and waited for the boat. It was a ferryboat, a big, rough hand-made wooden creation used mostly by the milkmen and farmers who brought their products to the city for sale. The ferryman stood high up at one end and used a pole to guide the boat across.

We were hoisted up and slowly taken across the calm waters. This was the summer guise of the river: during the monsoons it could rise and lash savagely at our cellar gates. On the other side of the Yamuna, we jumped down on our own, chased each other up the sand embankment, and made a run for the watermelon fields.

The watermelons seemed to grow right out of the sand. There they were, dozens and dozens of monstrous green balls, barely acknowledging the withered, browning vines they were attached to, just lying there, asking to be taken away from the burning sun and devoured.

We chose one, paid the farmer for it, and rolled it down the sand embankment to the edge of the water.

"Now," said Rajesh, "I will teach you how to swim."

He pushed the watermelon into the river. The giant fruit began to float. "Jump in after it and grab it with your hands," he instructed. "Keep your arms stretched and your head down. Kick your feet without bending your knees."

"I'll drown, I'll drown. The water is so deep in the middle of the river."

"No, you won't drown. We are all with you."

And so, with my cousins flanking me on all sides, I crossed the Yamuna River with the help of a watermelon. It was my first swimming lesson.

Jai Singh scooped me up on the other side. He threw towels on all our shoulders and carried the watermelon triumphantly home, where it was cut up and demolished. My grandmother pickled the rind. No signs of the fruit were left except the seeds, which were put in the sun and left to dry for future use.

It was during one of our summer trips to Delhi that I had my ears pierced. My finicky father would never agree to use one of the traditional women who came to the house and pierced ears with small gold hoops. They had done it all their lives, but my father insisted that they were untrained and unhygienic. He wanted us to go to a proper doctor who would use "clean instruments." So he marched all of us girls off to Dr. S. B. Mathur, the family physician, whose office was in Chandni Chowk, the heart of the Old City, and who knew as much about piercing ears as he did about existentialism.

The doctor took a deep, brave breath and got himself some needles and thread. He carefully sterilized these, dabbed our ears with antiseptic lotion, and shoved the fat needle and thick thread in. We screamed, as might be expected, each in turn, as our ears were violated.

When we arrived home, with the ugly knotted-thread loops dangling from our ears, my mother and grandmother immediately fell upon us with home remedies for "quick" healing. It was a process that went on three times a day for a month: Ghee (clarified butter) was heated in a *katori* (small metal bowl) with ground turmeric. The ghee turned a bright yellow color, but the aroma, I remember, was pleasingly earthy. Sticks taken from a clean broom were covered at one end with cotton wool and dipped into the boiling liquid, and the bright color was transferred to our ears under the guise of a hot fomentation. Turmeric was considered the best antiseptic that the heavens had provided. That it left an indelible color seemed to bother no one. For one month we went to school with cooked yellow earlobes, drawing the stares of all our schoolmates. My ears were so badly and unevenly pierced that I can barely wear earrings today.

TWELVE

The Drawing Room • Winter Evenings:
Family, Friends, Lemonade, Nuts, and
Pakoris *• Dining at the Long Tables*

O n each and every winter evening we spent in Delhi's Number 7, we would all gather in the drawing room, where Ishri, my grandfather's manservant, had already lit a fire. "It must have snowed in Simla," we would say, rubbing our cold hands and pulling shawls, cardigans, and coats closer to us. Simla, that much-loved Himalayan hill town where my sister Kamal had been born, was in the very distant North, but whenever it snowed there, icy blasts made sure we got the news.

No one in the Number 7 household had been blessed with much sense of style, so furniture bought wholesale at auction was shoved against all four walls. As you entered the drawing room from the gallery end, there was the radio around which we huddled to hear Hindi movie songs at midday and cricket commentaries in the afternoons. Beyond it, on the same north side, was a big sofa, above which hung a large framed print of Hope sitting, head bent, on top of the globe, playing a lyre. In the corner was a kind of organ that could only be played by pumping wind into it with a pair of foot pedals. Then, as you turned the corner to the east side, there were overstuffed chairs galore, of disparate designs. On the wall above them, attempting to give them some cohesion, was a tinted, rather nicely framed photograph of my grandfather, looking quite Edwardian—Raj Narain, Barrister-at-Law. Next, on a stand and enclosed in glass, was a miniature marble reproduction of the Taj Mahal, near a potted palm on a stand. On the south was the fireplace with a mantel that held a rather lovely Chinese cloisonné urn with dragons. On top of the mantel was a print of a young, free-spirited lady (European but with an Eastern abandon) gazing into a fishbowl.

Surrounding the fireplace was an upholstered bench. Farther into the room on the same south side was another large sofa, where my grandfather sat, and set around on the west were more overstuffed chairs. There was a Persian carpet of exquisite workmanship on the floor, which was also used as seating. The drawing room was, basically, a functional room that had been designed—or not designed—to hold a lot of people.

The evening routine in winter hardly varied, unless there was a religious festival, a wedding, or a music recital.

As sunset gave way to dusk, the air slowly filled with the perfumed smoke of *uppala*s, dried cow-dung cakes, which were being burned in hundreds of thousands of braziers throughout the city. This was, and to some extent still is, the winter smell of Delhi. As the cows mostly ate hay, that was what their dung smelled like: hay.

When the soft haze of *uppala* smoke began drifting through the glow of the setting sun, squawking birds by the hundreds, propelled by their own time clocks, would begin circling our trees in flocks, green-feathered parrots with red beaks, sparrows, yellow-beaked mynahs, and also the dreaded crows. They would fly round and round above the mighty tamarind, the umbrella-

Cousins Rajesh (left, here in my grandfather's favorite seat) and Suresh in the drawing room of Number 7.

shaped jujube, the mulberry near the gate, the medicinal neem, and the mangoes. As they circled, they would come lower and lower, disappearing, as night fell, into the darkness of the foliage. You could still hear them for a while, though, chattering noisily, and then there would be quiet. Outside, there would be darkness, perfumed faintly with *uppala* smoke.

Ishri would light the fire in the fireplace, then hobble off to prepare my grandfather's hookah, his hubble-bubble water pipe, a fairly formal floor-standing version. I would follow Ishri, because the odor of that wet, dark, manly-but-sweet tobacco drove me wild. Ishri would make a ball of the tobacco and deposit it in the top section, the chillum, of the hookah. Over this he would arrange small pieces of burning charcoal and blow on them repeatedly until they glowed, his cheeks puffing like a toad as he did so.

My white-bearded grandfather, supporting himself with his cane, would come through the door that connected his room to the drawing room and settle down in his accustomed place on the right side of the sofa. However old he may have been by this time, he was still king of the household. Ishri would put down the hookah and set a whiskey and soda on a small table near it. Babaji would draw on the hookah, and a roll of gurgling sounds would follow as the air went through the water in the pipe. He would then take a sip of his whiskey. It was the start of another winter evening at Number 7.

The women, freshly washed and changed into their evening sarees, would follow, coming in from various doors, one after another. The first two of them were generally commandeered by my grandfather to sit at his feet on the Persian carpet and play chess, or more often, Chaupar, a form of Parcheesi that used three long rectangular dice shaped like sticks of Kit Kat chocolate. He would direct the game; the women played it more to please him than each other.

The children, having finished their sports or their homework, wandered in as well. If we passed my grandfather, he would dip a finger in his glass of whiskey and give us a lick. We were known to queue up for these licks. The men returning from work would start dribbling in as well. If Shibbudada happened to come through the door—which was rare, as he was generally out at musical events or bridge parties or at the Roshanara Club most evenings—the air in the room would instantly get supercharged. He nearly always came in demanding our immediate attention. "Look what I have for you! These are dates from Iran. Sweet, sweet dates. Embedded in each one of them are the best walnuts you can ever hope to eat. Take a bite. Just take a bite." Yells and shrieks of delight would follow. Taiji would look up at Shibbu-dada with fresh hope, forgetting for the moment the years of unfulfilled expectations.

This was the social part of our day, and we never knew who might visit. No one needed to call before showing up. Mostly it was relatives, both close and distant. There was no formality, only familiarity. Om and Shant—green-eyed sisters and grand-daughters of Babaji's younger brother next door—might walk over to regale us with their wit or impersonations. Prema and Krishna, from Number 10, the daughters of my father's eldest and most beautiful sister, Bhuaji, might stop by. Prema and Krishna were about Lalit's age and identical twins. One wore glasses, the other did not. They were born as triplets, but only two had survived. I remember once when Prema and Krishna arrived, Prema was not wearing her customary glasses. As we looked quizzically, they told us that they had gone to a guru who had given Prema special eye exercises to do at dawn every morning while gazing at the rising sun. She had done the exercises religiously, and now she was cured! She was, indeed.

Other than the unassailable family rule that you always gave your chair to anyone older than you, seating was very much by the grab-what-you-can arrangement. Generally, the grown-ups settled into all the plump sofas and upholstered chairs while we cousins draped ourselves where we could, on the arms of the sofas, the carpet, and the bench by the fireplace.

All social occasions are fueled with food and drink, and our winter evenings in the drawing room were no exception. The men were offered whiskey-sodas, the women tea, and the children squashes and lemonade. Squashes and lemonades were not what the words might suggest. Squashes were fruit concentrates sold by the bottle. You poured some into a glass, added water and ice, and you had a tolerable drink. But I disliked squashes intensely. The Glacier brand that we drank was manufactured in the Himalayan foothills by close family friends. (My father had once wrested a superb marmalade recipe from them.) However, even that refused to endear these lifeless squashes to me. Now, lemonades were another matter.

In the mornings, as we sat sunning ourselves on the front veranda, we would hear a clip-clop of hooves and the cry of a hawker, "Lemonade-wallah . . . Lemonade-wallah." We would plead with our mothers to get some cases for the evening. A servant would be dispatched to the gate to signal to the lemonade-wallah that his wares were desired, and the lemonade-wallah, sitting atop his laden horse-cart, would come clip-clopping in.

Lemonades had nothing to do with lemons. They were carbonated drinks, sodas really, that came in special returnable glass bottles with marbles in their narrow throats. It was the marbles that held the fizz inside. Once the marble was pushed down with a stopper-shaped gadget, red or green or clear lemonade was there for the taking.

With the drinks were served the inevitable nuts. Nuts were warming, according to my mother, my grandmother, and all the ladies of the house, and winter was the best time to eat them. They were freshest then, too, having been harvested in the autumn.

These were not nuts you could grab by the fistful and shove into your mouth. No, you had to work for every one of them, as they came in their shells. The shells could be tossed into the fire-place, which was fun, but the peeling was sometimes harder. *Chilghoza*s (pine nuts) demanded the most time and concentration, and I liked them the best, especially the untoasted ones with their soft white flesh and green inner core. My preference then ran to walnuts, especially the *kaghzi akhrote,* or "paper-shell" walnuts. They could be crushed between two hands without the help of a nutcracker. As I picked out the flesh from the mess of crushed shell, my mother would remind me, "Always eat walnuts with raisins or you will get . . ." "I know, I know," I would answer, "a sore throat." There would be peanuts, too, freshly roasted in *karhai*s (woks) filled with sand, and pistachios from Iran, the best in the world.

The nuts were not always enough. So a servant would be dispatched to the distant kitchen for plates of *pakori*s, vegetable fritters made by dipping vegetables or slices of them in a spicy chickpea-flour batter and deep-frying them. We would shout in the general direction of the servant's departing back, "Ask the cook to make extra green-chili *pakori*s." The *pakori*s were eaten by most with fresh green-mint chutney, but for those of us who wanted to set our mouths ablaze, a bite into a hot-chili *pakori* after a bite of the sliced-potato *pakori* was the perfect pairing.

Soon all the guests who did not live at Number 7 would begin to depart, and my grandfather would take his last sip of whiskey and say to no one in particular, "Have the food put on the table." After a while, the servant who had taken the order would return, salaam my grandfather, and announce, "*Sa'ab,* the food is on the table." We would all get up and start ambling towards the dining-room annex in small groups.

In the dining room, there was a long, formal dining table and, joined onto it, two other dining tables of decreasing quality.

There was a chair for my grandfather at the head of the formal table, a chair for my grandmother to his left, and more chairs for the grown-ups on either side. Farther down, at the tables of lesser quality generally reserved for the children, chairs gave way to benches. We children were so far away from the head of the table that I did not know until I was told years later by my aunt Saran Bhua that my grandmother was a vegetarian and that she had invented the East-West dish spicy cauliflower with cheese that we all loved so much. We could hardly hear or see what was going on at my grandfather's end. We made note of Babaji's bobbing white beard, but we were too busy with our own discussions to pay the upper end of the table much heed. I did know one thing, though. My grandfather did not drink water with his meals. He drank club soda. We saw it being poured.

Whatever was cooked in the kitchen's large *pateela*s (pots), it came to the dining room in recurring serving dishes, two or three to each of the tables. There was hardly a question of courses. Everything savory was part of the main course and came to the tables at the same time. Fresh fruit, and sometimes carrot *halwa* in the winter, followed.

Winter dinners often included game, as the men were avid hunters. There might be duck or partridge or quail, some with pellets still inside them, cooked with rich cardamom-flavored sauces; or my father's favorite, leg of wild boar, cooked for a whole day in beer. But most of the time it was the usual goat-and-potato curry, a standard and much-loved staple. Accompanying it might be cauliflower with peas, carrots with fenugreek greens, and some spinach, all to be eaten with *phulka*s, little puffed whole-wheat breads. We rarely had rice at night.

Special needs were not overlooked. A sick child might need a soup, or once, when Taiji was on a diet to control her ballooning weight, her meat was boiled, and instead of eating it with Indian bread she wrapped each morsel in lettuce leaves.

I began to notice a disturbing pattern. Very often, choice pieces of meat were missing. Marrow bones, pieces of fish-shaped muscle—where were they? I would look around in the serving dish and find nothing I wanted. Then I would see Taiji emerge from the kitchen with a small bowl and quietly spoon out these choice pieces to just her own three children, Raghudada, Sheila, and Rajesh. Easily indignant and unable to deal with what I perceived as unfairness, I would look up at my mother, but she would blink her eyes, suggesting I be quiet.

At night, as I undressed for bed, I would complain bitterly to Bauwa, but she would hush me up—Taiji's room was just next door—and say something like, "You had enough to eat, didn't you?" or "Once we get back to Kanpur, you can have whatever you want."

If Taiji was trying to compensate her children for their emotional deprivations by giving them choice foods, this could be written off as one of the smaller ripples created by Shibbudada's behavior towards his family. As we all got older, the ripples would reach further and further and enmesh Shibbudada's family and ours in the worst tangle of human relationships.

THIRTEEN

*Family Picnics in Delhi • The Art
of Getting Thirty People into Two Cars •
Cinema Trips • Story Time*

We all looked forward to family picnics in Delhi. They helped to cloud nagging worries, to take our minds off the daily grind.

The best time was winter, when the days were sunny and crisp, but the monsoon season, with its romantic, cool, moisture-laden breezes, was just as attractive. Our chosen destination was rarely some glorious wilderness. No, when we were in Delhi, we preferred familiar territory, perhaps the well-tended garden of an eighteenth-century tomb or a twelfth-century palace on the outskirts of our own beloved city, which affirmed our deep connection to the land and its history, our sense of entitlement. The entire family would go on the picnic. During my childhood it did not occur to me that families came in sizes smaller than thirty people, swelling beatifically to a few thousand at the mere hint of a grand event.

Preparations for the picnic would begin at dawn. All the short ladies of the house—and they were all short—would begin scurrying around in the kitchen. One would be stirring potatoes in a gingery tomato sauce; another, sitting on a low stool, rolling out *poori*s (small puffed breads requiring deep-frying) by the dozen; yet another would be forming meatballs with wetted palms. Pickles had to be removed from pickling jars, fruit packed in baskets, and disposable terra-cotta *mutkaina*s—handleless cups for our water and tea—given a thorough rinse.

I would run from the kitchen, where the smells would serve as a reminder of future pleasures, to where the servants were packing the charcoal and the *ungeethi*s (braziers). From here I would make a dash for the garage, where the trunks of the cars were being coaxed to hold the dhurries, sheets, pots, pans—indeed, a whole *batterie de cuisine pique-nique*. The servants were all masters at it by now and carried on with military precision.

Two cars, the gleaming Dodge and the Ford, would stand at the ready in the brick driveway, with Masoom Ali, Babaji's fez-hatted driver, giving last-minute flicks with a dustcloth to the cars' exteriors.

The art of getting thirty people into two cars had long been mastered. The first layer consisted of alternating short ladies and teenage children, with the teenagers sitting perched on the edge of the backseat. On their laps went the slim ten-to-twelve-year-olds. The third layer, sitting on the laps of the second layer, consisted of those under ten. The tall men and servants sat in the front seat. On their laps sat the fat ten-to-twelve-year-olds, holding all the baskets and pots that could not be stuffed into the trunk.

The cars would grunt and groan but always start. The Ford would lead the Dodge through the northern Kashmiri Gate of the Old City, past the St. James Church, built by a nineteenth-century Anglo-Indian, past Shah Jahan's seventeenth-century Red Fort, and out of the Old City through its southern Delhi Gate. Soon we would be traveling along the wide, tree-lined boulevards of Lutyens's New Delhi. It was from here that British governors-general and viceroys, known by the Indians as "Laat Sa'abs" (Lord Sahibs), ruled from their own Lutyens-designed pink sandstone palace in a setting that one Englishman described as "the court of the Great Moghul run with the quiet precision of the court of St. James." Beneath the entire four-and-a-half-acre palatial building (the palace is now the official residence of the Indian president) ran a full Edwardian basement, a downstairs to the upstairs, replete with domestic offices, sculleries, bakeries, larders—even a press to spew out streams of menus. Bands played when these viceroys came down to dinner, with one particular ruler choosing "The Roast Beef of Old England." (We children *did* get something out of all this. Whenever someone was acting too grand, we would put him down with "Don't be such a Laat Sa'ab.")

Our cars would now head towards open fields of mustard and millet (the mustard and millet of my childhood have given way to concrete as the city has grown from fewer than a million to over twelve million). Well before we got there, far away in the distance, standing upright like a welcoming beacon, could be seen the tower towards which we were heading, the Qutb Minar, built in the early thirteenth century by the first Muslim dynasty to rule Hindu India.

The cars would pull up beside the gardens and unload their passengers. The short ladies, coming out last, would inhale the fresh country air and, with their hands, try vainly to iron out their now very crushed sarees. While the children rushed to climb the tall sandstone tower, the short ladies would amble to the base of the tower, touch it to establish that they had been there, and, having exerted themselves enough, amble back to the garden to pick a site for the picnic. A large blue-and-red-striped cotton dhurrie would be spread out, and a slightly smaller white sheet laid on it.

From the top of the tower, we children could survey all the Delhis below us with a certain degree of propriety. This was our city: there was the thirteenth-century Delhi of the Khilji dynasty, the fourteenth-century fort of the Tughlak dynasty, the fifteenth-century tombs of the Lodhi dynasty, the sixteenth-century tomb of the Moghul emperor Humayun, Shah Jahan's seventeenth-century mosque, and then British India with its elegant avenues and circular shopping center, Connaught Place.

Soon our eyes, impelled by our stomachs, would settle on something closer—a brightly edged cotton dhurrie over which hovered some familiar short ladies. We would think of the meatballs cooked with cumin, coriander, and yogurt and come thundering down the hundreds of steps.

As we settled cross-legged on the edges of the dhurrie, the servants would lay out the freshly heated food. We rarely used plates or cutlery for eating. Instead, we would take two *poori*s at a time, using the first as a plate, a kind of medieval trencher, and the second to make our little morsels.

Meanwhile, Jai Singh would be making tea in a kettle set on top of an *ungeethi* (brazier). After our meal, we would hold out our handleless, disposable terra-cotta *mutkaina*s towards him, making sure to wrap them in our handkerchiefs first so our fingers would not burn, and Jai Singh would pour: steamy hot tea, milky and sweet, so hot that we would have to start by breathing in tiny little sips.

Indian movies encouraged another kind of picnic, a mini-picnic of a more informal, impromptu nature. When we were in Delhi, we never saw movies with our parents, only with our cousins. An older cousin acted as escort and was given the task of buying tickets, generally for the upstairs balcony.

Movies were just an extension of storytelling, which was second nature to most of us in the quill-and-ink set. We did not grow up with bedtime stories: that sort of cozy intimacy was hardly possible with twenty or so bedded-down children. We grew up more with the family huddle in the middle of the day. We would drag an aunt or an uncle to a sofa and drape ourselves all around them, on the arms and back of the sofa, on the carpet below, on their laps, a little hillock of overlapping bodies, hanging on every word. "Please, please, tell us another story." My family's fund of riddles, poems, and anecdotes seemed endless. My aunt Saran Bhua's husband was an accomplished golfer who impressed us no end with his plus fours and beret. He was hardly home from a round of golf when we would corral him to regale us with several folksy tales told in the *purabia* dialect of his home state, Uttar Pradesh. One story that we loved to hear again and again had to do with the trip he'd made to England with an Indian athletic team. At a grand dinner, all heads of foreign delegations were asked to sing their national anthems in "their native languages." "What could I sing?" he would say. "Our national anthem then was 'God Save the King' and it was in English. So I sang this . . ." And he would proceed with his rendition of a folk song that he had taught us all, so we could join in: "*Bibi maindaki ri, tu tow pani may ki rani*" ("O lady frog, you are the queen of the waters").

My cousin Mahesh's paternal grandmother looked most dignified and formidable with her shock of white hair, her straight back, her peg leg, and her cane, but her whispered tales rocked us with giggles, as they were full of the naughtiest scatological humor. Shibbudada's yarns were either about musicians and the training of musicians—"So-and-so could not look his guru in the eye, he was not allowed to play a single note for ten years"—or about hiking across the Himalayas, another of his passions.

We children made up our own stories, too. Sometimes they took the form of plays, which we enacted for our enthusiastic elders, setting up curtains, arranging seating, and even selling tickets. No mean reviews here! Our very first play, when our proportions must have been diminutive, used the space between the four legs of a rolltop desk in Shibbudada's annex as a stage! This was still in the days of innocence, well before I had learned to question my contradictory uncle.

Filmgoing was just another step. We liked all movies, but going to Hindi movies had added benefits. These Indian films were particularly conducive to whetting our appetites and then to satisfying them. They generally lasted about four hours, and whole families, including infants, would come to view the mythological-historical-tragicomical musicals. There was a great deal of yelling, crying, getting up, singing along, and sitting back down among the audience throughout the show. Certainly no one minded the noisy unwrapping of paper cones containing *chane jor garam*, small chickpeas that had been flattened and roasted, then flavored with cumin, chili powder, sour mango powder, and black rock salt. We would munch on the chickpeas as we watched Hanuman, the Monkey God, fly across an indigo sky dotted equidistantly with hundreds of five-pointed stars, all cut from the same stencil.

During the long intermission, we would all go in a horde to buy potato patties, *aloo ki tikiya*s, from vendors who had carefully posted themselves just outside the cinema doors. These patties, a Delhi specialty, depended for their unique flavor partly on the way they were cooked and partly on the spices in the stuffing. They were not deep-fried, they were not shallow-fried. Instead, they were pan-roasted.

Each vendor carried a brazier on which he had set up a very large, barely concave, round cast-iron griddle (*tava*). Patties that were ready to sell sat waiting on the outer fringes, staying warm until needed. Those that were still cooking were in the center, sizzling away in the few tablespoons of oil that pooled in the middle. In one pot were the vendor's seasoned mashed potatoes, and in another the stuffing, made out of highly spiced split peas that had been cooked until they were dry and crumbly. To make a patty, the vendor would pinch off a ball of mashed potatoes, flatten it into a small patty, pinch off a smaller ball of the stuffing, place it in the center, and cover up the stuffing with the potato to make a ball. The ball was then flattened and slapped onto the griddle.

The squatting vendor kept turning each patty this way and that until it was reddish brown and completely crisp on both sides. By this time our mouths could almost taste the *tikiya*s. As soon as he got the order, the vendor would place a patty on a leaf, split it open into two parts, and smother both with sweet-and-sour tamarind chutney. We would carry these hot patties back into the dark cinema house and eat them as we watched Hanuman trying to rescue Sita, the good queen, from the clutches of the demon king of Sri Lanka.

FOURTEEN

*Summer Holidays in the Hills • The
Great Exodus • Grandmother's Magic Potion •
Mountain Picnics • The Taste of Ecstasy*

During the same eight years that we shuttled between our
homes in Delhi and Kanpur, our summer holidays, three
or more glorious months of them, were spent in "the hills." The
official version of this custom had started in 1864, when the
British government, unable to suffer the heat of "the plains,"
moved the entire administration up to Simla, in the central
Himalayas, for the "summer"—a good six months, from April to
early October. Seventeenth-century Moghul emperors, also
originally outsiders from colder climes, had set a precedent. In a
mighty cavalcade of elephants, horses, and camels, these Moghul
rulers had traveled annually even farther north, to a lake-filled
valley in the heart of Kashmir, Srinagar. Once there, they had
quickly declared, "If there be a Paradise on earth / It is this, it is
this, it is this." For the English, who governed India first from
Calcutta and then from New Delhi, a similar cooling respite was
provided by the hill town of Simla.

Known as Shimla today, the area, in the state of Himachal
Pradesh, once contained a few small hamlets and, on top of the

highest peak, Jakko, a temple dedicated to the goddess Kali. Though it was sparsely populated by humans, nature was fully represented in its resplendent glory, providing stately forests of deodars, pines, and oaks, and a profusion of rhododendrons that climbed all the way up to the snowline.

The early nineteenth century was to see a war here, first between local chiefs and the Nepalese Gurkhas, and then, when the British came to the aid of the chiefs, between the Gurkhas and the British. Leading the British to their final victory was Major General Sir David Ochterlony, the same gentleman who would insist on hiring my grandfather's grandfather in Delhi somewhat later. The first cottage was built in Simla in 1819 by an assistant political agent for the hill states, Lieutenant Ross. As more and more English officials visited, more and more British-style cottages with very British gardens sprang up to accommodate them. The main road was called the Mall, and the town developed the feel of a British transplant.

Around April and May, when scorching *loo* winds swirled hellishly in the plains, Britons began leaving in droves and heading north. Army battalions were stationed in the hills for the summer so they could rest and recoup. British businessmen tried their best to flee the plains, but if they could not, they sent their wives and children. In the government, everyone from the viceroy down to the petty officers packed their bags and traveled to the Himalayas. The viceroy had a domed sandstone palace in Delhi to stand up to the grand remnants of Moghul architecture. In Simla he took refuge in a more English mansion with a countrified name to match its countrified look, Viceregal Lodge. As the High Court moved up, too, my grandfather, an eminent barrister, followed. His business was now in the hills. Besides, it was cool and much more pleasant.

Babaji was the head of the family, and if he moved we all moved.

Oddly enough, he never built a house in Simla or in any other hill station. He rented, instead, not one large house but two or three adjacent ones, according to the number of people expected that year. These houses, nestling in the mountains and surrounded by sun-kissed dahlias and hydrangeas, with semi-British names like "Choor View" and "Pentland," came with only basic furniture. This meant that everything else, including the servants, had to come from Delhi. The contents of kitchens, bedrooms, bathrooms, along with toys and games, were all put in trunks, canvas "holdalls," baskets, and bundles. The whole army of forty or so people—all in a state of excitement, as we loved the hills—would then embark on the annual exodus. We would take the overnight train to Kalka, in the foothills of the Himalayas, which, at twenty-four hundred feet above sea level, already hinted at the pleasures to come. There we would have a British Railway breakfast in the waiting rooms—generally, slightly greasy eggs, toast, and tea served on heavy railway crockery—and then pile into the eight or nine cars that had been hired for the four-hour drive.

The first sight of the Himalayan peaks towering over the plains, range after purple range, was exhilarating enough. But as the procession of cars started up those hairpin bends, as the air got cooler, as we saw the first pines, the first ferns, the first waterfalls and gushing mountain streams, as we climbed to six, seven, then eight thousand feet above sea level, as the first mist licked our cars, all of us, separately and together, felt that this was our Paradise.

Some of us with delicate constitutions got a little nauseous on those hairpin bends. No need to worry—my grandmother had a cure. She would call a halt to the moving procession. "Jai Singh, Jai Singh, where is the lime pickle?" she would yell out. Everyone would start jumping out of the cars. A break felt good.

Jai Singh, who knew where every last spoon was located,

would quickly get his hands on the to-be-opened-on-the-journey basket. There, in a crock, would be Bari Bauwa's homemade lime pickle. Black with age and with black pepper, cloves, and cardamom, it was my grandmother's magic potion. When she ministered tiny portions of it, nausea just vanished. She had many such tricks up her sleeve. Once when I was stung by a bee, I yelled with pain and my grandmother came running. The next I knew, she was stroking my afflicted cheek and reciting some Sanskrit verse. I could not understand a word, but it cured me right quick. She was a useful short lady to have around.

As new houses were rented each time, the first thrills were provided by the exploration of their nearly always damp and musty, unaired interiors. How many bathrooms? What sort of toilets? Enough tables to play bridge and rummy? Oh well, the floor would do. Was there a glazed veranda? We could not live without a glazed veranda.

Glazed verandas were enclosed with glass windows to protect them, when necessary, from the cold and from monsoon downpours. When the sun shone, all the windows could be flung open. Most hill houses had them, either running on one side of the house or, if we were lucky, on all four sides. We children lived in the verandas and sometimes slept in them, too. They gained such a grip on our psyches that when my husband and I bought our country house in upstate New York, the first room I added, to take advantage of southern and western exposures, was a hill-station-style glazed veranda!

Once everyone had settled in and unpacked, the children were pretty much left to themselves, to explore mountain pathways, to

I (second from left) stand next to Veena, aged about eight. Sheila leans over me. Lalit is on the extreme right, with Santoshjiji beside her. We are at one of our Himalayan rented residences, with glazed veranda in the background.

hike, bicycle, ride, and walk. No cars were allowed beyond a base point on most hill stations, including Simla, so we all had to move our own bodies around. It was considered healthy and, along with the fresh air, the main reason for our going there.

We, my boy cousins and I, might decide to go to the Wood Bazaar (Lakkar Bazaar) and order new yo-yos. Here we would marvel as the carpenter, using just a lathe, transformed a block of wood, right in front of our eyes, into any size yo-yo we requested. He would then lacquer it in the colors that suited us that day. I could never twirl and unfurl the yo-yos like my boy cousins, or make them "walk" or "talk" or whatever else the boys did, but I could hold them in my hands and admire them, shining, smooth oranges and pinks and blues. We could take a walk past Scandal Point and the Ridge, past the Gaiety Theatre (where many years later I was to film the theater scene in the Merchant Ivory movie *Shakespeare Wallah*), go to the tallest peak in the region, Jakko Top, and stare at the hundreds of monkeys that gathered there around the Temple of Hanuman to stare right back at us.

The only organized activity in the "hills" was the mountain picnic, which was quite different from the city picnic.

The picnic site was carefully chosen weeks in advance, usually by Shibbudada, who was well versed in the terrain and remained our majordomo in the hills. Sometimes it was a distant mountain peak, several ranges away; at other times it was a thunderous waterfall in a deep valley; once it was a mountain stream rushing through a remote gorge. Ordinary picnic spots, where most mortals went, were never considered good enough. No, not in the hills. Our spots were picked not only for their natural grandeur but for their inaccessibility in terms of distance or the climbing required.

Preparations for the picnic would begin weeks in advance. Rickshaws and hill palanquins (*daandees*) were arranged for the old and the infirm, and horses for the riders. The ladies of the house, plus numerous servants, spent many days preparing the food. Baskets of mangoes were ordered from various North Indian cities: *langra*s from Benares for those who liked their mangoes tart; *dussehri*s from Lucknow for those who liked them sweet and smooth; and *chusni*s, small sucking mangoes, for those who preferred not to eat the fruit at all but, rather, to suck the juice straight from the skin. Litchis were ordered from the city that grew the juiciest, smallest-stoned varieties, Dehradun.

Boys wear pullovers and girls solar topees on a mountain picnic. Typical picnic fare would be curry patties and pooris, *the latter also used as plates.*

At sunrise, when the mountains were still shrouded in an icy mist, porters (*qoolis*), rickshaws, palanquins, and horses were all assembled. First the porters were loaded with baskets of food and sent off with a party of servants. The walkers—led by Shibbu-dada, who had a passion for hiking—would leave next. I chose to go with him but nearly always lagged behind, which made him very cross. Third were those who rode in the rickshaws and palanquins, and the last group consisted of those on horseback.

Clad in heavy sweaters, mufflers, and shawls, our large party moved slowly, making numerous stops along the way. If we passed an orchard, a stop would be called and the farmer asked if, for a certain sum, we might pick plums or apricots. My favorite

Family picnics in the Himalayas often involved long hikes. Here the walkers among us pose with Shibbudada (in the hat). I am in the front row, far left, resting on a very handy stick.

groves were those of almond trees. I loved green almonds, slit open and robbed of their tender white flesh.

We would generally arrive at our picnic spot around midday. If it was beside a waterfall or stream, the children were allowed to swim while lunch was unpacked. The mangoes were placed in nooks of the stream to cool, fires were lighted to heat certain dishes (and also to warm the children when they emerged from the freezing water). Then the meal, often including ground goat meat cooked with peas (*keema mattar*) and cauliflower cooked with fresh ginger, would be served, accompanied by tales of adventure and hilarious stories about our ancestors.

The best part of the meal was still to come. It was those mangoes, biding their time in the frigid waters. At the start of the season we had the choicest *dussehri*s and *langra*s, standard-bearers of the northern mango world, peeled and cut into slices by the women. By the season's end, all that was left on the market were the small, visually unprepossessing *chusni*s, the sucking mangoes. After lunch we would rush to the stream to peer at our final course, dozens of mottled yellow-green egg-shaped wonders, nestling on the pebbles just beneath the surface of the rippling, gurgling waters. We would each pick one out and roll it between our palms to soften the flesh and reduce it to juice. Then we would pluck off the very top, where the mango was once attached to a tree, put that top to our mouths, and squeeze. Cool and sweet, this nectar had the taste of ecstasy, the ecstasy of our summers in the hills.

Paddling in a stream on a picnic with Rajesh. I have
embroidered my shirt with a very stylish anchor.

FIFTEEN

A New School • Classmates in Burqas •
Hindi or Urdu: A Dreadful Choice •
A Lethally Sharp Pencil

Leaving Kanpur in 1944 had been hard, as we knew it was for keeps. None of us ever went back there except in our dreams. For months afterwards, I would wake up in our new, much smaller home at Number 5, crying. My mother would move from her bed to mine and say, "Were you dreaming of being in Kanpur again?" I would sob even louder. I felt I would never recover from the loss.

My life in our gardens, my shimmering Diwali oil lamps, my salmon-colored dining room, my intimate world—it had all come to an end. Verging on my teens, I had to face a bustling cosmopolitan city without my older sisters, who had been such calming companions. I did have my brothers now, but they were already in college, dealing with their own lives and loves. My baby sister, Veena, was too young for almost-teen conversation.

School, yet again, was a problem. My father first put me in what he thought might be a continuation of the tried-and-true convent school. He had me admitted into the Convent of Jesus and Mary in New Delhi.

I lasted a month. The school was cruelly segregated then. Education was carried on in two unequal "sections," the English and the Indian. My father must have got a guarantee that I would be put in the English section, which had better teachers and students, though the thought of my father wanting me to be there was demeaning enough for me. After just a few days in this English section, which had mostly English girls but a few Indian daughters of high government officials as well, the school decided on its own to transfer me to the Indian section. There were only Indians here, under an Anglo-Indian teacher named Mrs. Clock. I was even more confused and angry. No one in this section could read or write or add. Where was I?

I complained daily to my father. In the end, he pulled me out and put me into Queen Mary's Higher Secondary School. Even though not a convent, it was still a missionary school, run by lay Episcopalians for the rather unique purpose of educating "purdah girls," inner-city Muslim girls who wore the veil.

How such girls were educated at all was a wonder. Although our family was Hindu, we had, out of necessity, adopted many Muslim codes. Purdah, in its mildest version, had played its part. According to stories told by my two youngest aunts, my father's sisters Saran Bhua and Kiran Bhua, their father, my grandfather, had decided to send them to college, the same one he himself had attended, St. Stephen's College. Not so easy. First the girls had to get out of their house in the Old City, with its very Muslim sensibilities. My grandfather's grand phaeton was summoned to the nearest road that could accommodate it, and servants held up sheets on both sides of my aunts as they maneuvered the narrower lanes. Once they got to the college, where they were the only two female students, two chairs were placed for them as near the professor as possible. They could play tennis if they wished, but only with each other and after the courts were cleared of male students for the duration of their match.

By the time I went to Queen Mary's, Hindu girls certainly had much more freedom, but for Muslim inner-city girls, even getting to a good school was full of hazards. Queen Mary's solved the problem by sending a small, curtained horse-driven van to collect them. I remember that rickety van as it clattered back into the school grounds. A door at the rear would be impatiently shoved open from the inside, and a dozen or more girls—shadowy, unrecognizable forms swathed in white, dark green, or black burqas (body-covering chadors)—would burst out, hopping down one after another. Once inside the school doors, they would race down the hall, tearing off the constricting burqas as they ran. There was a special corridor leading to the back netball court where hooks had been strategically placed on both sides. This is where the burqas were hung—long, haphazard rows of shrouds.

Queen Mary's meant that in my schooling I was moving from a more Westernized Christian world to a more Indianized Christian one. The school was Christian in name and intent for sure. But because only the heads of the school were Christian, and Indian independence was already in the cards, Indians were more and more allowed to be themselves—Hindus, Muslims, Sikhs, whatever.

When I walked into the school, my first, seemingly insurmountable, hurdle was something else entirely. In the middle school, where I was to enter in the sixth class, all subjects— history, geography, mathematics, everything except English— were taught in either Hindi or Urdu, Indian languages that I had spoken at home since I uttered my first words but that I had never learned to write or read.

First I had to choose between Hindi and Urdu. Hindi was part of my Hindu inheritance, the language that had evolved from classical Sanskrit. Urdu was part of our Muslim culture, a hybrid that had actually developed in the bazaars of Moghul Delhi, my very own city. It used the grammar of Hindi but borrowed much of its vocabulary from Persian and Arabic. One was the language of my mother and the women of our house; the other, because of Delhi's peculiar history, the language of my father and most of the men I was related to. Partly inspired by Shibbudada's passion for Urdu poetry, I had actually studied the Urdu alphabet once with a *maulvi* (Muslim teacher) who would come to Number 7, make me whitewash a wooden board, and then, with a freshly sharpened *qalam* (quill) dipped in an ink that I made myself by dissolving ink tablets in water, teach me to write my alphabet— *alif, bay, pay, they, tay*. I had got as far as being able to read and write simple words.

It was a dreadful choice for me. I loved the elegant sounds of Urdu, but, employing perhaps the only gene for farsightedness I possessed, I opted for Hindi. Until then, to be among the brightest in my class had seemed almost a birthright. Yet here I was at barely twelve years of age, at the bottom of the class, struggling with a new alphabet. I was in the uniquely embarrassing position of not being able to read or write in school.

My father hired a Hindi master who came every other day on a bicycle. As our lives at Number 5 and Number 7 were hopelessly intertwined, it was decided that the best place for me to study quietly would be in one of the unused rooms in Number 7's south annex. Shibbudada's suite was at the river end; the room where I studied was at the opposite end. A table and chair had been set up there for the purpose.

The corner room of the south annex at Number 7, where I studied Hindi. The annex also housed extra bedrooms, the library (with the family history), and Shibbudada's suite. The garden is decorated with lights for a wedding.

I started with the Hindi alphabet—*a, aa, e, ee, o, oo.* I struggled. My masterji struggled. I was learning, but very slowly. Every now and then my youngest sister, Veena, who was about seven by now and in the same school as I was, would get on her bicycle at Number 5, ride through the Number 5 gate, cross the road, ride through the Number 7 gate, come down the long driveway lined with henna hedges, and wave at me through the door as I studied with Masterji. Masterji took to inviting her in, playing with her, and teasing her.

One day she came in and idly picked up my pencil as she and Masterji bantered. Masterji lifted her up and was teasing her when somehow, no one knew quite how it happened, the next thing I saw was the point of my pencil in his eyeball. I have always liked to keep my pencils lethally sharpened. He screamed in pain, Veena began to cry, and I felt miserable, because it was my pencil and my sister. He pulled the pencil out and dabbed his eye. I offered to call a doctor, but he insisted on going home right away. He did not return for several weeks. When he did, his eye seemed healed, but he remained so cross about the incident that he could barely teach. Soon he stopped coming altogether. That was the end of my Hindi lessons.

I was left too agitated to start again with another teacher. I told my father that I would manage. After all, anyone who knows the Hindi alphabet can read it. It is a completely phonetic, logical language. Of course my writing was pitiable, I read v-e-r-y s-l-o-w-l-y, and my knowledge of the more Sanskritized vocabulary that pure Hindi demanded was still nil. But I soldiered on. Within a year, I could just about keep up with my classmates.

SIXTEEN

Shibbudada continued to haunt my life with a presence I wanted and did not want. The seeds of the slow-developing rift between our families were also being sown.

It was not enough for Shibbudada just to ignore his wife and children. Every now and then he needed the warmth of a family, and he picked ours. We were all on the whole good-looking, well mannered, neat, and clean. He liked that. I remember him saying once to a roomful of listeners, hanging on his words, "He has such a thick, coarse neck, how could he possibly appreciate the finer things of life—poetry, music?" He made statements like that. Most people just laughed and went along.

All members of my father's family had thin, delicate necks. That must have been a plus. In my father he had an adoring younger brother who never learned to deny him anything he asked for. My mother was sweet, pretty, and pliant. We were his ready-made family when he needed us.

Shibbudada went further. Out of my parents' six children, he picked two to bless with his special glow, thereby driving small wedges into our family that would grow into bigger wedges.

Of the two brothers that my parents had left in his care, Shibbudada's favor was bestowed on the younger, Bhaiyyadada. My eldest brother, Brijdada, always a bit of an introvert, was quiet and thoughtful. He liked to paint and draw, not Shibbudada's interests. Bhaiyyadada was a total extrovert, full of jokes and fun, easygoing, and utterly charming. He was picked.

Among the girls, his eye fell on Kamal. Lalit was startingly beautiful, too, with wavy hair and dark eyes that glowed with intelligence. He liked her. But it was Kamal who had an unearthly, angelic innocence, and a face to match. I remember that, even at the age of seventeen, she thought babies came directly out of the stomach. Perhaps the convent's nuns could be credited with this bit of fantasy. She had shy, undemanding eyes, a fine aquiline nose, thin, well-shaped lips, and a firm chin. As her body began to fill out, it, too, followed a master plan of divine devising. Rather like the goddesses that cling to temple brackets, she managed a large bust, tiny waist, and rounded hips. She had it all. And, in our joint-family setup, she was Shibbudada's favorite.

Bhaiyyadada and Kamal could walk into Shibbudada's suite freely. He could be seen laughing with them, with his arms on their shoulders. They had an ease between them that few others shared. What his children and wife were thinking all this time can only be imagined.

Shibbudada had, some time back, given up his law practice. As he himself explained, his delicate constitution rendered him incapable of pleading the causes of thick-necked crooks forever. He had, instead, started a financing-and-leasing company of his own. The business was first quartered near Kashmiri Gate, and then, as it grew wildly successful, the family bought a building in

Kamal (left) and Lalit, leaning on the falsa *tree in the garden of Number 5.*

Lutyens-designed Connaught Place in New Delhi, and the business moved there.

On his way back from the office in the early evening, Shibbudada had taken to stopping off at Number 5, where my mother would ask him politely if he'd like some tea, even though we might have had our tea earlier. Our smaller meals were in Number 5 now, but for lunch and dinner we still went to Number 7. After his tea with us, Shibbudada would drive on to his suite in Number 7 to rest, change, and then go out for the evening. At this rate, his wife, Taiji, hardly ever saw him.

My brother Bhaiyyadada.

Once Taiji discovered that Shibbudada was making a habit of stopping off in Number 5 for tea, she started keeping a lookout for him from Number 7's front veranda. If she managed to spot his familiar two-toned cream-and-blue Chevy turning into our much smaller bricked driveway, she would begin walking slowly towards our house, a casual look on her face, as if she had just thought of coming over to greet our family. The weight of her large body would shift in heaves from one side to the other as she moved.

As Shibbudada settled down in our drawing room, I would look nervously through a window and see what I knew I would see, Taiji advancing along Number 7's red gravel driveway. My stomach would knot up in a state of the highest anxiety. I could barely get the tea down my throat.

When Taiji arrived, all bathed and freshened up for the evening, Shibbudada, as expected, would not greet her or look at her. He proceeded as if she were not there. My mother would sweetly pour some tea for her as well, while trying to ignore the prevailing tension. After tea, Shibbudada joked with us, asked us about school, told funny stories, and offered all manner of wonderful fruit—mangoes or cherries or litchees or loquats or whatever he had brought especially for us from the most expensive fruit shop in Delhi, Oriental Stores. I would be at a loss to know what emotion to project, the I-am-so-happy-to-receive-the-gifts look to Shibbudada, or the I-don't-want-them-take-them-for-your-children look to Taiji. My palms would begin to sweat. What I felt was acute misery.

After tea, Shibbudada would say a merry goodbye to us, get into his car, and drive off to Number 7, leaving Taiji to walk back slowly on her own.

My father had taken on the job of general manager at one of North India's largest sugar factories, in Daurala, just outside the city of Meerut, and so avoided this recurring scene in the family drama. Most of the time he was not there at all. My mother had stayed with us because of school, but we joined our father whenever we could.

In Daurala, my father, far from his powerful relatives, shut out that world and once again created one of his dream homes. The house was a sprawling but very basic brick structure, entirely surrounded for miles and miles by sugarcane fields. Way in the distance could be seen the outlines of a dense guava grove. Other than that, there was nothing but the blue of the sky, the chirping of birds, and the sounds of pumps gushing water out of the earth. The sugar factory was such a distance away that we could neither see nor hear it.

My father built a large chicken coop in the back courtyard, which was filled with plenty of baby chicks to greet us whenever we visited, and in the walled vegetable garden he had the gardener plant what seemed most exotic and desirable to us, strawberries. We visited Daurala only during our shorter holidays. My father missed my mother. He did not even know how to fall ill without her. If his temperature reached anywhere near a hundred, he would start moaning, "*Hai, hai.*" My mother's gentle ministrations were needed to calm him down. She tried to spend as much time with him as possible. Whenever she went, she took my sister Veena and me along. If it was vacation time, Lalit, Kamal, Brijdada, and Bhaiyyadada came, too.

Once we were ensconced in the house, our favorite destinations were the sugarcane fields, and, if we wanted a longer walk, the guava orchard. The sugarcane was so tall we'd get lost between the rows of stalks. The thin, long leaves scratched our arms. A field hand would cut us a cane, which we would peel with our teeth and proceed to crush the juice out as we chewed on one end. We could then wash our sticky hands at a water pump and perhaps wet our feet as well. Our brothers, if they were there, brought their guns along and shot at the little black *tiliyar* (rather like ortolans), which we all considered a rare delicacy.

Sugarcane was a winter crop, and so were the guavas. We grew some of the best guavas—large, round pale green balls—which my sisters and I liked to bite into when they were still jaw-breakingly hard. The softer, fully ripe ones we took home to my mother, who instantly made *chaat* out of them. It was easy enough to do. We would stand around, eyes glued to her hands, mouths watering in anticipation, as she peeled the guavas, the skin coming off in long snakes, and then cut them into dice. She put these into a bowl, adding salt, pepper, ground roasted cumin seeds, chili powder, lime juice, and just a tiny bit of sugar. She mixed all this thoroughly with her hands, sometimes sprinkling in a few drops of water so the spices would adhere better. Then she would serve the guava *chaat* to us on a plate and stick tooth-picks in as eating implements.

It was the toothpicks, used in the bazaars of Old Delhi in place of forks, that transformed homemade *chaat* into the illicit bazaar *chaat,* which my father had, with his repeated, ominous warnings, forbidden us to eat as it "carried diseases." Whenever we placed a piece of spicy guava in our mouths, we could taste the toothpick, taste the illicit bazaar. My mother knew just how to add extra flavor to a simple treat.

Sometimes my brothers, armed with their double-barreled guns and their twelve-bore cartridges, would hop onto the small sugarcane-trains that ran through the fields and head out for distant lakes, looking for ducks, or go on deer and partridge shoots. At night, after we had feasted on some of the game, I would go to sleep with the sounds and smells of my brothers cleaning their guns and talking excitedly to my father about the hunt.

One day my father asked us if we would like to go to the sugar factory. Sugar and sugar cubes were made here by the tons. This would certainly be more interesting than watching the making of hydrogenated cooking fat, though I must admit I did like seeing peanuts being pressed at my father's previous place of work. What Dadaji thought might draw our real interest this time was the tonnage of candy that the factory also churned out. He had always brought some home, and my mother had doled it out to us in small amounts.

At the factory, all such curbs vanished. Half the workers stopped working to greet the family, and each one pointed to hillocks of toffees, wrapped candies, peppermints, lemon balls, and said the same thing—"Take, take. Take as much as you want." We did. We kept eating candy as we saw the sugarcane juice being boiled and thickened, as we witnessed white sugar cubes neatly packaged into boxes, as granulated sugar came pouring out of large metal tubes, as we went up and down the factory's metal steps. In the end, we were so sick of candy that hardly any of us eat it now. Sad to say, in the course of that one single day I lost my sweet tooth entirely—or almost entirely.

My father, too, had probably had his fill of fat and sugar, as he eventually returned to Delhi and became the general manager of a cloth factory, Delhi Cloth Mills, also owned by family friends. From then on, instead of hydrogenated fat or bags of sugar, the household was never short of bolts of cloth acquired on the cheap.

SEVENTEEN

Visiting the Old City • The Lane
of Fried Breads • Monsoon Mushrooms

Whenever my mother wanted to visit her own family home, she said, "Come, *beta* [child], let's go to the City." We knew what that meant: a visit to our *nana ka ghar* (maternal grandfather's house). Her father and mother had lived and died in the Old City, in a house where her eldest brother's family still resided. I think that, to her, the orchard site of her in-laws, beyond the City's walls, beyond the northern Kashmiri Gate, would always be the suburbia of the la-de-da set into which she had, by good fortune, married.

It was usually just my mother, Veena, and I on these City visits. The ritual generally began on a Saturday morning. After breakfast, my mother would remove the big silver key chain clipped to her waist and open her locked cupboard. Inside was a State Express 555 tin, from which she would fill my father's silver cigarette case, tucking a row of cigarettes behind an elasticized band. The cigarette case would be clicked shut and handed over to my father, who hovered behind her. She would also remove some cash, whatever my father needed for the day, and place that in my father's palm. The cupboard would be relocked, and the bunch of keys tucked back in her waist. My father would stride off to the car waiting to take him to his office.

Freed of household duties, which my mother took very seriously, she would pull out her *attachee* case. Yes, that is how we pronounced it. I thought it was an Indian word. I did not discover its French connection until I was fully grown. Into this rectangular leather box, this *attachee* case, went a fresh cotton saree, my mother's knitting or sewing, a comb, and a few gifts. Then my mother would disappear into her dressing room with its three-mirrored dressing table, and change into a printed silk saree.

I never understood this. Some odd sense of propriety had convinced her that she should travel and arrive in silk, change into crisp cotton for the day, and change back into flowing silk to return home.

By this time my father would have sent the car and driver back for us, and my mother, smelling sweetly of Hazeline Vanishing Cream, would step into the car, *attachee* case in one hand, her handbag in the other.

My father almost never came with us or deigned to join us later in the evening. He had been raised in the Old City, but once he left it, it gave him no joy to return. A part of him viewed it as old fashioned, germ-infested, and dangerous.

The residential section of the Old City then, as now, was a maze of such narrow lanes that a cow and a human could barely pass each other. We would have to leave the car on a wider road at a fairly distant point with instructions to the driver about the time at which he could collect us at the end of the day. Then my mother and her two youngest children would walk. We would have to walk carefully, sidestepping sleeping dogs and oncoming

My mother, ever elegant, in the back garden in Kanpur.

cycle-rickshaws. If a shopkeeper decided to empty a bucket of dirty water onto the lane, we expertly hopped out of the way as we simultaneously dodged a man carrying a hundred cardboard boxes on his head. If my mother stopped to buy sweets for her family, she knew enough to keep an eye on her handbag at all times. If we saw a street-sweeper approaching with her wild broom, we held handkerchiefs to our noses so we would not inhale the dust she raised. My mother walked at a steady pace, one hand gripping the *attachee* case, the other (with the handbag) holding her saree a few inches off the questionable ground.

Our journey took us through the Lane of Fried Breads (Parathe Vali Gulley), where I always urged my mother to stop for a quick *paratha* (fried puffy bread) stuffed with fenugreek greens. There were two or three open-fronted shops, all with shallow *karhai*s (woks) set up almost on the street, right where passersby could be easily enticed. Inside the *karhai*s, bobbing in a lake of hot ghee, were three or four big, fat, puffed-up *paratha*s.

A word here about nomenclature. In our family, a small ball of whole-wheat dough, rolled into a flat round and deep-fried into a puffball, was called a *poori*. If it was stuffed with spiced split peas, it was called a *bedvi*. A *paratha*, on the other hand, was a flatbread, made on a *tava* (a griddle), somewhat like a pancake. Why, in this lane alone, a *bedvi*—or stuffed *poori*, if you will—was called a *paratha*, I do not know. And why, in this lane alone, was the *karhai*, however shallow, called a *tava*? Delhi was an ancient, idiosyncratic city. I never asked the questions, and my mother never explained. My preoccupation then was that the *paratha*s, or whatever anyone wished to call them, came stuffed with a choice of green peas, potatoes, fenugreek greens, chickpea flour, spiced split peas, cauliflower, or grated white radish. Which one, or ones, would I choose? To make the choice even harder, combinations were also possible. All were expertly spiced, all were utterly delicious.

The peculiarity of these shops was that they charged only by the *paratha*. This had been the tradition since time immemorial—time immemorial, in this case, being 1875, when the first of these shops-cum-restaurants opened. The vegetables and condiments served with the *paratha*s were free.

As my father frowned on all bazaar food, my mother at first

denied my request. But she herself was tempted by the smells and, if asked enough times, capitulated with a certain relief. "Just don't drink the water," she would whisper, convincing herself that now she had dealt with my father's fears. We climbed up a few steps, went past a billboard reassuring us that only the purest "real" ghee was used on the premises (as opposed to the kind my father had churned out in his factory), and took our seats at the rough wooden tables. A young man whizzed by dropping *pattal*s (plates made out of semi-dried leaves) in front of us. He came by again, ladling out the chutneys and pickles with equal speed: sweet chutney, made with dried green mango, dried pomegranate, and dried jujubes; sour chutney, made with fresh mint, green coriander, and grated white radish; and carrot pickle, made with carrots, yellow chilies, crushed mustard seeds, and tamarind. Already on the table was some salt seasoned with ground roasted cumin and crushed red chilies.

Before any real food arrived, we would start dipping our fingers in the condiments and licking them. Then came the vegetables—meats did not belong in such places—carrots stir-fried with young fenugreek greens; potatoes, and peas cooked with cumin, asafetida, and tomatoes; cauliflower with ginger and green chilies. As soon as the vegetables were on our plates, the hot, hot *paratha*s floated in, whichever we had ordered, all puffed up, ready to be deflated and devoured even before all the steam had hissed out.

My mother never allowed us to eat too much, as we were, after all, on our way to spend the day with her family. This was just a taste to tide us over until lunchtime. But what a taste it was—vegetarian, pure Old Delhi, and exclusively Parathe Vali Gulley.

We crisscrossed a few more narrow lanes before coming to the portals of our mother's family home, our *nana ka ghar*. There was no way anyone could gauge from the outside what the inside might be like. The well-worn wooden double doors were always shut. We would knock, and a servant girl would come to unlatch them to let us in. As the doors closed again behind us, the pace of life slowed instantly, and we seemed to enter an earlier world.

My *nana ka ghar* was of the same basic design as other attached houses in the Old City. All the rooms, on several floors, were built around an inner courtyard that served to let in light and air. Wealthier homes had several intricately carved stone courtyards, one leading to the next, some even with gardens and trees in them. But my mother's home was modest. One courtyard, plain, undecorated, and treeless, sufficed. The rooms were simple, too, with Moghul-style arched niches for closets, and seating either on low divans covered with white sheets or on the floor, with bolsters to lean against. The office room did have a desk, but it was the short-legged kind that required the writer to sit cross-legged behind it.

I must confess I thought then that my inner-city family and I had very little in common, though their undemanding, noncompetitive nature made them unusually comfortable to be with. What attracted me there was the food, which was uncommon, and, of course, witnessing my mother's relaxed pleasure at being "home." As in Kanpur, she seemed to be in control of her own life once again, falling into the pace of her childhood days with ease. Veena and I would climb up the narrow stairs to the roof. From here we could hear the hum of the city. If we spun around, our eyes could look down on family life in hundreds of courtyards that receded into ever-smaller sizes as they stretched into the distance. If we looked straight ahead in a southeasterly direction, our gaze would meet the grand dome and minarets of Jama Masjid, the seventeenth-century mosque. We could hear all the calls to prayer. Meanwhile, my mother changed into her cottons and settled down to knit or hem or attach a border to a saree—she rarely sat idly—and to catch up with family news.

There were few servants in this household, and the cooking was done mostly by my aunt, my mother's brother's wife, though all the women and girls pitched in, scraping bitter gourds, shelling green chickpeas, and pinching off small fenugreek leaves. My sister and I were rarely allowed to join, as we were considered "guests." We hung around, unable to tear ourselves away from the aromas.

One of the specialties of the house was a sauced dish of monsoon mushrooms. I never had them as good anywhere else. These were not the common white mushrooms now sold all over Delhi, though they were white in color. Called *khumbi,* they consisted of very slight three-inch edible stems topped with elongated narrow caps that closed in on themselves so no gills were visible. These mushrooms chose to spring out of the earth only when the rains poured during the monsoon season. They were so delicate—and expensive—that they were sold in baskets, heaped into little piles. Their texture was smooth and satiny, not unlike that of the fresh straw mushrooms I have since eaten, but only in the Far East.

My aunt Mainji, with her large protruding teeth, knew how to cook them to perfection. She always said, "There is nothing to it." There must have been something to it, because even my mother's *khumbi* were not quite like hers.

Mainji would take off her shoes, step into the kitchen, and squat on the floor in front of a brazier, blowing on the charcoal until it glowed to her liking. A pot would go on top of the coal, some oil next, and the cooking began. The mushrooms took but ten minutes and seemed to require only cumin, coriander, turmeric, and chili powder, but in some magical proportion that she alone had mastered. She prepared one dish after another. There was meat—all the men in her family required it, just as those in ours did—and several seasonal vegetables, each one more delicious than the last, tiny stuffed bitter gourds, okra with dried green mango, green chickpeas cooked in a pilaf, and pumpkin cooked with fennel seeds.

The pièce de résistance, for me at any rate, was the mushrooms. But would I get to eat any? Lunch was served quite late, and the men were always served first. Striped dhurries were spread out on a shady end of the courtyard, topped with a fresh white sheet. The men took off their shoes and sat down in a circle. The women served them, placing all the food in the center.

I would watch the mushrooms disappear, wondering if there would be any left for us. As the men served themselves generously, I would hold my breath. When it was our turn to eat, there were fewer mushrooms and more sauce. By that time I hardly cared. The sauce was delicious, too. I scooped it up with bits of my *poori* and just devoured it.

After lunch, some grown-ups napped; others sat in groups and talked. My sister and I went up and down the stairs, in and out of all the rooms, breaking off and eating a leaf of holy basil (*tulsi*) whenever we passed the plant near the prayer room.

For tea, Mainji sent out for some roasted white sweet potatoes (*shakarkandi*), some star fruit (*kumruq*), and some roasted water chestnuts (*singhara*s). These she made into a spicy *chaat* to serve with our sweet, milky tea. Then it was time to leave. My mother gathered up her needlework, freshened up, and changed back into her silks. *Attachee* case and handbag in hand, she walked out of her family portals, and we followed. We always returned a different way, partly because of where the car could park and partly because my mother still had some unfinished business in the Tinsel Bazaar (Kinari Bazaar) and in Dariba, the Street of Jewelers. In the first she picked up spice mixes like *chaat masala* from a specialty stall that has existed in the same spot for all of my life, and in the latter she checked on pieces of jewelry that she always seemed to have on order, bangles, rings, and necklaces. We made our last stop right at the end of Dariba, just where it met the main street, Chandni Chowk. This was at the shop that sold *jalebi*s, the squiggly, pretzel-like sweets filled with syrup. We liked them hot and crisp, straight out of the wok, and freshly dunked in syrup. The *jalebi*s would be served to us on a leaf, which we would carry to our car. Our sticky hands and sticky mouths would be quite busy throughout the journey home.

EIGHTEEN

I was settling into my life in Delhi. My father had joined the Chelmsford Club, the only advantage of which for me was its swimming pool. Rajesh and I would hop onto a bus at Alipur Road and slowly make our way there on most weekends. He would disappear into the men's changing room, I into the ladies', then we would meet to jump into the pool. Here he continued his swimming lessons, teaching me how to float and then to do the crawl. With my thin, weak ankles and wrists, I was indifferent at all sports. My body lacked muscular tone and strength. Physically, I was a weakling. At school, I had already been nicknamed the dreaded "bookworm." The only strength I possessed lay in my single-mindedness and in my dogged determination. The brain just pulled the body along. I managed not only to learn how to swim, but to love being in the water. I still do.

Something similar had happened with dance. Because of Shibbudada's deep love for Indian classical music, Number 7 had turned into a haven for India's foremost singers, sitar players, *sarangi,* sarod, and *shehnai* players. Shibbudada was an old-fashioned patron of the arts whose money went to support his passions. The artists were encouraged to stay with us, evenings were set up for private recitals, and all of Delhi's music-loving glitterati were invited to attend.

Some summer evenings, if there was a full moon and the light reflecting off the Yamuna River could add its own special brilliance, the recitals were held on the roof, but normally they were in the drawing room. Overstuffed chairs and sofas were pushed against the wall, and large white sheets spread across the Persian carpet for most people to sit on. A special area was set up at the fireplace end for the musician of the day to sit like a monarch— on the floor, of course—and pour out his enchantment. As these recitals generally started after dinner—musicians preferred to start late and then, if they were inspired enough, play into the early hours of the morning, ending with morning ragas—tea, cigarettes, whiskey, juices, ice cream, and betel leaves were served. Interrupting the music for anything more than that was considered déclassé.

At Number 7, music teachers had always been available to anyone wishing for them. I could not sing at all and gave up early. My older sisters had sweet voices and could carry a tune and so had been cast in every convent musical, whereas I, after a stint at the age of five as the Brown Mouse in *The Pied Piper of Hamelin*, had given up on the theater. All that St. Mary's Convent did in Kanpur were musicals, and I was not good at them. Out of all my grandfather's grandchildren, the most musical turned out to be the three that Shibbudada had produced.

They were angrily, passionately musical. Raghudada, the oldest son, played the violin. He was going to end up as a renowned statistician at the University of Chicago, but his love of both classical Indian and Western music would continue through his life.

Indeed, when my American husband, then a violinist with the New York Philharmonic, visited India, it was Raghudada who guided him in his purchases of classical Indian recordings. Rajesh, the youngest, played the tabla (hand drums). Sheila sang. Sheila may have reminded her father of her mother in her looks, but he must surely have been startled by her singing. He began to notice her for the first time.

Shibbudada's interest in music had not extended to dance, but one year, when I was thirteen, a South Indian troupe that performed temple dances, Bharata Natyam, an energetic, devotional form of dancing that North India had never before seen, was to perform in Delhi for the first time. The unknown dancers, with their troupe leader, Ram Gopal, needed a place to stay, and Number 7 was offered. I saw them practice each day and was entranced. I fell in love with Bharata Natyam.

It just so happened that some American tap-dancers were staying with us at the same time. At Number 7, a system of open hospitality was the norm. Poor relatives and artists (who were generally equally poor) could stay as long as they wished. One blind uncle—I never did understand exactly how he was related to us—came to us with his five daughters and did not leave until each of his daughters had been married off on our premises. Counting his blessings, he had married off two of them at one go. He lived in the same room that I once used for my Hindi lessons.

One magical summer night, while the Bharata Natyam troupe was still staying with us, we—and I mean the youngsters, as all those of my parents' generation were in bed—were all sitting outside on a lawn perfumed heavily with jasmine and Queen of the Night flowers, when an American tap-dancer, speaking to a South Indian drum (*mridangam*) player, said, "I am sure I can tap to any rhythm you can play." To which the *mridangam* player replied, "And I am sure I can play anything you can tap." And so began a night of friendly East-West competition that was to last until dawn. This was around 1945–46, well before Yehudi Menuhin came to India and any rapport between Eastern and Western music was established. The large *takht* (divan) outside was cleared of its mattress and sheets, exposing the bare wood, and the two "competitors" jumped up on top. It was an exhilarating, inspiring night. As the two goaded each other towards even more complicated rhythms and greater glory, all I knew in my heart was that I just had to learn how to dance.

And I did. Unfortunately, no one in the Delhi of that time could teach me Bharata Natyam. I had to settle for one of the two styles performed commonly in North India: Kathak, a dance form that developed in the Moghul court, and Manipuri, a soft, rhythmic, almost folk form that had developed in the Far Eastern Indian state of Manipur.

In the end, I learned both, one in school and the other through a private teacher at home. Once again, I was plagued by a lack of strength and stamina, but I learned enough to perform in minor recitals and to love dance forever.

For my first public dance recital, a school friend, Promila, and I were to do a duet in the Manipuri form. What should we wear? I suggested that we dress as local milkmaids. I, for one, knew exactly what they wore. After all, I crossed the Yamuna River in the same wooden boat they used, and many of them came to work in Number 7's cowshed or could be seen squatting on the lawns, weeding and cutting our grass with scythes in the monsoon season. They were earthly apparitions, with their topknotted hair, over which they flung a bright veil that fell to the back, their short, equally bright forty-yard skirts that came to mid-calf, and their masses of silver jewelry that covered their wrists, arms, ankles, necks, and hair. These were our local village women. Much of their personal wealth was in the silver they wore about their bodies.

We started to dress for our recital. I opened up the large bundle of silver loot I had borrowed from our own rather large *gwalan* (female cowherd). As I began putting it on, Promila ventured a quiet remark: "Are you sure you can dance with so much jewelry?" "Of course I can," I replied, determined to dazzle. I danced well enough. But as I spun and flung my arms around, first my bracelets, then my anklets, all too large for my thin bones, began to fly off, one at a time. As we danced faster, there were bracelets flying all over the stage. I hardly knew if I should stop and retrieve them, carry on, stepping on the jewelry as I did, or fall down in a heap and burst into tears. I carried on, but wept buckets at my own foolishness as soon as I was home.

Twelve and thirteen were not easy ages for me. I was struggling at school and, without my older sisters, struggling at home. There was no niche I fit into with any comfort. I was not pretty, I excelled at nothing, and I sighed a lot. Quite naturally, I had developed pathetic crushes on my cousins' friends, all to no purpose, as I was too shy to say anything. I spent my time wrapping myself around Number 7's elegant white pillars and moping. Or weeping. The monsoon season in particular brought out all my deepest despair.

Monsoons in India are a romantic time. Just as literature in the West suggests that it is with the arrival of spring that all thoughts turn to love, Indian literature, music, local customs, and even food all make a similar case for the monsoon season. With good reason.

The monsoons arrive with such drama, especially in the North. The summer starts in April with the hot *loo* desert winds, blowing hot air and sand with cruel ferocity. Temperatures rise to 104 or 105 degrees Fahrenheit. If you get into a car, the leather burns your skin; if you touch metal, you get a rash or blister. The trees are subjected daily to such thick coatings of dust that you want to disown them. The grass turns brown and then starts to disappear. The earth cakes and cracks. You drink cooling green mango juice or lime juice with salt or sugar, or with both, or try to decompress with the juice from the watermelon-rind pickles that sit in large round terra-cotta pots. Nothing cools you down for long.

My sister Veena and I would run the distance between Number 5 and Number 7 in the summers as if demons were chasing us. Number 5 had air conditioners. Number 7 had thick vetiver (*khas*) curtains on the outside of every door or window, which were constantly kept wet. Hot winds blowing through them magically cooled down, picking up the remarkable perfume of these prized roots as they did so. But between Number 5 and Number 7 there was only a roiling hell.

The summer seemed endless. It went on through May, June, and part of July. Mangoes that could be eaten out of hand came and went, as did cherries from Kashmir and litchees from Dehradun. Summer vegetable gardens yielded only soft marrows and squashes, the bowling-pin-like *ghiya*s, the tennis-ball-shaped *tinda*s, and the slightly glutinous *tori*s, and we tired of them easily. The earth and sky remained broiling and menacing. After lunch we all tried sleeping through the long hot afternoons. There was a

*Veena plays in the well-equipped garden at
Number 7. Part of the annex is in the background.*

takht (divan) covered by a giant white sheet (*chandini*) in the big
east-facing room at Number 7. With pillows placed all down its
center, it was large enough to sleep about twenty people lying in
two rows, side by side. But our sleep was restless, since chirping
birds, seeking respite in all our verandas, kept up a noisy chatter.

Then, one day, quite suddenly, there was a change in the air. A hint of some momentous possibility went through it like an electric charge, though the heat remained. Far, far in the distance, dark clouds began appearing on the horizon. Majestic and threatening, like a dark army on the move, they got closer and closer. We all rushed to the veranda and began to inhale that anticipated smell of freshly wet earth, the one that Indians have tried to capture in an attar called, rather simply, "earth" (*mitti*). It was a faraway smell, almost as if we were imagining it. Soon the entire sky was dark with black clouds. Thunder boomed from all sides, accompanied by zigzags of lightning. The earth seemed hotter than ever. First one or two fat drops of rain fell, then more and more, until there was a deluge. Suddenly the heat broke, as if some shell encasing us had been cracked open. We all rushed out onto the paved driveway just outside Number 7's front veranda, held our faces up to the sky, and allowed ourselves to get thoroughly soaked. The monsoon season had finally arrived. We could now feast on monsoon sweets, the squiggly pretzel-shaped *jalebi*s, dunking them in glasses of cold milk as we gazed dreamily at the downpour.

The first cooling breezes went through the hearts of most young people, awakening or intensifying their yearnings and joys. Whether we were just following the suggestions of an ancient tradition that had proclaimed the monsoon season to be the most "romantic" one, or whether there really was a collection of elements that provoked and egged on the romantic spirit, is hard to say. All I know is that around the ages of twelve and thirteen I was a self-conscious, bespectacled bundle of misery, and the monsoon just made it worse. It set before me all the possibilities without offering any hope.

Nothing in school interested me enough. I did well by dint of hard work, but my heart was not in it. I knew, I just knew that a world existed into which I would fit some day. It just was not the world I was in right then. Boys I had crushes on, boys at the swimming pool, completely ignored me, mostly because I could not summon up the nerve to say one word to them. The irony was that I was not really shy: I could be quite bold when I wanted to be. I lacked tact and softness, I was too much a mixture of insecurity and arrogance to flirt, and had the awful habit of watching and instantly analyzing myself and all others around me, so that I allowed no action to be entirely carefree or spontaneous.

Shibbudada, whose validation, however contrary that seemed, we all craved, did not seem to care much, but he did notice. Once he complained, "Why are your eyes so dull? At your age they should be shining like those of a wild animal, like those of your cousin D———." I wanted to shout back, "But Cousin D——— does not read all day or write all day or THINK. Cousin D——— is an idiot." But I said nothing. Cousin D——— was pretty. I was overcome with insecurity.

Another time, during the winter, I just happened to be sitting by the fire in the drawing room next to Shibbudada when my boy cousins walked in with a particularly good-looking friend. My heart began to beat so fast I thought it would pop out of my mouth. To cover my confusion, I turned away towards Shibbudada and started up some innocuous conversation, but he saw right through me and stopped me in my tracks, saying, "You don't really want to talk to me right now. Why don't you keep your eyes where your interest really lies?" I could have died of shame and inadequacy.

As I grew older, I had begun to tolerate Shibbudada's behavior less and less. He sensed this and began to return the favor with a regimen of quiet cruelty. He demanded nothing short of adoration, and I was not providing it. Always of two minds about him, Shibbudada's children seemed to be getting ever more prickly, contrary, and unpredictable. I never uttered a word against their father to them, especially not to Rajesh, who was my friend, as I suspected it would only lead to a spirited defense. I could never talk to my parents or brothers and sisters, who all seemed either to adore or to forgive Shibbudada much more easily than I could. I berated myself endlessly for being hardhearted, not "deserving" and "good" like my sisters Kamal and Lalit. Even in our very large joint family, where we were rarely physically alone, I felt very alone.

(I have now, almost sixty years later, found out that I had company. As I was going around collecting photographs from cousins for this book, we began recounting old times, and I discovered that Shibbudada had tormented most of them. "You, too? You, too?" I said to each one of them in disbelief. He was their god, too, family-anointed and permanent. They had all hungered for his approval, just as I had, and hardly ever received it. They, too, had been subjected to the games he played with his favors and his power. What if we had just talked to each other? Not one of us knew what the others were feeling. For some reason, we had all held our separate tongues.)

To add to my woes, I soon came down with a severe case of chicken pox. This happened at Holi, the Spring Festival of Colors. We had always celebrated our Holi holidays in Delhi, even when we were living in Kanpur. The women of the house would start off the Holi season with the preparation of *bara* pickles. These were rather like Jewish cucumber pickles, except that instead of cucumbers it was dumplings that were pickled, in a spicy brine flecked with plenty of crushed mustard seeds.

It was an uncommon pickle. We knew no other community that pickled dumplings. But we did, and delicious they were, too. *Urad dal,* the most ancient of Indian legumes, was soaked, seasoned, ground into a paste, beaten to allow the infiltration of air bubbles, and then formed into patties on a piece of muslin with a wetted hand. Each patty was carefully transferred to a *karhai* (wok) filled with hot oil and fried before it was dropped into the pickling solution. The combination of liquid and dumplings was then ladled into *mutka*s, round-bottomed—and rounded—terracotta pots with narrow necks. These were covered with terracotta lids and left in Number 7's northern courtyard on wooden stands to "mature" in the sun. If my grandmother, who gave it a swish and a taste now and then, declared that it was not quite ready, this just meant that it had not soured sufficiently for her taste.

Once the *bara*s were firmly ensconced in their brine, the family's collective attention turned to other Holi foods: there were *papri*s, crisp chickpea-flour poppadums nicely spiced but hard to roll out, as the dough needed to be really hard; *gooja*s, turnovers filled with coconut and sweetened nuts; and of course there were those *pakori*s, fritters that had to be made at the last minute. They were certainly not ordinary fritters—laced as they were with *bhang,* or hashish.

Some aspects of my life in India seem, in retrospect, difficult to reconcile. We were a conservative, buttoned-down Kayastha family but with forward-looking, intellectually liberal leanings. We could question anything we wanted to, and did, but we followed family Hindu traditions to the letter, almost by rote, as if they were some form of indelible background musical beat. We even took full advantage of the license these traditions allowed on certain days without much thought. For example, on the other major religious festival, Diwali, tradition suggested we gamble, so that the clinking of money would entice the goddess of wealth into our homes. Thus we, grown-ups and children, gambled and loved it. We never gambled or played the pokerlike card game Flash at any other time. It did not have a seal of approval at any other time.

At Holi, tradition suggested that both sexes throw inhibition to the winds, mingle freely, throw colored waters and powders on each other, dance, sing, and, yes, for the adults, drink and even partake of hashish. The couplet that we chanted with some frequency on Holi Day, *"Kahay, sunay ka bura na mano, / Aaj humari Holi hai,"* could be translated as "Don't be offended by anything we say or do, / For today is our Holi." For one day in the year, we had been "freed."

Holi's origins probably lay in India's distant pantheistic past, when the spring harvest must have been celebrated with a certain abandon. In India, you rarely lose a tradition. You simply layer one on top of another. We still recognized its harvesttime beginnings. On the night before Holi, we would build a bonfire and throw into it sheaves of newly picked wheat from our faraway farms and, better still, sheaves of freshly harvested stalks of chickpeas. As soon as they had roasted sufficiently, we dragged them out with long poles and fell upon them, separating the wheat grains and peas from their blackened skins. Our fingers and mouths turned sooty as we ate, but we could not stop munching until the last chickpea had been found and devoured.

The next day we let go. We played Holi. Preparations for the "playing" had already begun. The *mali* (gardener) had scrubbed out the cement water tank in the garden, plugged it, and filled it with about two and a half feet of water. Into the water were emptied several baskets of dried *tesu* flowers, which, when soaked, released a yellowish orange dye and a pleasantly musky aroma. The flowers floated to the top, swelled, and, looking rather like large bumblebees, covered the surface of the water.

The children's preparations were less benign. First we made sure that all the *gulaal,* the colored powders, had been ordered, the reds our parents preferred and the more vile and newfangled yellows, greens, blues, and purples that we liked. Then we went into the garage and asked Babaji's driver, Masoom Ali, for the darkest grease he had lying about. He tried to put us off with "You children are always eating my head. Go away. Don't bother me." But in the end he always relented. The grease was put into jars and reserved for those we disliked. And for those we liked or even loved? Ah, there was the gold powder, carefully mixed with oil and hidden in a special spot from where it could be whisked out to transform the faces of the desired ones into those of gods and goddesses.

We awoke at dawn on Holi Day, made sure our brass water-squirters were ready for ambush and pails of colored water and colored powders hidden strategically. The first people to be attacked and overwhelmed were all the cousins themselves. We had already planned our moves. As our parents shouted, "Not inside the house. Go out. Holi must be played outside the house," we tackled each other and were not content until we were all fully wet, had received a dunking in the *tesu* tank, and had had our faces smeared with a variety of powders.

Once we had finished with each other—the elders got a more polite version of the treatment—we, old and young, gathered on Number 7's driveway to march on to all the neighboring houses: Number 16, Number 14, Number 12, Number 10, Number 6, Number 4, Number 2 . . . Each household was equally prepared and gave as good as it got. Everywhere we went, we were offered food and drink, the same *papri*s, *gooja*s, *bara* pickles, whiskey, and the hash-laced drinks and fritters. Our numbers and raucousness increased as members of households we had attacked joined us. We ended up in Number 7, a few hundred of us, sitting under the jujube tree on the front lawn, right on the grass. A harmonium and a set of tablas (drums) were brought out, and the singing and dancing began. *"Holi ayee ray kanha, / Bruj kay basiya,"* we sang. These were mostly hymnlike medieval songs about Lord Krishna playing Holi with the milkmaids—hymnlike and lusty.

I remember one particular Holi when I was about twelve years old, neither child nor woman, my hair all smeared with green and purple, my face golden, and my body wet with *tesu* water, an unrecognizable creature shivering on the grass under the jujube tree. My head was aching, I remember, aching so it felt as if it might explode. Everything had gone into slow motion. I remember someone turning towards me and saying, "Who is she? She looks quite pretty." I wanted to explain, "It's only the gold paint. This is me. I don't have my glasses on." My mouth opened to speak, and then shut again without uttering a word. Then my parents got up and started dancing. I must have begun fading away, for the next thing I heard was my brother Bhaiyyadada's voice: "Are you all right? You seem feverish."

Bhaiyyadada walked me to Number 5, where I had a quick bath and crawled into bed. Big blisters had begun appearing—on my face, my arms, my body. I had a severe case of chicken pox.

NINETEEN

*Chicken Pox • Soup-Toast and Sewing •
A Fancy-Dress Party*

The chicken pox lasted a good three weeks. I was convinced that I would come out of it severely deformed, as many of the blisters had filled up with pus and some were a good three-quarters of an inch in diameter. No one was allowed to visit: I was completely quarantined. The blisters first hurt, then itched, never allowing me to lie in comfort. My father's eldest sister, Bhuaji, offered me little food packets over the Number 5 wall filled with *mutthri*s (savory cookies). I devoured these quickly with thick layers of my grandmother's *meethi* chutney (sweet chutney made with shredded green mangoes and ginger). One good thing that came of this long illness is that our family began eating all its meals in Number 5. Our much smaller kitchen was humming all day now, and we were ecstatic.

My mother, whose calm ministrations had so comforted my father during all his minor illnesses, now turned her full attention to me, but her tactics were entirely different. Besides spoon-feeding me "soup-toast," simple chicken and meat broths with slices of toast for dunking, which I loved, she approached me with another of her talents. She began teaching me how to sew. She had already taught me knitting at the age of five. By now I was knitting the most complicated designs, many of my own devising, requiring several colors that snaked their way across and up the insides of cardigans, vests, and pullovers.

Sewing was another matter. We had a tailor, Ram Narain, to do the simple stuff. He came to us from the Old City on a bicycle and worked at one end of the Number 5 dining room for weeks at a time. We bought the fabrics and sketched out the designs. He sat on the floor on a mat with my mother's Singer sewing machine and did his best to interpret our thoughts. If there was a wedding on the horizon, he stayed for months. He irritated us, because he never followed our designs to the letter, and because his finishing was hurried and careless. His buttons were never aligned, and his hemming was slipshod. Besides, he always cut the thread with his teeth. My mother kept reminding us that any help was hard to find and that we should be grateful to have him at all.

I considered myself highly stylish and was not content with Ram Narain's bumbling approach. There were no ready-made clothes in India then, so, with my mother's expert help, my chicken-pox days were happily employed with sewing. In this period I made two *kameez*es (shirts) to go on top of the *shalwar*s (baggy trousers) that we wore. One was a delicate white poplin with a turtleneck, and the second was a cream silk. The first I boldly embroidered with an anchor placed just above the left breast. A "rope" (which I made by twisting some silk threads) wound around the anchor, going in and out of the white poplin through strategically placed buttonholes. The second shirt had embroidery placed in the same spot, above the left breast, but it was much more elaborate. It consisted of the ace, king, and queen of hearts fanned out prettily.

Encouraged by my skills, I began preparing for my twelfth birthday—and the start of my thirteenth year—in the coming August. It would be a fancy-dress party, and I would think up and make something really grand. Cousins and friends were duly informed. Everyone's dress was a secret. Enthusiasm poured in from all quarters, even from Shibbudada. He insisted there be a photographer to cover the event. He would arrange for one. My birthday would be held in Number 7, he said.

Suddenly the stakes had got higher than I wanted, and I was nervous. I still did not have anything to wear. I thought up and rejected idea after idea. It was already early August before I settled on being a hula girl with a grass skirt and a short blouse. The blouse seemed easy enough. I already had decently large breasts. I would wear a white blouse and tuck it up so my waist was visible and my breasts were defined. The skirt I would make. I would cut up hundreds of strips of paper and sew them onto a waistband. My hair? My hair was long, and I would just leave it loose.

The day dawned, and I began to dress. I put on the blouse. It just looked like an ordinary blouse. I rolled it up at the waist, but it kept rolling down, and the bulk hid all definition of my newly formed breasts. There was no time to worry about that. I tied on the skirt. Every time I moved, a few of the paper strips tore off. I undid my two long braids and combed out my hair. I still looked just like myself, not like a hula girl at all. I cried. My mother insisted that I looked just fine and that I hurry on to Number 7 before the guests arrived.

My cousins and friends came—girls dressed as boys, boys dressed as girls; there were Arabs with daggers and Japanese damsels with fans and milkmaids with a ton of silver jewelry. I

*My twelfth birthday and the start of my thirteenth year. The party consisted
mostly of cousins, with the honorable exception of my friend Sudha (front row,
fourth from left), her young sister, and two of Sheila's friends. Fancy dress was
the order of the day. I am seated on a* moondha, *a cane chair, in the center.*

blew out the candles on my cake from Wengers, helped pass
along the slabs of three-in-one (chocolate, strawberry, and
vanilla) Kwality ice cream, and nibbled on the spicy samosas
from Ghantaywallah in Chandni Chowk. Finally, I posed in the
center of my group birthday photograph. But my heart was not in
any of it.

TWENTY

I think that I started growing up right about then. School, Queen Mary's, helped. I was out of middle school, and Hindi was no longer the medium of instruction. Even though I had mastered it, I felt easier with the English we would use through the upper classes. Instead of plodding, I could now fly. The school, a dour, gray stone building with Gothic arches, had changed.

The summers, for one, had been quite unbearable until then, as none of the classrooms had been armed with electric ceiling fans. The shirts that we wore on top of our *shalwar*s (baggy pants) did not help, either. Even if made from the thinnest voiles, they did not stop the perspiration from trickling down our bodies and down our legs. When we picked up our pens to write, sweat trickled down our arms and over our pens onto the notebooks. The pens slithered about in our fingers. Wearing all white did little to inspire a sense of cool well-being in that stone school building.

What the school did provide to all classes were cloth pulley fans. Imagine, if you will, a long rod or beam suspended above the length of a classroom near the ceiling, almost bisecting it. Imagine a curtain with many pleats, about two and a half feet in length, hanging from the full length of this rod. Now imagine a simple pulley system attached to the rod that allows someone to pull the entire contraption back and forth, thus "fanning" the whole classroom as a handheld fan might. Ingenious? The operative words, of course, are "someone" and "handheld."

The "someones" that the school hired were our local village women, who came to their fanning jobs every day wearing their bright forty-yard skirts, provocative brassiere-sized blouses, and head-to-toe silver jewelry. Their job was to take the pulley rope in their hands, extend it through the classroom door to the veranda just outside it, sit down on the veranda floor, and start pulling and releasing, pulling and releasing.

The first few pulls were quite exciting. But the weight of their clothing, the sheer boredom of their jobs, and the numbing heat slowly lulled the women into ever-slower and then nonexistent motion. First they could be seen half sitting, then half lying down, then lying down and pulling the rope with their toes, then lying down and snoring. Every now and then one of my schoolmates would give the rope a tug, which would waken them briefly, but to no long-term purpose.

We would rush out for a drink between classes, but the only water we could get was from the tap at a small tank in the courtyard. We cupped a hand and drank it straight from the source. It was always too warm and offered no respite.

There was one bit of relief, though. Every day at midmorning, there was, if we signed up and paid for it in advance, a break for *do phal, do biscuit,* or "two fruit, two biscuits." The English school nurse, in full uniform, dispensed these from a special table, checking us against her list as she did so.

I was always of two minds about signing up, as I did not care for biscuits (having lost my sweet tooth in Daurala) and the fruit was always a mediocre orange and an unripe banana, the only variation being two mediocre oranges or two unripe bananas. What I really loved, and what I could have only if I splurged on the biscuits and fruit, was a glass of cold, cold milk.

This was no ordinary milk. It did not come straight from the cow's udders, as ours did at home. It had not been boiled in a kitchen pot and cooled. No, this was homogenized milk from a proper dairy and came in a glass bottle. I just loved it. Sometimes I paid for the whole package just to get the milk, but most of the time I gave up, as the fruit was not even good enough to give away and ended up rotting slowly inside my desk.

It must have dawned on the school at some stage that pulley fans were a losing proposition all the way around. By the time I was thirteen, they had been replaced by ceiling fans.

Many of the teachers had been replaced, too. I was blessed with Mrs. McKelvie, a Parsi lady of about the same height as I was, perhaps even shorter. She was married to a Briton, which accounted for her name. With a sweet, round, light-skinned face, and brown hair that she wore as a braided wreath around her head, she could easily have passed for an Englishwoman. In a school where there were both English and Indian personnel at that time, she wore only sarees to class (though with European blouses), so there would be no mistaking who she really was. She wore her sarees oddly, though, as if she had lived in England too long and lost the grace of wearing them well. What struck me when I first saw her was the combination of her laughing, intelligent eyes and her small, even teeth, which were caked with nicotine.

Mrs. McKelvie was my history teacher. She didn't just teach me Indian history and British history, which were part of the set curriculum; I also learned from her that any subject could be fascinating if I delved into it deeply enough. She showed me how history, for example, could be researched from a hundred angles, some obscure and seemingly unrelated; that the study of maps and drawing of maps led to ever-greater clarity; that understanding the character of emperors and generals was sometimes as important as memorizing the dates of their battles. She wanted me to read everything, *1066 and All That,* Shakespeare's plays, Emperor Akbar's biography by Abul Fazl, Nehru's books written in jail when the British had imprisoned him. She wanted me to see everything, the Red Fort in Delhi, the paintings of Turner, Moghul miniature paintings, Buddhist art. Because I loved drawing, she set me to making monstrous maps that the school then framed and hung up in the library.

When the school decided to do a performance of Shakespeare's *A Midsummer Night's Dream,* she suggested my name for the role of Titania, Queen of the Fairies. Until then I had acted seriously only once, at St. Mary's Convent, playing the brown mouse in a musical version of *The Pied Piper of Hamelin* at the age of five. Because I could not sing, I pursued acting no further, chalking it down as another great disappointment. Of course, I fooled around with my cousins, writing small plays and performing them for the family with rigged-up curtains and make-believe clothes, but I knew I could never be like my older sisters, who sang and were given leading roles in all the school musicals. I could perform under Shibbudada's rolltop desk before an audience of aunts and uncles, but the real stage was for others.

Titania—and Shakespeare—opened up the possibilities of a future I did not think I had, or deserved. Here I was, floating outdoors on the lovely grass stage of Queen Mary's School, eyes outlined with black, lips a luscious scarlet, body swathed in shimmering green robes, declaiming in righteous anger to a slippery Fairy King:

> *These are the forgeries of jealousy;*
> *And never, since the middle summer's spring,*
> *Met we on hill, in dale, forest, or mead,*
> *By paved fountain, or by rushy brook,*
> *Or in the beached margent of the sea,*
> *To dance our ringlets to the whistling wind,*
> *But with thy brawls thou hast disturbed our sport.*

I felt elated and at home. Every atom of my being felt energized and utilized. My cup, suddenly, was full. That constant, critical chatter in my head stopped. Whatever was missing in me had been completed. I was consumed with purpose.

I knew enough to say "pave-ed" and "beach-ed." Another new and excellent teacher—Miss Dutt, who taught us English— had just been covering iambic pentameter. I was prepared for Shakespearean niceties. Besides, the college of my grandfather, father, aunts, and now my brothers, St. Stephen's College, had been doing performances of at least one Shakespeare play every winter for as long as I could remember. I not only could be found in the first row year after year, but was known for my firm opinions on the niceties of the performances, such as that of Joyce Christian as Rosalind. Joyce, a tall, shapely Anglo-Indian, was one of the few women at St. Stephen's. This college seemed unable to decide whether it wanted women pupils or not, and seemed to reverse itself every other year. Joyce got in during one of the "yes" periods but was one among a very small minority. All the boys were half in love with her, and so was I, especially when she was on the stage.

When I was asked to play the lead in *Robin Hood and His Merry Men* at school, I was ready for that, too. Already half a boy since early childhood, I donned my tights and tunic with glee, picked up my bow and arrow, and entered the fray in Sherwood Forest as if I had been born in Nottingham.

There were other infusions to the blood. Out of the haze that separates juniors from those in more senior classes, one face kept asserting its presence. It was that of a girl, about three or four years older than I, called Amina Ahmed. For someone like me, who came from a staid family of fully documented ancestors, a family in which kind married kind, Amina's history alone was enviable, and she repeated it with a certain pride. She was a Muslim girl from the inner city whose father was the illegitimate son of a prostitute. It could not get much better than that!

But it did. This father, Nuruddin Ahmed, had managed to educate himself enough to become a lawyer and, when in England, met and married a half-Jewish woman named Bertha Boam, commonly known as Billy. Amina was the offspring of this unusual couple, who still lived in the inner city, near a disreputable movie house that we had been warned to avoid, Novelty Cinema. She was as blond and light-skinned as her mother and sported her father's long, prominent nose. She wore her silky blond hair in a fashionable pageboy. Quite fearless, she could outswear any local ruffian in street lingo but also spoke the most chaste, elegant Urdu when it was required. (Later, as the wife of an Indian ambassador, she was to master Russian and Persian as well.) None of the Anglican supervisors in our school could control or suppress her.

Miss Devi Ditta, our principal, tried. Each morning started with an assembly of all the students for prayers. Here we stood in rows according to the class we were in, with the younger children standing in front. We began with hymns, accompanied by the nurse on the piano. These were Christian hymns, but because most of us were Hindus, Muslims, and Sikhs, certain concessions were made. Instead of singing, "Onward, Christian soldiers," we sang, "Onward, onward soldiers." I did not realize until I heard my father-in-law singing in a Brooklyn church some decades later that our words in India had been altered. After hymns and prayers, announcements were made about trips to interschool games, or "*chaat* parties" to raise money for a charity, or about new teachers. This was followed by a cursory inspection to check if our clothing was neat, our hair was tidy and free of lice, and our nails were clean and unpolished.

It was absolutely forbidden to use nail polish. Amina's nails, squat and bitten, were nonetheless always polished. Varnished a bright red or bright pink. Her name would be called out, a common occurrence.

"Amina Ahmed!" Miss Devi Ditta would say in an exasperated voice. "You have been asked again and again *not* to wear nail polish. Kindly go with Nurse and remove it."

Amina: "I can't."

Miss Devi Ditta: "What do you mean, you can't?"

Amina: "I can't. I am not allowed."

Miss Devi Ditta: "Who is not allowing you?"

Amina: "Doctor's orders. I have to keep the nail polish on to protect my nails."

Miss Devi Ditta: "I have never heard of such nonsense."

Amina: "I have shimiitis [or some other invented name]. If I remove the nail polish, my nails will fall off."

And so Amina would get away with it again. I would stare back at her and invoke my Hindu gods in awe. My admiration for her knew no bounds.

Amina behaved with equal gumption in the drawing class. Not that she and I went to the same class, but I knew the drill. Miss Aloo MacAdam, the art teacher, taught only two things, object drawing and painting, and in the same way, year after year.

For the object drawing, she placed wooden blocks, one or two of them, perhaps a bottle as well, or a vase with flowers, at the front of the class on a table. We sat in semicircular rows at a little distance with our drawing books open on our desks, well-sharpened pencils beside them, and drew the objects.

In order to get the proportions right, we had to keep measuring. "Hold your pencil out in front of you. Keep it straight. Close one eye. Now measure the length of the box on your pencil. Mark that point. Now measure the height of the box. Mark that. On your pencil, how many times does the height go into the length? Follow those proportions. Then use your watercolors and paint the objects in. Use the colors you actually see, making them paler where light hits the objects."

I had no trouble with any of this, because I could draw and paint anyway. Miss MacAdam's directions only helped me double-check what my natural instincts already knew. She always rewarded me with the highest marks and showed my work around as an example.

Somehow, it was not enough. I needed Amina's approval. I had heard that she was an "artist." So, one day, I waited for her outside the art room, drawing book in hand.

It took her a while to come out. Most of her class had already left when she and Miss MacAdam emerged. Miss MacAdam looked cross. Amina looked nonchalant. Miss MacAdam went back into the art room and banged the door shut behind her.

"Amina," I said, "I want to show you my drawing."

She looked at it.

"What do you think?" I persisted.

"Do *you* like it?" she asked me. "The most important thing is that *you* should like it."

I was suddenly insecure. Unsure. "May I see what *you* did in class?" I managed.

She held out her drawing book. She had broken up her blocks, bowl, and vase into bits and pieces, scattering them about her page, and then colored them in nail-polish colors, magentas, reds, fuchsias, and oranges. The objects and colors were unrecognizable—that is, if you tried to match them to anything real in the art room—but the painting was beautiful.

Here was another dawn, another awakening. West European painters of the late nineteenth and early twentieth centuries had already left their mark on us. On one of my birthdays, my family had given me a book of the paintings of European masters. I would sit with this heavy tome in my lap, drinking in the images on its thick, glossy pages day after day. Rembrandt, Holbein, and Leonardo da Vinci were there, but so were the more fragmented, angular worlds of Cézanne and Picasso. Just below this book, on the same shelf, I kept a thinner volume containing the turn-of-the-century paintings of Jamini Roy. A Bengali, he painted stylized folk-arty figures in few strokes and bright colors. This, too, was well thumbed. My favorite painter, though, whose work I loved with a passion then, was Amrita Sher-Gil, a half-Indian, half-Hungarian woman who had studied in France in the early 1930s, returned to India, and died at twenty-nine, but not before leaving the most graceful images of fluid Indian figures, often draped in striped clothing.

Until then, I had never been to an exhibition of paintings and did not apply the lessons I might have learned from my art books to myself. I admired the freedom of painters but did not realize that the freedom could apply to me, even at the age of thirteen, even while I was a mere student. In the end, I was not as bold as Amina. I painted as Miss MacAdam wanted me to in the art room, but bought myself some oils and painted in furious blobs at home.

TWENTY-ONE

The Sisters Return • A Taste of the Future •
Mother's Shawls • Kamal's Illness

My sisters Lalit and Kamal spent nine months of the year in their unheated boarding school, the Himalayan convent in Nainital. They came home only for the months of January, February, and March, when the mountains turned uncompromisingly frigid. By this time their slender fingers were already red and raw from chilblains. My mother had spent months furiously knitting woolen mittens with openings for the fingers so they could hold their pens and pencils. These, as well as hand-knitted cardigans, socks, and mufflers that had made their way up to the mountaintop school in package after package, hardly helped. My sisters suffered dreadfully from the cold. Of course they did not complain. Delhi must have seemed downright balmy to them. I was ecstatic to have my older sisters back for the winter holidays. We celebrated in big ways and small.

On those winter weekends, the men were free by lunchtime on Saturday. We all congregated under the *beri*, our beloved umbrella-shaped jujube tree, which each of us had climbed as a child. Weekend lunches were always preceded by beer—for the men. But many of the girls were in their teens now and permitted shandy, a mixture of beer and our carbonated "lemonade." Those who wanted to sit in the full sun pulled their chairs away from the *beri*'s shade, but most chose to have their heads in the shade and much of their bodies in the sun, and so kept adjusting their chairs. It was here that Bhaiyyadada, my very courtly brother, carefully poured me three-quarters of a glass of lemonade and added just enough beer to allow me to feel grown-up. The very first sip tasted of a future that lay in waiting.

During this period, I cannot quite pinpoint the exact time or the reasons for it, we sisters began addressing each other by our initials. We probably thought it was "cool"—some sort of Indian "cool" of the period. I became M, Kamal became K, Lalit was L, and Veena was V. When writing, we all spelled the initials differently. I addressed all letters to Lalit "Dear L" and signed them with an "M." Her letters to me began with "Dear Emm," and were signed, "Ell." My parents never fell into the game, nor did my eldest brother. But Bhaiyyadada went along, and so did our closest cousins and friends. It soon stopped being a game. Our initials *became* our names for each other, names we still use. Today, the group of people who call me M is a limited club, and I, for one, guard membership to it jealously. Besides my sisters, my children call me M and so do many of my cousins, nieces, nephews, and dear, close friends. Recently, in Los Angeles, on the way to a film location, when a young actress I hardly knew, quite out of the blue, addressed me as M in a casual sentence, I was at first too startled to say anything. But the very next day I had to let her know, as gently as possible, that only those who had known me for at least forty years or were members of my family could address me that way.

(I was reminded then of a story told to me by a young director working for the first time with the legendary and formidable English actress Dame Edith Evans. Not knowing how to address her, he took the easy way out for the first few days by not addressing her directly at all. Then, one day, screwing up his courage, he ventured, "Edith, would you . . ." Dame Edith rose to her full height. "Edith?" she barked. "Edith? It will be Edie next.")

Winter was when my mother bought her Kashmiri shawls. Delicate pashminas (the real ones, not the imitations available cheaply in the West), fine *shahtoosh*es made from the softest mountain-goat hair, and *jamevaar*s, handwoven antique paisleys, were all the stuff of dreams, sold only by itinerant shawl-wallahs, who traveled, generally on recommendation, from house to house. Kashmiri shawls were to Delhi women what furs are, or were, to women in the West. Pashminas, *shahtoosh*es, and *jamevaar*s were the rarer sables and ermines of the trade. They established a woman's credentials as soon as she walked into a room. Unlike some furs, a good Kashmiri shawl could never look cheap or tarty. It always enhanced the wearer, encasing her in solid dignity.

My stylish mother bought a few such shawls each year, adding to her already large collection. Now that her two older daughters were blossoming, she was keeping them in mind, too. The itinerant shawl-wallah, most often a Kashmiri, traveled with an assistant. He himself walked in front, carrying a small bundle. The assistant walked behind him. Both were directed to Number 5's back veranda. There my mother and older sisters would sit down on chairs. They were serious. Veena and I hung about. We, too, would turn into serious shawl-buyers one day. The shawl-wallah spread a bedcover on the floor and began opening his bundles.

The reason my mother chose the back veranda was that it was

possible to be discreet there. After all, our relatives were every-where. How many shawls we bought and what we paid for them was *our* business. Besides, she wanted to take full advantage of the southern light. Good light was essential, as these shawl-wallahs, according to my mother, could not be trusted. Sometimes, she said, they took several old, fraying *jamevaar*s, cut off the dam-aged bits, and pieced the good bits together, dyeing sections to make them match. Sometimes a beautiful shawl was riddled with the tiniest moth holes. Only if the shawl was held up to the light would they be visible. Light was needed to check on the fineness of the embroidery, the exact colors, and whether there had been any fading.

The shawl-wallah would unfold a shawl and hold it up to my mother. My mother might shake her head and say a firm "No," in which case the shawl would be thrown in the direction of the assistant, who would refold it and put it away. Or my mother would say, "Put it aside, I will think about it," in which case the shawl would be put to one side. My canny mother knew that almost as important as the light needed to examine the shawls was the poker face needed to fool the shawl-wallah. On no account was he to get the slightest hint of which shawl she was really interested in, as that would jack up its price.

The shawls were never ticketed with prices. A shawl-wallah could ask for whatever the market would bear, and that, of course, varied. If, at the end of a day, no shawls had been sold and the shawl-wallah needed money, prices could come way down. If the shawl-wallah had got a hint of the one shawl that was most desired, he could hold off until he got the price he wanted.

Soon there was a heap of "possible" shawls that my mother might want. Then she would start all over with this heap, win-nowing them down by making a second selection from the first selection, again saying "No" and "Put it aside." The heap of possibles got smaller and smaller until there were only a few left. She asked for their prices and began haggling. She was very good at it. Sometimes she presented the shawl-wallah with so many options that he got confused and forgot the ridiculously high prices he had originally quoted. "If I take this one and this one and this one, how much would it cost?" "What if I removed this one and added that one?"

Once, a shawl-wallah came to us with the most stunning green nineteenth-century *jamevaar*. It was a rare color, and the hand-loomed paisley workmanship was incomparable. It was the only shawl we wanted. Yet my mother went through her usual "No" and "Put it aside" for hours, until the poor shawl-wallah sold it to her for a price she was willing to pay.

March came to an end before I wanted it to, and my sisters went back to their convent school in Nainital. I began to feel lost the second they headed north.

The twin, seemingly contradictory, elements of dependence and resilient independence were being etched into my character. My brothers were absent for much of the first decade of my life; my older sisters were missing for most of my crucial early teens. I used to write to my oldest brother, Brijdada, from Kanpur, and he would reply, reassuring me sometimes with letters and sometimes with drawings. Lalit had assumed a semi-maternal role. She was certainly my mentor for all intellectual matters and was the only one who seemed to understand my insecurities enough to try to draw me out of them. Once she and Kamal left for school, I felt bereft.

*My father, me (standing to his left), aged about thirteen, and
Veena on holiday in Poona. These were difficult years.*

Since private traumas were never discussed in my family, only
smoothed over whenever necessary, these feelings of loss just
stayed within me and festered.

At the end of 1946, Lalit graduated from her mountain convent school and returned to Delhi for good. In the following
year, she was admitted to Indraprastha College, an easy bicycling
distance from our house.

Around this very time, I began to notice my father and mother
whispering to each other with a worried look. Somehow Kamal,
who was still in Nainital and still everybody's favorite, was
involved in this worry. At first I could not understand any of it,

and my parents would not explain. What I did know was that something had happened during sports. Had she fallen down and hurt herself? There were calls to the school, talk about X-rays, calls to doctors. It seems that Kamal had noticed swelling and pain in her ankle and had found herself unable to compete in their summer sports meet. The nuns had called in doctors who had pronounced it serious. There was talk of a malignant bone tumor in her leg.

Kamal was brought back to Delhi in June 1947. Doctors poked around doing biopsies and then deep radiation. It was felt that the problem had been brought under control. She would do her final school exams, her Senior Cambridge, from Delhi.

TWENTY-TWO

*The Muslim Twins • Sudha's Vegetarian
Delights • Punjabi Promila • Our Shared
Lunchtime Feasts • Contacting the Spirit World •
The Icy Hands of Partition • Mahatma
Gandhi • Spinning for India • Independence
Day and the Bloody Aftermath*

There were other changes in the air. World War II was finally over. Whereas Europe and East Asia looked forward to peace, India could look forward only to a wrenching partition. Partition, as it was called, with a fearsome capital "P." This Solomon-testing breakup of its being into two entities had already caused mayhem. The British, with Lord Mountbatten as their viceroy in India, were granting India its freedom, but not before splitting the country, taking two chunky ribs out of India to form Muslim Pakistan to its east and its west. All the secular dreams of nationalists like Jawaharlal Nehru and Mahatma Gandhi that saw Hindus, Muslims, Sikhs, and Christians coexisting in a newly independent nation were being crushed into the ground.

The Partition drama was being played out at all levels. The Muslim League, under the guidance of Mohammed Ali Jinnah, had already endorsed the idea of a separate nation for India's Muslims. Nehru and Gandhi were using all means possible *not* to give in to that idea, to keep the country whole. The British were leaving anyway. How much did *they* really care? They were being accused of a history of divide-and-rule tactics that were culminating in Partition. Hindus and Muslims, encouraged by their own fanatics to be ever more mistrustful, were now pitted against one another. Riots were breaking out throughout the country, and Gandhi was rushing around trying to quell them with his policy of nonviolent resistance.

Until then, our school, Queen Mary's Higher Secondary School, had been a haven of tolerance. Our class was fairly evenly divided between Hindus and Muslims. We picked our friends on the basis of intellectual companionship and common interests, not religion. My intimates included the Muslim twins Abida and Zahida; Sudha, a vegetarian Jain; and Promila, a Hindu Punjabi.

Abida and Zahida came to school wearing the most exquisite *gharara*s as their lower garments, with short *kurti*s (shirts) on top. *Gharara*s were worn only in Muslim families and resembled culottes. However, they were unlike the *i*ʐ*ars*—the wide, floor-length pajamas—of my mother's childhood. *Gharara*s were so full of gathers that they gave the appearance of being floor-length, ample skirts. As all the gathers were pushed to the back and collected there, the general effect was that of an elegant bustle. Very smart, I thought. I wanted to wear them, too. I borrowed a *gharara* from Abida and had our tailor, Ram Narain, copy it several times over. Now all I needed were the long scarves, *chunni*s, the two-and-a-half-yard cloth pieces we draped across our bosoms and then threw back over our shoulders—not ordinary *chunni*s but the hand-dyed, hand-pleated ones, often with sparklers in them, that my Muslim friends wore.

I dragged my mother to the market to get a whole bolt of the finest *mulmul* (muslin). I cut this up into two-and-a-half-yard sections and left the pieces in a shop that specialized in covering them with the tiniest embroidered silver stars. Then I rushed them to the dyer and picked the shades I wanted—aqua, a soft spring-leaf green, maroon, cobalt blue, peach—and left clear instructions that the muslin needed to be heavily starched. Once this was done, I was left to do the hand-pleating myself. Each *chunni* took about two hours if I worked fast. The highly starched fabric wore down my fingers to the bone, but I was determined to do it. Abida and Zahida had taught me how.

It needed two people. My mother, or my younger sister, Veena, could always be drafted. The second person held a comfortable length of the *chunni* in front of her, as if she were playing the thread game Cat's Cradle. I sat opposite them with my hands closed in loose-fist formation. I grabbed one edge of the fabric between my thumbs and curled fingers and proceeded to form the pleats, one at a time, in a kind of horizontal milking action, one hand moving quickly after the other, until I had gone across the whole width. I did this a million times for each *chunni,* then twisted the *chunni* like a rope several times over, so the pleats would firm up and hold. I could now float through school just like some of my friends, holding up the folds of my *gharara* elegantly to one side when I ran, my newly dyed, pleated, sparkling *chunni* dangling from my shoulders. I never did manage to look quite as elegant as Abida and Zahida, though. They had single, thick, ever-moving braids going down their backs all the way to the bottom of their hips. My two thinner braids, ending in ridiculous black-ribbon bows, ruined the entire effect.

Abida and Zahida excelled in mathematics and embroidery. I could barely even say the word "mathematics" without having clouds of confusion descend upon me. Mathematics and I were born on two separate planets. When given a choice in the upper school of higher or lower mathematics, I had quickly opted for the lower kind, which allowed me to drop algebra and geometry altogether. Lower mathematics, on the other hand, was a startling composite. It consisted of arithmetic, which I could just about manage, and domestic science, a catchall subject that must have drawn its inspiration directly from *Mrs. Beeton's Book of Household Management*. I found myself learning some turn-of-the-century British "Downstairs" refinements, like how to use a scrubbing board and how to make food for invalids, such as blancmange. (I just made it and threw it away, it being totally alien to Indian sensibilities.) I also learned how to tie a tourniquet and assorted head-to-toe bandages, how to remove stains, basic embroidery stitches, and the names and number of bones in the human body. There are 206 bones in the body. You must always remember to count the six in the ears.

In arithmetic, when the very words "If it takes a train six hours to travel 145 . . ." made me desperate to reach out for a good novel, Abida and Zahida took firm charge of me, guiding me through a labyrinth of ratios and square roots. The genius of these twins, for me at any rate, lay not so much in their mathematical abilities as in their fine embroidery. The school was teaching us the British standards, embroideries using the cross-stitch, the chain stitch, the herringbone, and others that I already knew, but Abida and Zahida could do *kasheeda*. Perfected probably in purdah homes, where veiled Muslim women were isolated for hours at a time, this was a form of magical embroidery that allowed both sides of a fabric to end up looking exactly the same. There were two right sides and no wrong side. I *had* to learn it, and there were no better teachers than my twin friends.

They also taught me some games. *Gittay* was a picking-up-stones game similar to jacks, except we played it with pebbles, and *pitthoo* was a two-team game rather like baseball. They were both street games, a world away from the more formal badminton, tennis, and cricket that I'd grown up with. But I loved playing them in my newly donned *gharara* and *chunni,* as it allowed me to enter into the inner-city life of my peers that I desperately wanted to share.

There was one other way at school of sharing—and actually tasting—the inner city, not the inner city that my mother had introduced me to, but the inner city of my growing group of friends: that was at lunch, which we ate together, as far away from the stone school building as possible. We all brought our lunches from home.

The moment the bell clanged for lunch, we would lift up our many-tiered tiffin-carriers by their handles and make a dash for the outdoor area at the back of the school. We'd run through the corridor where burqas hung on either side in desultory rows, down the back steps, past the ancient neem tree with stone seating built around it, and past the netball courts. We kept running even beyond the second old neem tree, where our Girl Guide classes were held, and where our little fingers had been drilled in the art of perfectly executed reef and sheepshank knots. We were aiming for the back of the school grounds, where the land sloped upwards, and where the heat of the day was kept at bay by the soft breezes wafting under rows of tall shade trees. Here we stopped, took a few deep breaths, and sat down on the ground to picnic.

Tiffin-carriers were taken apart, tier after tier. What wonders did they contain today? Abida and Zahida could be relied upon to bring meats—and what meats they were! Goat cooked with spinach, browned onions, and cardamom, or goat with potatoes, cinnamon, and cloves. It was not so much the ingredients—the ingredients we used at home were not all that different, though we did use less chili powder—as the hand that put these ingredients together, and the order and timing it chose to use. That hand had a different rhythm, a different energy from my mother's, and from our own Hindu cooks from Himalayan villages. It produced a Muslim result.

That was the peculiarity of India's cuisines. There were dozens of traits, habits, and traditions that could be used to define regional foods. But such definitions were never entirely satisfactory, as there also hovered over each dish an air of indefinable religious sensibility that could be seen and tasted but eluded pinpointing. This stamp was present even if the dishes had the same names but were being prepared by families of differing religions. These families might even have lived in the same city for centuries.

Abida and Zahida's food was inner-city, Delhi, and Muslim. As my fingers tore off a small piece of meat from a bone, formed a morsel with the *roti* (flat whole-wheat bread), dipped the morsel in the spicy meat sauce (*shorva*), and then placed it in my mouth, I could taste all three influences. In the winters, when fat from the meat dish formed a stiff yellowish red icing over its surface, the twins heated up that particular container of the tiffin-carrier over a small kerosene stove, which they lit with a match. Those smells—the cardamom, cinnamon, kerosene, and the freshly lit match—would swirl around my head as I sat through the next class, whatever it was.

Sudha was also a Delhi girl. Her family, like mine, had moved out of the Old City and gone straight to Lutyens's New Delhi, to Firoz Shah Road, a road named after the same emperor whose ruined battlements had provided the foundation stones of my great-great-grandfather's inner-city home. Sudha's food was as

Jain as Abida and Zahida's was Muslim. It was completely vegetarian, devoid of onion and garlic, as those bulbs were thought to
arouse base passions; devoid of tomatoes and beets, as their color
was reminiscent of blood; and contained no real root vegetables
(though rhizomes were acceptable), as pulling out roots killed the
entire plant. The preservation of life demanded by her religion did
not stop her food—green beans, peas, chickpea-flour dumplings,
or cauliflower—from being scrumptious in a haughty, austere
way, nor did it stop her from sharing her food with us.

Promila's family were relaxed Delhi Punjabis. A few "modern" Punjabis had begun giving their children Western-sounding
names, hoping to propel them fully into a modern world they
were only half in then. Their food, though, would never change.
They did not want it to change. It would always stay Indian—
Punjabi-Indian at that. They were proud of it.

Promila lived within the inner-city walls but at one end, in
Daryagunj, an area that used to lie by the Yamuna River, before
the river idiosyncratically moved farther east. It was less
crowded there than in the heart of the inner city. Here roads and
houses had at least some room to breathe. She, too, lived in a joint
family, in a house as large as Number 7 but without the countrified gardens. We visited each other often.

She brought *paratha*s (griddle breads) stuffed with cauliflower, and mango pickle to eat with them. In the winters,
Promila's tiffin-carrier was crammed with *makki ki roti* (corn flatbreads) and *sarson ka saag* (mustard greens), all so buttery-rich
and mouth-wateringly good that she knew we would devour
every last bit.

I always found my own food the least interesting and barely
touched it. It was all too familiar. The others might enjoy my
poori (fried bread) and *aloo* (potatoes with ginger), at least at

those school lunches, but I wanted the contents of *their* tiffin-carriers. After we ate, sharing what we could, we either played *gittay* or wrote the letters of the alphabet in a circle on the dry earth or on the floor of the art-room veranda, making an instant Ouija board, and, using an ink-bottle top as a guide, called the spirits. We were big into spirits then, into Life, Death, Love, even Elopement. Shahida, a Muslim girl in my class with pale green eyes, was crazily in love with a first cousin and was contemplating running away. We were following that story closely.

The school, we had been told, was built on an old graveyard, and spirits seemed to be there for the asking. We pestered the spirits with questions about exams, about our crushes and loves, and about our futures. Most of the answers were spelled out without hesitation, but sometimes the ink-bottle top refused to be contained within the Ouija circle. It rose upwards by itself and flew out angrily, landing yards away. We did not know whether to be alarmed or to giggle.

Most of our teenage friendships withered and died as soon as talk of Partition began. It was as if two icy hands had descended and split our class into two, Muslims on one side, fully armed with appropriate arguments, demanding a partition of the country, Hindus on the other, with their own much-repeated counterarguments, saying, "Never." Not surprisingly, I was left in the middle, trying to hold the two sides together. And, not surprisingly, I was mistrusted by both sides. I did not belong to the one, and I seemed to be a traitor to the other. The hurts and angers were such that we had turned into a class of righteous fanatics. I would not, could not, allow all Muslims to be condemned, as some of my

Hindu friends wanted, but I also could not bear to see India divided and, as I saw it, a great country frittered away in bits and pieces. Tolerance and nuanced thinking had been shoved out of the window. It was an unbearable time of hardheaded black and white, them and us.

Without giving it much thought, at that somewhat tender age, I had become a firm follower of Mahatma Gandhi, with my dear softhearted father and mother serving as my guides. I had initially become agitated with their descriptions of the Salt March. This was not in our school history books and predated my birth, but I already knew all the details of Gandhi's Dandi Salt March on March 12, 1930. At that time our British colonial rulers had decided to impose a draconian law that prohibited salt production by anyone they did not control. This law affected every single Indian. We all ate salt, and it felt like a salt tax. Gandhi decided not only to make his own salt in a seaside town named Dandi, but to stage a very public 240-mile march to get there.

In my earlier years, Gandhi had begun advocating that we stop our reliance on foreign fabrics and that we spin, weave, and produce our own handloomed cloth as a symbol of our independence struggle. By now, I was determined to participate. I bought myself a spinner. At least I would spin the cotton thread. The simple spinning gadgetry, sold to millions of eager Indians, was housed in a black box, similar in shape to the portable wind-up gramophone I also possessed. Instead of a spinning wheel, it held a simpler spinning turntable that I could rotate with my left hand while my right hand expertly pulled a ball of cotton wool into a fine thread. Every week, I delivered several large spools of freshly spun thread to a central collection center.

As anticipated, the British soon drew final lines through the India they were partitioning. Produced in some faraway office, the newly formed boundaries cut right through the middle of farms, villages, rivers, and homes. A wail went up from the nation. Fear and uncertainty ruled. Would the new Muslim Pakistan allow Hindus to coexist? How would a Muslim minority really fare in the new secular India?

Independence Day for India was August 15, 1947, two days after my fourteenth birthday. My father took me to watch the transfer of power at India Gate, where a statue of Queen Victoria stood guard right in the center of a wide Lutyens boulevard called Kingsway at that time. I cannot remember where we parked our car, but it must have been quite far away. We walked and walked through dense crowds—hundreds of thousands of us had collected there—and stood near enough to Kingsway to have a clear view as Jawaharlal Nehru and Lord Mountbatten, both exceedingly handsome in all white, came riding down in an open horse carriage. The Union Jack was formally lowered, and the Indian tricolor went up. We screamed our lungs out. Thousands of caps were flung skywards. I felt giddy.

In what was the new West Pakistan, the joy did not last too long. Muslim fanatics began butchering Hindus and Sikhs and appropriating their houses. Hindus in the truncated India began butchering Muslims, whom they blamed for the breakup of their country. Neighbors who had trusted each other now betrayed each other. Some neighbors who had never paid much attention to each other now hid and saved each other. Mobs marched through villages, towns, and cities, killing those of faiths other than their own. Cornered men would be asked to drop their pants to distinguish circumcised Muslims from uncircumcised Hindus. If what came into view did not suit the viewers, daggers, guns, and knives put a quick end to precious lives.

A massive multidirectional migration began: Hindus crammed

trains headed for India, clinging to doors and roofs; Muslims jammed trains headed for the two Pakistans. Sometimes the trains arrived at their destinations filled with nothing but dead bodies, having been intercepted by a mob with massacre on its mind. A million people died. Several million lost all their belongings as they ran or were chased from their homes. Angry, hapless refugees were piling up on both sides of the new borders.

Until then, I had seen the men in my family pick up guns only to hunt, to hunt for delicacies of the edible sort—venison and partridge and duck and quail. But there was fear in our houses, too. Unruly gangs, some bent on religious mischief, some just old-fashioned looters taking advantage of the chaos, were on the attack. This time family guns were being picked up and patrols organized to protect our neighborhood. I could hear my father say, "You two take the 2 a.m. shift. Patrol from Number 5 to Number 8 on Jumna Road, and walk back on Raj Narain Road the Number 4 way." All the men, our fathers, brothers, uncles, and cousins, oiled and polished their guns with no sense of adventure or enjoyment. One night, the mob got so close we could hear the wild cries and shouts. We barricaded ourselves indoors, fearing for our men still patrolling the streets. But the mob melted away before doing us any harm.

This was not the case with the mob advancing on the house of Dr. Joshi, Shibbudada's close friend and uncle to one of Lalit's dearest friends. As it marched menacingly through the gate, Dr. Joshi thought he could reason with the leaders and approached them in friendship. They shot him dead. When Shibbudada received the call, he jumped into his two-tone Chevy. We begged him not to go, as he would have to drive through dangerous sections of the Old City, but he paid no heed. I remember so well seeing the back of his car as it sped out of the Number 7 gate and fearing that he, too, would be shot and that we would never see him again.

The Old City had erupted. Hindus and Muslims, who had for centuries lived there cheek by jowl, in the closest proximity, were now turning on each other. Mainji's son, my inner-city first cousin, was in his late teens at the time. He left his house for some minor shopping and did not return for several days. By then he had lost his mind. Literally. Was he beaten? Raped? Tortured? He never spoke coherently after that.

Delhi's Muslims began disappearing, making their way to Pakistan. All of my Muslim classmates left without farewells. I can only assume they had safe journeys. I have not seen even one of them since. Amina's father, rightly gauging the roughness of the Novelty Cinema area and Delhi's general instability, bundled up his family and deposited them in London. He, however, chose to stay in India, rising much later to be mayor of Delhi. My father's dearest friends, Bashir Zaidi and Zakir Hussain, also chose to stay. One would become vice-chancellor of Aligarh University and a member of Parliament and the other the president of India. But other Muslim friends of his did leave. Badr-ul-Islam had a large, grand house on Curzon Road (now Kasturba Gandhi Marg) in Lutyens's New Delhi. His sons were friends of my brothers, often going on hunts with them or playing bridge at their homes. They all left for Karachi. One of the sons would marry into the politically powerful Bhutto family of Pakistan. Once they had moved out, a family of desperate Punjabi refugees, the Bhagats from Lahore, moved in, not into Badr-ul-Islam's mansion but into the servants' quarters at the back, upstairs, over the garage. By the oddest coincidence, we would get to know this family with its several young daughters as well. One of the daughters would become my sister Kamal's best friend, and her older sister, the personal secretary to Prime Minister Indira Gandhi.

Shibbudada did return safely from Dr. Joshi's home, only to report that most of the city had turned into a hell. That did not stop him from riding out in his Chevy again and again to escort his Muslim musician friends from the inner city to planes and trains headed for Pakistan. Like many others, Bundu Khan, master of the *sarangi* (a bowed string instrument), left India with the greatest reluctance, after much urging from his family.

Delhi as we knew it ceased to exist. Its vibrant Hindu-Muslim culture, its nuanced rules of etiquette, its unfailing politeness, and its unique sense of hospitality began to fade away. Urdu, the language it had given birth to, went into a fatal decline. Depleted of many of its original inhabitants, and in a spirit of "the king is dead, long live the king," Delhi began filling up with new citizens, refugees from the Punjab.

No refugee center could contain them all. They poured in by the thousands. Once a modest-sized ancient city of a little over a million people, Delhi was to bustle with more than thirteen million. The refugees took over all open spaces to set up little shops, markets, and shanties, anything to help them survive. The city began expanding haphazardly in all directions and without any of Lutyens's innate sophistication or the Moghuls' guiding principles of symmetry and grandeur.

On January 30, 1948, Mahatma Gandhi was shot and killed.

A few days before, my mother had asked me if I wanted to accompany her to one of Gandhiji's prayer meetings. These meetings were held with some regularity at the grand residence of one of India's richest industrialists, Birla. One edge of the landscaped garden was at some height and looked down, after a sheer drop, upon a large open field, forming a natural "stage" and "audience hall." Gandhi came to this "stage" in the early evenings to pray and talk.

The prayer meetings were nonsectarian, nondenominational. Gandhi believed not in one nation under God but in a world, a universe under God—under the same God, whatever different names people chose to address Him by. He embraced India's Untouchables and included all faiths in his hymns. His lectures were about tolerance and man's common humanity.

Of course I wanted to go, I told my mother.

We set off in the late afternoon. The driver had warned us that huge crowds attended these meetings and traffic would be slow. It was worse than slow. Delhi dust mixed with January's *uppala* smoke swirled around thousands of unbudging cars that honked and beeped as if that would somehow facilitate a forward movement. All order had broken down. Instead of one neat lane, cars had angled themselves to the left and right, hoping to escape to a nonexistent magical, fast-moving path. There was no going forward or backwards. I feared that Gandhi's prayer meeting would come to a close before we could reach the field.

But we inched forward and got there. There was a sea of people. We joined them, taking our place, cross-legged, on the ground, just like everybody else. Gandhi came, in a white dhoti (loincloth) and shawl, escorted by two young women. We looked up at the stage. He folded his hands and bowed, and the hymns, sung by his followers onstage, began:

> . . . *Ishwar Allah taray naam*
> *Sub ko sanmati dey bhagwan* . . .
> (Ishwar [the Hindu name for God] and Allah
> [the Muslim one] are but names for You,
> O God, grant us some wisdom/tolerance)

We all knew the hymns and sang along. When Gandhi himself spoke, it was in a toothless whisper, amplified as much as possible by a microphone. We listened raptly. The sea of people—taxi drivers, farmers, carpenters, sweepers, film tycoons, and business moguls—was silent.

Just a few days later, Gandhi was shot three times. He was on his way to a prayer meeting with his usual escorts, walking towards the same "stage" at Birla House, where I had so recently seen him, when the shots rang out. He sighed "*Hey Ram*" ("O God") and died. We heard of it on the radio. The whole city heard of it. Our family was in Number 5. We rushed out onto the street, as if an earthquake had struck. All our relatives were on the street, too. Number 7, Number 16, Number 14, Number 12, and Number 10 had spilled out all their inhabitants for an impromptu wake. We cried, sharing our shock and disbelief. Our fear, too. At that time, we did not know who had done the shooting. If it were to turn out to be a Muslim, more killings and riots would surely follow.

That night, our first prime minister, Jawaharlal Nehru, spoke to the nation on the radio—"The light has gone out of our lives and there is darkness now . . ."—his voice rising and falling in the soft, warm cadence that only he possessed.

The assassin was a member of an ultra-orthodox Hindu party that demanded a Hindu India, not the secular, tolerant country of Gandhi's and Nehru's dreams. In our family, there was some indefinable sense of relief, but great anger as well, at any version of religious certainty that could lead to such a senseless murder.

We were all present at Kingsway to view Gandhi's funeral procession, standing at the same spot where, just a few months earlier, my father and I had seen our new national flag unfurled. We wanted to attend the cremation at Rajghat, by the river, but the crowds were so thick we just got close enough to watch the white smoke from his funeral pyre dance upwards to meet the clouds.

TWENTY-THREE

*Punjabi Influences • Food with New
Attitude • Bazaar and Tandoori Foods •
A Taste of Spam • Sunday Lunchtimes*

Refugees from the Punjab settling in Delhi had brought with them their own language, Punjabi, their unique entrepreneurial spirit boosted by a hearty physical energy, and their own culture. Delhi succumbed and became, to a large extent, a Punjabi town. The martial Sikhs, who were once Punjab's fearsome horsemen, monopolized another kind of vehicle, becoming the movers and shakers of the newly created Delhi taxi service. Because it was the capital city and housed a central government that drew civil servants from around the country, Delhi began to develop a national consciousness. As new embassies slowly established themselves, Delhi picked up the heady air of international sophistication as well.

There was a major change, a revolution really, in the city's food. Before Independence, most upper-class and middle-class families ate at home. Among Hindu families like ours, cleanliness was certainly next to godliness. We bathed at least once a day in the winter and at least twice a day in the summer. And always in flowing water. Bathtubs were anathema. "How can those people sit in dirty water!" my mother would exclaim, gesturing her head in the general direction of the West.

We ate only home-cooked food and washed our hands and mouths before and after meals. Eating out was not condoned. As my father said repeatedly, "Who knows what germs lurk about in *outside* food? Perhaps a dirty finger has been poked into a bowl, or perhaps clean food has been removed with a *jhoota* [previously used] spoon."

"*Jhoota*" was a big word in our home. If someone's mouth had touched a food, it was taboo to anyone else. It was now considered *jhoota*, or tainted by the mouth. I never shared a whole apple or pear or peach with anyone, not even my sisters. Once one of us had taken a bite, it was definitely *jhoota* and unavailable to all others, even if the person who started on the fruit could not finish it. My mother then just said, "Oh, how could you waste it like that," and threw it away. If one person drank from a glass of water or soft drink or whiskey, it was theirs. No one else could take a sip. Not a soul in our family was ever heard to suggest, "Taste mine. Take a sip of mine." (Even today, if a friend in America or England says innocently, "Taste my Bloody Mary. It is wonderful. It has something unusual in it. Tell me what it is," I am at first paralyzed into a Hamlet-like state of inaction. I then fall on my sword and taste it as every atom of my body yells, "No, no, noooo.") As children we played dirty rotten games with each other, one of us quickly licking the fruit or chocolate or sandwich we all had our eyes on and then singing wickedly, "It's *jhoota* now. You can't have it."

A few strange contradictions did, however, manage to work their way into the fabric of our pure, clean lives. They took the form of special bazaar foods. There were, of course, the aforementioned *paratha*s our mother let us eat on the quiet—these definitely slipped under the radar—but others were officially sanctioned, too. The first of these was the *aloo bedvi* (sauced potatoes and stuffed *poori*s) we got on the odd weekend from Ghantaywallah Halvai for breakfast.

This *halvai*, or sweet-maker, who had his shop in the very center of Chandni Chowk, the Main Street of Moghul Delhi, specialized in sweets and savory snacks. It was the savory snacks I was interested in. Most of the time in Number 5, we had eggs for weekend breakfasts, with ham or bacon or sausages from the English shop, Spencers, in Kashmiri Gate. But every now and then my mother prevailed, and my father let the driver go out to procure a breakfast of her choice from the Old City, the very Hindu *aloo bedvi*. My father justified this indulgence by saying, "At least the food is cooked and hot, and therefore free of germs. Besides, we serve it on our own clean plates, which have not been washed in filthy bazaar water."

My father's own choice of bazaar foods, and he certainly had his indulgences, were far more questionable, especially in light of his own articulated standards. He—and my brothers, for that matter—all loved Muslim foods from another inner-city bazaar area, the one that surrounded the Moghul emperor Shah Jahan's seventeenth-century mosque, Jama Masjid. They liked the kebabs, especially the satiny, crumbling-at-the-touch, tubular *seekh* kebabs, made by wrapping very finely ground, perfectly seasoned meat around thick skewers and grilling them on charcoal braziers. They also enjoyed the hamburger-like *shami* kebabs, made by boiling ground meat with spices, making a pâté-like paste with the mixture, forming patties, and browning them. But *shami* kebabs could be made at home; our family excelled in them. What we did not do was the grilling that *seekh* kebabs demanded, or the baking that the accompanying Muslim breads required.

Over the centuries, Kayastha families like ours had acquired the dubious reputation of being *sharabi kebabi*s, lovers of liquor and kebabs. That applied only to the men; the women almost never drank, they imbibed only "soft drinks." My mother spoke no English but she did know how to say "soft drink," two words that were required frequently in company. Even though they did not partake of the liquor, many of the women had taken to relishing their meats. One rather large, exquisitely beautiful, green-eyed cousin of mine was asked if she cared for sweets, to which she replied languorously, "Nooo, not realleeey. If I have any roooom left in my stomach at aaall, I just eeeat another *kofta* [meatball]."

Whenever we had a big party—and sometimes it was just a large family gathering—the men demanded that their much-loved kebabs and Muslim breads be sent for. A driver was dispatched, but not before he was given clean platters, clean tablecloths, napkins, and dishtowels, so that when the food reached us it upheld the family's standards of cleanliness, at least outwardly.

The driver made sure that the breads, the *roomali roti*s (handkerchief breads, breads as thin, soft, fine, and large as a man's handkerchief) and the *bakarkhani* (dense, thick, multilayered, buttery flatbreads), were wrapped in the tablecloths. He handed our clean platters to the Jama Masjid kebab-maker and supervised as the *seekh* kebabs were arranged in neat rows and paper-thin red onion rings spread generously over the top. The onion rings were not only a much-loved accompaniment but helped to keep the kebabs moist. The onion rings were raw (my father supposedly mistrusted raw bazaar food) and they had been soaked in water—filthy bazaar water?—to erase some of their sharpness. Yet the finicky men in our family devoured them without a care.

Until then, that was the extent of the "outside" food we ate, other than the odd pastries and cakes we bought from Davicos and Wengers, English teahouses, or the semi-Western meals we ate at our parents' clubs. Then a restaurant called Moti Mahal opened on a main road in Daryagunj, on the edge of the Old City. More a set of rough-and-ready stalls than a real restaurant, it had embedded in its floor a set of large clay ovens shaped like vats. These were known as tandoors. Delhi was entranced. It had never seen the likes of them before, or eaten the tandoori foods these ovens produced.

Young, whole roasted chickens emerged so tender and moist they could be pulled apart and devoured in seconds. Light, bubbly *naan* breads, made by slapping elongated teardrop shapes against the heated tandoor walls, were pulled out with long hooks. These could be torn and wrapped around the meat. *Kali dal* (whole black beans) provided the accompaniment. It cooked overnight in an earthen vessel partially buried in the tandoor's fading embers. The only condiment offered at the table was a bowl of small, whole pickled onions. This was food with a new attitude. Its very simplicity and freshness was modern and enticing. There was nothing like it in Delhi. Moti Mahal was packing them in.

This was Punjabi food, from what had once been India's North-West Frontier, near its border with Afghanistan. When India was partitioned, fleeing Hindu refugees from the newly formed West Pakistan gathered their valuables and ran in an easterly direction. They carried their tandoors with them so they could cook along the way. One such family that fled all the way to Delhi had decided to open Moti Mahal and offer its plain village cooking to a city of culinary sophisticates. The rest, as they say, is history.

Tandoori food—good, bad, and mostly indifferent—has been produced by almost every major Indian restaurant since then. The trend started first in Delhi and then spread throughout the globe. In Delhi, other Punjabi entrepreneurs took note of Moti Mahal's success and felt they could do better by serving tandoori food on starched tablecloths. They would add Moghul delicacies, even Western hors d'oeuvres of baked beans and sardines to the menu, and have a fancy bar that served all manner of liquor, including hard cider. They would also offer the occasional week-end dinner dance. Gaylord in New Delhi was one such place. It, too, was very successful. The new, independent Delhi was in an extroverted, celebratory mood, and restaurants became the place to express this new freedom. The more conservative, effete Delhi-wallahs were soon following the more outgoing Punjabis and eating publicly. New restaurants, coffee shops, and *dhaba*s were opening daily.

The *dhaba* was entirely of Punjabi origin. Once a simple routier for truck drivers on the road, or any passersby, it turned into a fixture in the small shacks and stalls of Delhi's newer markets set up by refugees. It served Punjabi staples such as *chana bhatura*, spicy chickpeas with deep-fried leavened breads, as well as quick stir-fries made in the *karhai* (Indian cast-iron wok) with *paneer* (very freshly made cheese) and tomatoes.

Punjabis, like Texans, did everything bigger and better. If the entire nation had a passion for dairy products, the Punjabis indulged in them even more. They preferred rich milk with cream floating on the top and drank it in large amounts. When they made yogurt, they used water-buffalo milk, with its higher percentage of fat, often reducing it over low heat until it had the texture of cream. This they set into the richest—and tastiest—yogurt you can ever hope to eat. If they made *lassi* (a yogurt drink) with it, they added some cold milk for extra richness and then served it in tall glasses, each with the capacity of an average blender. (I use the few Punjabi *lassi* glasses I own as vases for long-stemmed flowers.) They not only used ghee for all their cooking, frowning on oils, but smeared the most generous dollops of homemade white butter on their *roti*s (flatbreads) and greens. One of my twin cousins had married a Punjabi, who impressed me greatly by telling me that as a child he was given a spoonful of ghee in the morning to make him big and strong. *Paneer* dishes were also Punjabi specialties: *mattar paneer* (*paneer* with peas), *saag paneer* (*paneer* with spinach), and *paneer bhurji* (shredded *paneer* stir-fried with onions, ginger, green chilies, green coriander, and tomatoes). The first two of these would become a firm part of the Indian-restaurant repertoire, in Delhi to begin with and then around the world.

Most grocers now carried big wheels of *paneer,* made by curdling milk with the previous day's whey, collecting the curds in a cheesecloth, and pressing down briefly on the bundle. Anyone could buy a chunk of the fresh cheese, along with the peas, onions, and ginger they needed.

World War II was over, but we in India were belatedly being bombarded with its leftovers in the form of mysterious boxes known as K rations. Delhi was awash in them. It was almost as if the rectangular brownish khaki boxes had been dug up from some forgotten hoard and then floated down to us on a million parachutes. This may actually have happened, as we were also awash in parachute "silk," which was being transformed quickly into blouses, skirts, sarees, and curtains by Delhi's masses.

I never thought then of checking the expiration date on the K rations. All I remember is that my cousins and I tore them open as if they were Christmas presents, pulling out each carefully fitted can or package with the greatest glee. Thus I was introduced to my first olive, my first fruit cocktail, and my first Spam. I rolled mouthfuls slowly around my tongue and pronounced each of them to be exotic and wonderful. I had never eaten canned fruit or canned meat before.

Although we, the younger generation in our family, now routinely picked up tandoori foods from Moti Mahal for our picnics, stopped now and then at a *dhaba* for a snack of *chana bhatura*, and regularly patronized restaurants like Gaylord, our meals at home, controlled by the adults, remained steadfastly the same. No Punjabi influence filtered in. K rations stayed out of the dining room and, like doll's food, were dismissed as children's rubbish.

All our meals were in Number 5, and our little kitchen there was humming busily from morning until night. Sunday lunches provided us with two of our most beloved dishes. One had a Hindu pedigree, the other a Muslim one. My mother and I preferred the very local, Hindu *karhi-chawal*—by a few degrees. Made with chickpea flour and buttermilk, *karhi* was soupy and sour, filled with light, bobbing dumplings. It was always eaten with plain Basmati rice. The men preferred the very Muslim pullao (pilaf)—by a few degrees. So we alternated between the two—unevenly—somehow always ending up in favor of the men.

By midmorning, the aroma of boiling Basmati rice would spread through the house, and I found myself drawn towards the kitchen to watch my mother make the dumplings. She would put the chickpea flour in a bowl and slowly add water, mixing away until she had a thick, smooth paste. She would beat it with her little hand, my father's signet ring firmly on, until it fluffed up and turned quite pale. "This is the step that makes the *pakori*s [dumplings] light and fluffy," she explained. She carried the bowl to our simple, hand-built brick-and-earth stove, lit with charcoal. A *karhai* with hot oil already sat on a burner. My mother would pick up a lump of paste with her fingers and then release it with her thumb. It plopped into the oil, sank, and then quickly rose to the surface, creating a frenzy of little noisy bubbles. She dropped in another dumpling and another and another, until the surface of the oil was covered with them, all bubbling away. When they were golden and cooked through, she scooped them up with a slotted spoon and released them into the hot, soupy *karhi* to soak and soften. Her dumplings, the heart of a good Delhi *karhi*, were always perfect.

Pullao Sundays were another matter. They were, without a doubt, a product of our Muslim heritage. The proper name for our pullao would probably be *yakhni* pullao, *yakhni* being the flavored stock used for cooking the rice. (Even the name of the dish was derived from Arabic and Persian sources.) That flavor was heady. Pieces of goat, from the neck and ribs in particular, were boiled with whole spices—cardamom, cumin, cinnamon, cloves, bay leaves, fennel seeds, black peppercorns, and coriander seeds—as well as a whole onion and chunks of ginger. The stock simmered slowly. We would inhale aromas of the feast-to-be as it cooked for hours, getting hungrier by the minute. Once the meat was tender, it was removed and the soup strained to produce the precious *yakhni*. The rest was easy. All that was needed was to brown the meat with sliced onions and some black cardamom pods, add Basmati rice and *yakhni,* and allow the rice to steam through. A *yakhni* pullao was earthy, basic, and honest. Rather like a good pasta or risotto dish, it required only choice ingredients and perfect timing.

Pullao days were good, because my mother indulged my father completely. She would include the *kofta*s (meatballs) he so loved, some gingery green beans, a potato *raita* made with yogurt that had just the right degree of sourness he was partial to, and a spicy salad made with tomatoes, onions, and cucumbers. The table was always graced with scallions stuck, green side up, in a Waterford cut-glass filled with water. They did double duty and served as our floral—green, at any rate—centerpiece as well. We chased each mouthful of pullao with a bite of the scallion, and then went on to the *kofta*s and green beans. After such a meal, bodies naturally turned lethargic, so pullao-Sunday lunches were invariably followed by serious pullao-Sunday naps.

TWENTY-FOUR

Until I was well into my teens, my father's beige-and-chocolate two-toned Plymouth had dropped me off at school. I now insisted that I was old enough to travel by myself on a bicycle. I had a basket in front for my books, and my three-tiered tiffin-carrier dangling from the front handle. Extra tennis shoes or clothing required for school plays or sports could be clipped to the carrier at the back.

My father had taught me how to bicycle on our rear lawn in Kanpur. Holding from the back the small-sized lady's bicycle he had given us, he had pushed me around the badminton court, along the rose beds, and up near the rear wall, until one day he just gave a big shove and let go. I was bicycling by myself and did not even know it, bicycling hard and fast, the little wheels turning like a dynamo.

That is how I bicycled throughout my childhood years in India, afraid that if I slowed up I would lose control and fall. I had a million fears, the first being the looming banyan tree that stood twenty bicycling-seconds away from our house. It was an ancient specimen with the dimensions of a cathedral, its many branches drooping to the earth and rerooting themselves again and again to form hundreds of crazy Gaudi-like arches. It was home to so many creatures that passing under it presented a world of hazards. Bird droppings were one of the more palpable ones. If I did not hit the pedals, I could receive a virtual shower.

Less palpable was a presence that lingered there imperceptibly, one I had been introduced to by our ayahs, the nannies who cared for us. Each successive ayah, whether Hindu or Christian, whether illiterate or semiliterate, had a similar stash of stories set in a pantheistic world filled with ghosts, spirits, giants, and fairies. We loved hearing their tales and, quite wisely, refrained from repeating them to our parents, lest this source be silenced. We quietly added the heroes and demons of these tales to our own growing lists drawn from Greek and Hindu mythology, from the Bible, from comics, from films, and from the books we read daily. One of the ayahs had impressed on me again and again that I should beware the spirits that peopled banyan trees. Then she had told me a "true" story that would haunt me for the rest of my life.

There was a young man, she had said, who traveled to work every morning and had to pass under a banyan tree to do so. A female spirit who lived on the tree watched the young man on his daily journey and fell deeply in love with him. She begged the Leader of the Spirits to let her assume a human form so she could meet the young man. The leader at first refused but relented in the end, saying, "I will grant you a human form for only as long as you live a proper human life, performing only human actions. The moment you do anything extraordinary and spiritlike, this boon will end."

The spirit was transformed into a beautiful damsel, who appeared before the young man repeatedly in different settings until he fell in love with her and married her. They had a joyous life together, eventually producing a son. She lived as a human, cooking, cleaning, and caring for her son in a small second-floor apartment. On weekdays, the husband went to work and the boy, eventually, to school.

One day, when the husband was still at work, the boy, who was about ten now, asked his mother if he could go downstairs to play in the common garden. The mother gave her permission but sat at the upstairs window, watching. She noticed that the local young bully had picked up a large boulder and was approaching her son from the back. She watched as the bully raised the boulder to smash it down on her son's head. Without thinking, she stretched out her arm—and stretched it and stretched it—until she was able to reach the bully and push him aside. Then, of course, she had to disappear and become, once again, a spirit in the banyan tree.

The road, as it passed under the vast edifice of the banyan tree, was on a slight upward incline. I lowered my head and, with my heart throbbing and two neatly beribboned pigtails flying behind me, raced uphill at top speed. No birds or long-armed spirits were going to get me.

From there onwards, I traveled mostly on back roads, choosing to enter the school through its front gate, which was on a quiet, narrow lane, and not the back gate, which was on an unsavory, busy thoroughfare. Sometimes I was followed by lecherous *goonda*s (petty hoodlums) in loose pajamas and fitted shirts, who came too close and whispered what good little girls were not supposed to hear, but I looked straight ahead and bicycled away.

The school was still reeling from the upheavals of Independence and Partition. Perhaps to provide an overlay of order, it had been decided that all the schoolgirls would wear uniforms. The uniforms would not be the traditional navy blues or browns of most schools. Ours were to be mauve. Not a nice mauve, but a vile one that even Mother Nature might not tolerate. Our *kamee*ẓes (long shirts) and *chunni*s (long scarves) would be mauve, while our *shalwar*s (baggy pants) would be white.

There were hardly any Muslims left, none at all in my class. Newer girls had poured in. We were just getting to know them. Manoranjana, a refugee, was a tall Sikh who had fled small-town Punjab. Hindi was not her language at all, so, given the circumstances, our school had made an exception and given her permission to study Punjabi instead, with a private teacher who came for her alone. English was not her language, either, though she spoke it well enough. She sighed frequently in the English classes. She had not grown up with any of the books we had been absorbing since childhood, from English nursery rhymes to Dickens—or the everyday proverbs we used—and felt like an alien. But, like Abida and Zahida, she was brilliant at mathematics. With mathematics, which required no language skills, or, better still, was its own language, all her awkwardness vanished, and she became serene and confident.

My Hindi, meanwhile, had improved by leaps, and all because of a new teacher. He was a tall, slightly pockmarked, bespectacled male, the only one of his gender among our teaching staff. I was shocked that Queen Mary's had hired him at all. At first, our relationship had been somewhat distant and wary. I was, on the surface, this Westernized, bold know-it-all, and he, in his Indian kurta and pajamas, was shy, hesitant, and seemingly ultra-conservative. When I was asked to read in class from a book we were studying, I watched his eyes glaze over at the slowness of my attempt. Reading Hindi was still an effort for me; I could not just zip along. Then, whether I was doing the reading or someone else was, I could not let a sentence pass by without making sure that I knew the meaning of every word in it. With my Hindi vocabulary still deficient, I was the cause of many stoppages. He frowned at me repeatedly for slowing down his class.

His attitude towards me changed entirely after one homework assignment. It was the kind of assignment that was usually given out only by our English teachers: Write an essay about your holidays . . . Write about someone you admire . . . Write about the happiest day in your life. Most of the children hated such subjects, as they seemed too vague and general. I, perversely, loved them, as I felt I was being granted the freedom to write whatever I wanted, create a holiday I had not had, conjure up a "person to admire" who did not exist, or turn what had been a tedious day into a "happy" one.

For homework, our Hindi teachers until then had stuck to questions raised in our textbooks. This new teacher—Masterji, as we called him—asked us to write an essay on our relatives.

Here was a subject I could handle, or at least manipulate to my own design. What had been becoming clearer to me as I was getting older was that there were two distinct types of Indians. There was my kind of Indian—a privileged product of British colonial India, who spoke English fluently but also spoke Hindi. We ate at a table with napkins, knives, and forks, but would eat with our hands when we wished. We were avid filmgoers who watched both Western and Indian films, and we could talk about

Tudor England just as easily as about Moghul India. One part of us was completely Indian, but there was this sophisticated Western overlay, a familiarity and ease with the West, that set us apart.

If my father had decided to send us to Mahila Vidyalay, the Hindi-language school in Kanpur, we might have become the second kind of Indian. Most of India consisted of this second kind of Indian, whose mastery of English was nil or limited; who, like my mother and her relatives in the Old City, like Manoranjana, and, yes, like Masterji, my Hindi teacher, lived much more traditional, unbifurcated lives. Were they the real Indians and we just hybrids created by a particular time and place, and would we now, after Independence, just be plowed under or left with no standing in our new society?

I did not really want to write about any relatives. I wanted to write about the relationship between the two different types of Indians and to pass that off as an essay on "my relatives." I devised a short story about a poorer, more traditional man (someone, say, like Masterji) coming for a dinner at the home of his richer and more Westernized relatives (to a family, say, like ours). I decided that I would view this encounter through the eyes of the youngest two children of the Westernized family. This way I could comment and analyze, be rueful, compassionate, or rude, whatever I wished. I did not need to dig up big Sanskritized Hindi words. After all, the story was being told from the point of view of children. My own vocabulary would be sufficient.

I wrote the story and added my book to the pile of homework exercise books on Masterji's desk. The following week, we got our homework back. Masterji handed out one book at a time, making small comments as he did so—"Good effort," "Watch your spelling," and the like. My book was last. He slapped it on his table, took off his glasses, and just looked at me as if he were seeing me for the first time. "Brilliant," he said, "that was just brilliant." He handed me back the book, still staring. I opened it up just a little bit to peek at my marks. I had received a ten out of ten. Across the top of the first page was scrawled in English, "Excellent. Brilliant psychological analysis."

Our relationship underwent a dramatic overhaul. He stopped looking at me with dismissive eyes, and I soon became his devoted follower. Instead of staid textbooks, he made us read the *Bhagavad Gita*, the ancient treatise, a dramatic speech really, given on the battlefield by Lord Krishna, on the subject of duty and action. He had us study the sixteenth-century poet Mira Bai's devotional love songs, and Tulsidas's version of the *Ramayana* of the same period. Looking directly at me, he stopped to translate the more difficult Old Hindi words, because he knew I would demand an explanation otherwise. Knowing I loved to read, he suggested Hindi novels and poems quite out of our curriculum, such as Premchand's rural novel, *Godan*, and Harivansh Rai Bachchan's poem about our struggle for independence, *Madhushala*.

Academically at least, I was now riding a crest. I was comfortable in all the subjects needed for high school. English, history, and drawing were old friends. Hindi had become an exciting new one. That left only lower mathematics—i.e., arithmetic combined with domestic science. I could manage the arithmetic, the needlework, the removing of stains, the naming of all 206 bones in the human body, and the tying of bandages wherever required. What I absolutely could not stomach was the cookery. Oh yes, I could light a charcoal fire and set a pot on it. What I could not bring my body and soul to do was cook the food. The textbooks had not changed suddenly after Independence. We were still being asked to prepare British invalid foods from circa 1930 and not much else. Blancmange still loomed large.

The foods I was actually eating at lunchtime in school were far more tantalizing. They had changed considerably since Partition. My new friends were bringing new foods from much farther afield. Manoranjana brought very thick, large, earthy Punjabi-village *paratha*s (griddle breads) stuffed with white radish. The accompanying condiment was a rough-cut sweet-sour pickle made with jaggery and mustard-laced cauliflower, turnip, and carrot. Leela, another new student, a Syrian Christian from what is now the southern state of Kerala, intrigued us with her food, *idli*s (steamed rice cakes) and coconut chutney flecked with whole brown mustard seeds. She left us with our mouths agape as she described her tropical home state, which none of us had visited. "There are coconut palms everywhere," she said, "and we all—everyone, rich and poor—walk barefoot, as the roads are so clean. . . ." A second, even more orthodox Jain girl from Rajasthan, also named Sudha, brought just boiled potatoes and some mixed spices in a newspaper packet. As we watched, she peeled the potatoes and crushed them coarsely. She then opened her newspaper packet, lifted some spice mixture with the tips of her fingers, and sprinkled it over the potatoes. I was never able to work out what that magical mixture was. I have not been able to re-create it, perhaps because it has attained mythical proportions in my head. Her potatoes were divine.

TWENTY-FIVE

Exam Season • Brain Food • The
Honey-Seller • Sweetening the Mouth

As soon as I got home, hot and sweaty from bicycling, my mother would produce cold *phirni* from the refrigerator. This was a very light cardamom-scented pudding made with coarsely ground rice that my mother set in shallow terra-cotta bowls (*shakoras*). A layer of *varak*, real silver tissue, was laid over the surface, and pistachios, slivered into *havaiyans*, airy nothings, sprinkled over the top. I would slide the spoon in and begin eating. The sweet, cool, milky pudding, tasting of the cardamom and pistachios, with an earthy aroma of terra-cotta, went down smoothly. It was worlds away from blancmange!

There was no time to rest afterwards. May was the time for our annual exams, and all of April had to be spent doing revision work. Indian history was the most demanding, as it started in the early B.C's. Battles, sieges, dates, planting of trees, emperors, ever-changing maps, kingdoms expanding and contracting, planting of trees, new laws, statutes, declarations, acts passed, planting of trees. Indian emperors planted a lot of trees. India probably needed them for the shade they provided. We seemed to

I pose by the neem tree at Number 5, aged about sixteen.

be always writing sentences like "King Ashoka gave alms to the poor, spread Buddhism, and planted many trees. . . ." The British-history textbook was somewhat thinner than the one for Indian history. As I struggled to retain the causes of the Wars of the Roses or remember the cast of characters championing the Spanish Armada, my mother brought me cooling glasses of *chha*, buttermilk flavored with salt and roasted cumin.

While I studied in my hot back room, my mother sat knitting for my sisters in their frigid Himalayan convent. In the superheated Delhi of April, I could hardly even look at wool, let alone touch it. My mother just carried on heroically.

Each examination was three hours long, starting and ending promptly at the designated times. On most days there were two exams, with a break for lunch. Before I left in the early morning, armed with sharpened pencils, pens freshly filled with ink, ink bottles, rulers, and erasers, my mother would appear with a plate containing two almond balls (*badaam ki golian*). She made these by soaking the nuts overnight, peeling them, then grinding them with sugar and cardamom, forming soft balls, and finally covering the balls with the silver tissue. They were the most elegant two balls you could ever hope to see. My mother firmly believed that almonds were brain food, and that any child sent off to write two examination papers for six hours unfortified with almond balls was surely suffering from the grossest form of neglect. I would take a bite of the *badaam ki goli* and savor it on my tongue. Meanwhile, my mind would be thinking: There are 1,760 yards to a mile, that is 5,280 feet to a mile. . . .

Blank sheets were handed out, and we began. Teachers patrolled the rooms to catch cheaters. I wrote as fast as I could, barely stopping to think. I would lift up a hand—"More paper, please"—and keep writing. Most questions, except, of course, for arithmetic, had to be answered in an essay form. For example, the question "What were the causes, main events, and results of the battle of Panipat?" would require regurgitating a couple of chapters I had crammed about the founding of the Moghul Empire, with all relevant dates duly stated. There was no sliding into fiction here.

I would return home, ink-stained and exhausted, and immediately begin to start studying for the next day's exams. My mother never asked me how I had fared. She always assumed that I would do well.

Often she would try to distract me from my studies if she thought I was working too hard. One afternoon when the servants were off duty, she called me, saying, "Come, come, there is a man here selling honey." By the time I came out of my room, the man was well into his sales pitch: "Purer honey than this, you can never hope to find. Look at its fine golden color. See, see, it still has pieces of honeycomb suspended in the middle. Smell it. The odor of nature's flowers . . ." My mother cut right through to the chase: "But how do I know it is pure? What proof do you have?" She was hoping that she had stumped him right there.

He turned out to be wilier than that. "What proof, you want to know? The oldest proof in the world. It has worked since the beginning of time. First you catch a fly, and then you throw it into the honey. It will sink. If the honey is impure, it will keep sinking and die. If the honey is pure, it will rise to the surface and fly away." At that he swung his hand in the air and caught a fly, flinging it immediately into the honey. It sank. Then it started to rise, higher and higher, until it reached the surface and flew away. My mother was so impressed she bought several jars, and I went back to my studies.

That evening, when our cook returned from his afternoon break and my mother recounted the honey story, he said, "*Arey memsa'ab* [Oh, lady], you have been completely duped. I can do exactly the same thing with sugar syrup." Our cook seemed as adept at catching flies with his hand as the honey man. He caught one and threw it into a jar of sugar syrup that my mother kept for sweetening our fresh lime juice. The fly sank, then rose to the top and flew away. We teased our mother mercilessly.

Soon after the exams, the results were announced. If they were good, it necessitated an immediate mango-and-ice-cream party, sometimes with *rasgulla*s (cheese balls in syrup) as well. As it was the height of summer, it also meant that it was the height of the mango season. Our grandparents, as well as our neighboring aunts, uncles, and cousins, were immediately summoned for a celebratory sweetening-of-the-mouth. My mother never called this simply a party. People were being invited to sweeten their mouths. Sweetening the mouth was auspicious and had the hallowed ring of tradition to it; a party was just a party. "Come around five, five-thirty?" my mother would say.

Boxes of mangoes were hurriedly sent for from a Kashmiri Gate fruit stall. *Rasgulla*s came in terra-cotta crocks from Bengali Market—Bengalis made this sweet better than anyone else—and three-flavored, three-colored blocks of strawberry, chocolate, and vanilla ice cream from Kwality in New Delhi. Before Partition, our thick, creamy homemade ice cream had come from a small Muslim family-run restaurant in Kashmiri Gate named Idris, after its owner. We could actually taste its main ingredient, clotted cream (*malai*). But that was all in the past. We could not linger on what used to be.

We would all bathe and change. The women wore flowing white voile sarees, embroidered for them especially in Lucknow with white thread. Jasmine from the garden, also white—and fragrant with summer's promises—was the only ornamentation in the hair. The men wore similarly embroidered white kurtas. As the party started, a mother whose child had scored particularly spectacular marks would try to dull her eyes with feigned clouds of humility. "Have more mango," she would say to her guests.

As good ripe mangoes were full of juice, there was a simple trick, now well mastered, of eating them without spraying your crisp white clothing with squirts of orange. You just had to lean over your plate and have napkins handy.

TWENTY-SIX

*First Jobs and First Loves • Ballroom
Dancing • Dressing for the Dinner Dance*

Our social life was evolving, too. Not mine, really, as I was
still in school and destined to remain a mere voyeur for a
while, but that of my older brothers, sisters, and cousins. The first
year that followed Independence had been full of elation and sor-
rows, but Delhi had settled down and was in a celebratory mood.

My brothers were now out of college and starting their first
jobs. My eldest brother, Brijdada, was working at the same cloth
mill as my father. Bhaiyyadada, devastatingly handsome, at least
in my eyes, and puckish in his humor, had tried to join the Indian
Army after his master's degree and had gone through several of
their tests. I understood why he might want to join. National
feelings were running high. India had been forcibly truncated
and felt embattled and threatened. China loomed to the northeast; Pakistan gnawed at the northwest. I did not want him to go
into the army. With belligerence between India and Pakistan
soaring, I wanted him at home. In the end, he joined my middle
uncle Shibbudada's very successful firm as second-in-command.

*Me with Lalit, some friends, and Lalit's future husband, Madan
(far right), on the wall of the beer garden at the Cecil Hotel,
Simla, three years after Partition.*

It seemed a natural extension of their relationship, which had remained very close and trusting through the years.

My older siblings and older cousins were of an age to fall in love, or to at least have deep emotional leanings. They were living up to expectations. Since we, the younger generation, and our friends did everything together as a large, friendly gang, it was hard at first for me to comprehend that stronger, more intimate relationships might be forming among those in our midst. Such things would never be discussed, so I had to keep my antennae up and focused.

My grandfather still insisted that we all come over to Number 7 for a dinner or a breakfast or a lunch. If we had friends visiting, it was expected that we would just bring them along. We never knew who might be filling up the benches in the dining room when we arrived. Besides the assorted first, second, third, and fourth cousins, there were all *their* college friends, who came and went, too. Sometimes there were so many people we had to eat in relays. Our picnics now consisted of just the younger set and were thought up frequently on the spur of the moment. No demands were made on any household kitchen, as there was no long-term planning. All of us, brothers, sisters, friends, and cousins of assorted ages, would pack into cars, pick up food from Moti Mahal, and drive off to the same historic sites or dammed rivers that we were already familiar with. Only this time all participants were young and included those for whom Delhi was new—refugee college-mates.

Even visits to the hills—to Simla, for example—might be undertaken by a similar collection of siblings, cousins, and friends. Instead of renting houses, we just stayed at a hotel.

Who was developing feelings for whom? Love, or something like it, seemed to be blooming right before my eyes. It was quite clear that Lalit and a student at St. Stephen's College, a tall Hindu called Madan from northwestern Pakistan, were getting close. They went for walks together. Among the refugee friends he had introduced to us was a young girl from Karachi whom Bhaiyyadada seemed to like. Lalit's best friend at college, a young Kashmiri girl, had a brother who seemed to dote on my cousin Santoshjiji, whom we called Tosh. Tosh and her family had been living in Lahore at the time of Partition and had been forced to flee. All around me there was an entanglement of relationships, bubbling and heaving with varying degrees of intensity.

One Holi, I discovered that my dear sister Kamal was perhaps developing a crush as well. There was a young, handsome youth who visited frequently. I did notice, however, that whenever this young man walked by our house he whistled a jaunty tune, which ended after he had passed our second gate. He was a good whistler.

That Holi had been like any other, a free-for-all with cousins, friends, aunts, and uncles all participating in assorted hijinks, most ending up in the tank of *tesu* water. I watched this youth circle Kamal and then grab her and rub red powder all over her face. She laughed and covered his face in return with the golden paste she was carrying in a jar. She seemed to be anointing him. Their play was innocent, and yet I could sense their attraction. Of course Kamal did not say one word to me about it.

Shibbudada's own eldest son was studying statistics in America and had met an American girl. There was talk of marriage. Sheila, Shibbudada's daughter, was thought to be in love with an economics professor at Delhi University. Was it true? It was all hush-hush, as the gentleman in question, it was said, already had a wife in Kashmir.

I watched and listened as I felt attractions and tensions straining the air, but I stayed at arm's length. Sometimes my brothers, sisters, and their friends would go dancing at the clubs. They had already started dance lessons with a Madame Varda, who was reputed to have Russian blood. What Madame Varda taught them was nothing particularly Russian. It was ballroom dancing that was highly popular then, the rumba, tango, quickstep, and waltz—both the slow one and the fast-twirling Viennese. When they came home from their lesson, my brothers and sisters danced with each other, winding up their gramophone and dancing to 78s of Victor Sylvester and His Band.

They had become very good by now. Bhaiyyadada and Lalit were particularly smooth at the tango, holding each other tightly and going pum-pum, pum-pum, pumpumpumpum, pum-pum, with their swaying and sliding feet.

I would hear them make reservations for a Saturday dinner dance. Dinner jackets would be sent out for pressing to the *dhobi* (laundryman). My sisters would look through their collection of sarees again and again. Would something they already owned suffice, or did they need to go shopping? By now they had starting wearing sarees frequently, both for everyday and formal wear. We had been convinced—mostly by Lalit, who guided our tastes—that ordinary silks were common and bourgeois. We were to wear rare handloomed cottons, some from far-off villages, others distinguished by fine work in real gold thread. In the summer, only the sheerest cream Chanderis, see-through cotton-and-silk mixtures from Central India, would do. If silk was to be worn at all, then it would need to be some exquisite antique, perhaps once worn in South Indian temples by nineteenth-century dancing girls. When a new saree was purchased, it did not come with a matching blouse. The blouse would need to be sewn, and Ram Narain, our tailor, hurriedly sent for.

It was equally gauche to wear any of my mother's heavy jewelry. Only small, rare pieces were stylish. We went to the jewelers again and again with our mother, searching through their storage boxes for old Moghul tidbits. There was the tiger's claw that we found, set in the most delicate gold filigree. It could be strung and worn around the neck. Then there was the *hauldali*! Years later, when we were grown up enough to have our own children, my mother, smart woman that she was, decided to distribute all her sarees and shawls and jewelry among her daughters while she was still alive. The two things we all wanted were the green *jamevaar* shawl and this *hauldali*.

The *hauldali* was a white jadeite tablet set with precious stones that had been arranged in a delicate floral pattern, each flower and leaf outlined with gold. Its workmanship was not unlike that of Emperor Shah Jahan's wine cup, now in London's Victoria and Albert Museum. My mother had it strung with a simple black thread so it could be worn modestly around the neck. (Veena got the *jamevaar*, I have the *hauldali*.)

The great hullabaloo in the days preceding a dinner dance had me all worked up, too. I could not go, but at least I would watch my sisters dress. They sat in their petticoats (long half-slips) and blouses before my mother's three-mirrored dressing table and put on their makeup—nothing much, just some rouge and lipstick, a little kohl for the eyes, that was it. They coiffed their hair in buns. If any hair ornaments were to be worn, they would consist of jasmines from the garden, made into a thick rope that was wound around the bun. Heels were out. Gauche, gauche. It was only proper to wear flat *chappals* (slippers), perhaps the natural leather ones from Kohlapur in Maharashtra. Finally, the saree, all ironed by the ayah, was wound around and my sisters were ready. How very beautiful they were.

My brothers, smelling of Old Spice, and my sisters, of fresh jasmine, drove off into the night. They would meet their friends and eat and dance. I wanted so much to grow up fast but was afraid that I would never end up with their grace or looks.

When they returned late at night, I was up and waiting. They would talk among themselves and I would listen. My eldest sister, Lalit, would say merrily, the joy of the evening still singing inside her, "You want to dance? I'll teach you." She would take hold of me as if she were the man. "Here we go. This is the waltz. . . . *One* two three, *one* two three . . . Dip and take a long slide on the *one*," or "Here is the quickstep. Forward quick-quick slow, backwards quick-quick slow." We would practice, she leading me around the bedroom furniture, twirling and sliding, until we fell down on the bed in a heap of giggles.

TWENTY-SEVEN

Future Planning • The Radio Station •
The Last Large Picnic • Wildflower Hall
and an Encounter with the Police

I n my last years at school, I was happy enough. But something deep inside me knew that the life I was living was not my real life. I was convinced that I belonged in another world. I had no idea what that world might be, I just knew that I had not found it yet. One day it would happen. I would step out of one life and into another one—the one I was meant to be in. I was oddly calm and optimistic about it.

I had begun thinking about college and what I might want to do with my life. I thought that I wanted to be a painter and that I would apply to the J.J. School of Art in Bombay.

Naturally, I discussed this with Lalit. "You could do that," she said, in her thoughtful, practical way, "but why not go to J.J. later? Go to a regular college now and get a proper B.A. degree, and once you have that as a backup, you can do anything else you want."

It seemed far too practical. I just wanted to fly away somewhere. Quickly. And paint with blobs of oil paint.

"Get a degree in what? What else am I interested in?" I wanted to know.

"You could do an Honors [major] in English," Lalit suggested. "That is my subject. It is Sheila's, too. Or you could do an Honors in history, like K."

Kamal was in a new all-girl college that had just opened, Miranda House. Even its brick buildings were not yet fully in place. But, partly because it was just behind the hallowed St. Stephen's College (now going through a males-only phase), and partly because it had begun to attract the hottest young ladies in town, it had become a highly desirable destination for Delhi's graduating schoolgirls.

Unfortunately, Miranda House, just like all of Delhi's colleges, was bound by Delhi University rules and offered a most limited range of subjects. In the arts category (mathematics and the sciences were obviously quite out of the question for me), we could do an Honors in English, Hindi, history, philosophy, or economics with a minor in one other of the same subjects. Or we could get a general bachelor-of-arts degree in some of the above subjects without specializing in any of them. The general degree carried much less cachet. I postponed thinking about it: I did not have to apply to any college until after I had graduated from school. The J.J. School of Art seemed to be drifting further and further away.

I had started taking on odd jobs at All India Radio. Even as a young child, I was quite familiar with the soft thump of recording-studio doors and the musty, enclosed smell of radio-station corri-

Lalit (right) and I on the gate of Number 5.

dors. Delhi's first radio station was barely five minutes away from Number 7. Whenever children were required for radio plays or children's programs, our gang of cousins was summoned. Where else could just one phone call produce such a variety of children, all of whom could be counted on to read fluently and, as was said in general praise of our abilities, "with expression"? The call always came to Number 7—to the one phone there, located in a corner of the gallery. Whoever answered it then buttonholed a servant and asked him to make a round of all the surrounding houses to convey the relevant information.

I had been taking part in radio plays almost all the years since I could read. Now that independent India's new All India Radio had been established in New Delhi, I was asked to come in several times a year. As I was paid a small fee for each session, this could be considered my first professional work. It felt more like play than work. A car was sent to pick me up, I met other schoolchildren I had never met before, we were offered tea and samosas, then we stood around a microphone and read our lines while invisible goblins in the recording booth made sounds of doors closing, cars starting, thunder, and rain. We knew how to dip our knees slightly and drop the page we had just finished onto the floor without a rustle, and to refrain from fidgeting noisily while someone else was reading. Radio was fun—and easy. Already, the allure of work that felt like play had begun to infiltrate my being.

My grandfather, far too old to work now, had stopped his annual trips to Simla some time back, but we still went, sometimes to Simla and sometimes to other hill stations, sometimes with elders of our parents' generation and sometimes without. I hardly knew where I belonged. At Hackman's Hotel in the hill station of Mussoori, I sometimes felt grown-up enough to attend the dinner dances there with my older brothers and sisters, to eat the never-before-tasted cream cheese on crisp breads as I watched scantily dressed European cabaret artists slither along the dance floor accompanied by the glow of a spotlight, but at other times I just felt too awkward in my glasses and my pigtails and chose to skip them, and to accompany my mother on her shopping expeditions the following morning instead.

All major saree shops had branches in hill resorts. My mother was their much-welcomed patron. I would sit with her for hours at Leela Ram and Sons as she examined bolts of French chiffon.

In chiffons, she never seemed to pick pure colors. She might pick a blue with a hint of silver, a salmon pink dulled with gray, or a maroon so dark it was almost brown. Then she looked for matching borders, thick Benaresi brocaded borders that came in rolls of wide ribbon, made with real gold and silver thread. She laid one border after another on the chosen chiffons to see how well they matched. Once the decisions were made, she still could not take anything home. The borders needed to be sewn onto the delicate chiffons by hand. Fabrics for the blouses and petticoats had to be picked out, and then everything left at Leela Ram's for stitching and finishing.

We had not stopped going on our hill picnics, but, just as in the city, their character had changed. The older generation, if they were in the hills with us at all, stayed at home now, exerting themselves just enough for gentle strolls and shopping on the Mall. It was the youngsters who picnicked. One year, in Simla, about eighteen of us, ranging in age from the mid-twenties down to me, still in high school, and including college-mates of my brothers and cousins—lovers, friends, and relatives—decided to create our own kind of picnic by bicycling from Simla to Mashobra, a good eight miles away, all of them uphill. We were heading towards a destination at least a thousand feet higher than Simla, standing tall at 8,250 feet above sea level.

Mashobra was a tiny hill town on the India-Tibet Road. Now part of the national Shimla Reserve Forest sanctuary, it was always devastatingly beautiful. High up on a spur that fell down sharply into deep valleys, it was ringed by snow-covered peaks. Its glades were massed with wildflowers, its steeply sloping sides thick with deodars (Himalayan cedars), oaks, pines, and rhododendrons where pheasants, musk deer, partridges, and eagles darted, leapt, and soared. There were plenty of gushing streams for those who wanted to wet their feet, and orchards for those hungry for apples or apricots plucked straight from the trees.

All members of my family knew Mashobra well. We had picnicked and trekked there, year after year. Aside from simple local dwellings, there were a few remaining turn-of-the-century British homes from the Raj days, the most famous of which was Wildflower Hall. Built originally in 1866, it had become a cooling haven for the rest and recreation of British India's rulers, its viceroys and commanders-in-chief. Lady Dufferin, writing in her book, *Our Viceregal Life in India*, declares, "This country villa of ours is 1000 feet higher than Simla. It is on top of a hill and in the midst of the most sweet-smelling pinewoods where the mountain views are magnificent."

Wildflower Hall's most famous resident in the early part of the twentieth century was Lord Kitchener, the great warrior of Khartoum. Indians referred to him as the Jungy Laat Sa'ab, or the Warrior Lord Sahib. Having made a name for himself in North Africa, he had been posted to India as commander-in-chief. Thwarted in his hopes of being appointed viceroy, he found great solace and comfort in Wildflower Hall, where he gardened and worked on an ingenious ice pit. Winter snow was pushed into a dark, covered hole and left there all through the frigid months. By the summer, its own weight had converted it into ice, which could then be used by the Wildflower Hall kitchen for the rest of the year.

Kitchener left India in 1909, and Wildflower Hall was sold to a hotelier whose wife eventually tore it down and, in 1925, built a hotel with the same name. It was considered quite grand for its time. This was the hotel, the Wildflower Hall, we had known and frequented. Our family had grown up with it. We often stopped there for lunch or tea when we were out on family treks or picnics. We wanted to show it off to our new friends.

The day of our picnic we rented our bicycles, picked up some sandwiches and drinks, and, in one large group of wild bicyclists, left Simla through the Sanjauli tunnel.

We would have to bicycle uphill for most of the outward journey. That hardship seemed a fair trade for the return trip, which we knew would be a joyous glide home. We pushed our pedals and sweated along the hairpin bends, all stubbornly pointed upwards, stopping often to drink at the small waterfalls. When we reached Wildflower Hall, we found it eerily quiet. All the vegetation seemed unkempt and overgrown. We tried a door. It was locked. We knocked. Where was everybody? We tried another door. It, too, was locked. We so wanted our new friends to see our beloved Wildflower that one of us probably pushed on a door too hard, and it flew open. We all entered a familiar dining room, happy and laughing. It was then that the few lone caretakers approached us. They accused us of breaking into the hotel, which was now closed, and said that we should wait right where we were, as they had called the police.

The police, when they arrived, were in no mood to accept any explanations or protestations of innocence. We, with our bicycles, were loaded into the back of an open truck for an immediate trip back to the Sanjauli police station. "Could we not return on our bicycles and just meet you at the police station?" we asked, thinking of the downhill ride we were being deprived of. They were unrelenting.

We sat in the police station for hours, answering the same questions again and again, until it was dark. What had seemed quite funny was now getting seriously worrisome. At that stage it occurred to one of our friends that he was closely related to a very senior member of the Himachal State government. He made a telephone call, which was followed almost instantly by apologies and release.

This was possibly our last large picnic. The number of attendees had been dwindling. We had in our collection posed turn-of-the-century photographs of family picnics attended by three hundred or more formally dressed family members, with my grandfather and his brothers seated grandly on chairs in the center. Later photographs showed forty or fifty people, then thirty, then twenty. We were all growing up, and our lives were never going to be the same.

TWENTY-EIGHT

*Kamal's Journey • Shibbudada Interferes
Again • Cookery Exam*

Kamal was ending her second year of college when her leg, the same left ankle, began troubling her again. My parents were distraught. Fresh X-rays were taken and sent off by air to Harley Street specialists in London and the Memorial Sloan-Kettering Cancer Care Center in New York. One biopsy after another was done. These results were also sent abroad. The specialists still suspected a bone tumor but wanted to examine her before recommending a clear course of action. She needed to go to the West.

Shibbudada thundered back into the center of our lives. Perhaps he had never left. *He* would take her. Raghudada, his elder son, had recently married the American girlfriend we had been hearing about. Shibbudada could now meet the new bride, Thelma, and also make sure that Kamal's medical problems were thoroughly examined. He made the decision, and it was not questioned.

I do not know what my father felt about this arrangement. He certainly said nothing, though his eyes looked more lost than ever. And what did Shibbudada's wife and children think? Not a word was said. We all seemed deeply unsettled, though not perhaps for the same reasons.

While preparations were being made for Kamal's long journey—we were not at all sure what its duration might be—I was getting ready for my final school exams.

The hot *loo* winds blew viciously that year. I hid in my back room, working hard on my revisions. My mother came in daily with a plate holding two beautiful *badaam ki golian*. We said little, just quietly dripped our salty tears over the sweet almond balls. Every evening, as soon as it became tolerable to leave the air-cooled house, I went outside and picked some jasmine flowers. With a needle and thread, I strung them into a thick rope. I kept this rope near me as I worked. Its aroma, filled with the India I knew, wiped out the rest of the world.

My mother pulled Kamal's warm clothes out of mothballs. Her coats and cardigans were aired. New silk sarees were bought, as it was thought that crushable cottons, which could be worn just once before needing special cleaning, light starching, and ironing, would be most impractical, however much we loved them. She already had several pairs of slacks, but more were sewn. My mother was learning. This was her first child to leave for distant shores. When Lalit and I left, some years later, she would know exactly what to do.

My exam time arrived when our hearts were focused on Kamal. I had been able to concentrate on my schoolwork through the wretched years of Partition, and I must have done so again with my final exams, as I had no difficulties with the English, Hindi, history, or drawing tests. Lower mathematics, my bête noire, proved the most exacting, but for reasons I could hardly anticipate.

I had worked at the arithmetic up, down, across, and sideways.

*My father and mother prepare to say goodbye to Kamal (her
arm linked to my father's) as she sets off for the West in search
of medical treatment. Shibbudada stands behind my mother.*

I had practiced doing every possible type of sum or problem that
could be thrown at me. I had done it once. I had done it twice and
thrice. When the exam questions were put before me, they
seemed quite accessible. I finished the exam and checked my
answers a dozen times. I handed in my paper well before my three
hours were up. When the results came, I had some of the highest
marks in arithmetic.

It was the domestic science that let me down.

When I arrived for the "practical" test, there were no stains for
me to clean, no herringbone stitches for me to do on a small piece
of cloth, and no bandages to tie. I was a master at bandages. I could
crisscross them over the head or the ankle to beauteous perfection.

For this test, we were asked to congregate in what appeared to
be the dusty ruins of some old municipal property, not at all
encouraging for my morale. Then the hapless students were led

to a dark corner, where, piled on the floor, were sacks of potatoes, tomatoes, onions, garlic, ginger, and assorted spices.

"Use these ingredients to cook a dish. Here are the matches. Here is the wood. Now . . . go."

Go where? Excuse me, what happened to the blancmange?

Over the next few years, I tried to understand what might have transpired that disastrous day. Perhaps some wise-guy examiner had said, "Why are we asking these poor Indian children to cook something they have never eaten, like this boring European blancmange? Why do we not ask them to cook some everyday Indian food, like simple potatoes?"

But to change course without any advance notice? For someone like me, who could not cook at all, it was a frightening proposition. Given a chance to prepare, I might have worked on a few Indian dishes. But just when I had mastered every last detail of British invalid cookery, circa 1930, why were we being presented with Indian spices?

I did the best I could. I cut up everything I found—potatoes, onion, garlic, ginger, tomatoes, chilies, and green coriander—into even-sized pieces, and threw them into a pot with a little water. I sprinkled a few spices and salt over the top, put the lid on, as I could not bear to look at my bubbling creation, and prayed. It did no good. The only reason I passed lower mathematics was that my marks for arithmetic were so high, they made up for the cooking I must have failed.

I did well enough in the other subjects to pass school in the First Division (the top grade). I applied for admission to Miranda House, Kamal's college, and on my form stated that I wished to do an Honors in English with a minor in philosophy.

Meanwhile, Kamal and Shibbudada got on a plane and flew off to London.

TWENTY-NINE

*A Joint Family in New York • Grandfather's
Decline • A Riverside Cremation*

The summer of 1950 was relentless. We stayed in Delhi to await letters, telegrams, phone calls, any communication from abroad. The news from the first stop, London, was not heartening. The Harley Street specialists seemed to confirm the Indian diagnosis, bone cancer. New York was the next stop. Sloan-Kettering doctors agreed, and suggested two long sessions of radiation treatments.

Kamal and Shibbudada, who were staying at New York's Barbizon Plaza Hotel for the first month, now needed to find longer-term accommodations. Shibbudada decided to rent a large house in Flushing, Queens, where there would be room enough for Raghudada and his new wife, Thelma, as well as for Thelma's mother, Kamal, and himself. He was creating a little joint family in New York.

Thelma and her mother were doing most of the cooking. Kamal's letters were full of praise for them and for the new foods appearing daily on the table. She seemed particularly enamored of upside-down cakes, and whole hams glazed with pineapple. We could not even imagine what they might taste like.

In Delhi, my grandfather, now in his late eighties and already enfeebled, took a turn for the worse. Until then he had used a walking stick to help ease himself first onto the front veranda and then onto the Number 7 front lawn in the evenings. Here he enjoyed the few passing breezes, smoked his hookah, and drank his whiskey. Of late he had felt too weak to make this effort. He chose to stay in his room, generally in his bed. He soon began complaining of the heat. Large ice blocks were sent for and spread under and around his bed. I remember taking my shoes off and sloshing into his room to give him a kiss. A haze rose from the ice. My grandfather looked so thin. Several women in their white summer sarees hovered around him.

Soon he was unable to get out of the bed at all and seemed asleep most of the time. The doctor, the same S. B. Mathur who had pierced my ears, had recommended an oxygen mask. The women were taking turns holding it up to his face. In the heat of the day, he was kept in his room, but if the evening was reasonably cool, the entire bed, with my grandfather in it, *and* his oxygen tank were carried out onto the lawn.

One day, when it was my mother's turn to hold the oxygen mask, she beckoned me and said, "I have to run to the kitchen. Could you take over for a few minutes?"

My hand replaced my mother's. The mask stayed over my grandfather's sleeping face. I must have got distracted and shifted my position, as I felt my grandfather raise his arm and, with a

*Kamal and Shibbudada on their grand tour of Europe, traveling in
style to Britain on board the RMS* Queen Mary.

powerful move, pull my hand back into place. He was dying, but this once-powerful man was not going to go easily.

Kamal had begun her first radiation treatment, but her letters remained upbeat. They were not going to return directly, she wrote. Shibbudada was going to take her on a grand tour of Europe first. They would sail from New York on the *Queen Mary*, stay in London at Grosvenor House. Then travel to Paris, Rome . . .

Shibbudada, just like all of us, was worried about her future and was offering her the world, now. He seemed determined to keep her smiling.

My grandfather continued to deteriorate. One day, as I cycled into Number 7, I saw small groups of people walking silently towards the house. He must have died, I thought. I berated myself for not having been with him at the time, but he would not have noticed anyway.

He lay on his bed with his eyes closed. The sunlight coming in through the window was making strange shapes on his chalky face. His arms, lying outside the top sheet, were covered to the wrist with the crisp starched sleeves of a muslin kurta. The hands—those aristocratic hands with the long, tapering fingers and perfectly oval nails, hands inherited by my father and most of my father's children, except me—were facing down in a slightly cupped position.

I could hear my father and eldest uncle, Taoji, talking.

"We must send for the barber."

"The body must be bathed . . ."

". . . and put on the floor. Shall we use the big room?"

"That will be best—there will be so many people."

Most men had personal barbers to cut and shape their hair, but in our family we also had ceremonial barbers. A ceremonial barber had many functions, some involving hair and some not. This gentleman was an official matchmaker and carrier of horoscopes, a service he had performed for my parents. He was also responsible for shaving the head of the oldest son of a deceased father in a semi-religious ceremony. It was only after this purifying shaving had taken place that the oldest son could light the funeral pyre, as custom demanded.

A chair was put on the lawn. My uncle sat down, and the razor approached his head. He just stared at the grass.

The big room, across the gallery from the drawing room, was cleared and cleaned. Once he had been bathed, my grandfather was moved there and laid on the floor on a clean sheet. He was now in a fresh kurta with mother-of-pearl buttons. Relatives and friends began to congregate, sitting down cross-legged on the floor all around the body. Some dabbed their eyes, others talked. They filled up the room, even overflowing onto the front and side verandas and the gardens beyond.

The cremation had to take place that very day, so there was no time to dally. The body was enshrouded in a white sheet, and the sheet secured. As Babaji was being lifted onto a bier, my father, who until then had been performing his tasks perfunctorily and quietly, let out two deep, echoing sobs—like a wounded animal—and then abruptly collected himself and went on with the business of tying the body to the bier. But the escaped sobs, like large waves, reverberated through the big room, through the verandas, and out across the lawn. Everywhere they passed, there was sobbing and wailing.

Then the two sons who were present and two grandsons heaved the bier up onto their shoulders and began walking in the direction of the river. We followed, chanting:

Ram nam Satya hai
Satya bolo, Satya hai
(The only Truth is God's name
Speak Truth for Truth Is)

Normally, only men went to the riverside cremation grounds. But we were considered a very "modern" family, known for changing the rules. After all, had not Rai Bahadur Raj Narain sent his own daughters to St. Stephen's College? Still, the older generation of women, following older rules, stayed home. But we youngsters followed the bier.

At the cremation grounds, the body was put down several times so priests could chant and pray over it. After a final, purifying immersion in the Yamuna River, the bier was placed on the sandalwood pyre. Incense and perfumes were sprinkled, and more wood piled on top to form a "roof." My eldest, shaved uncle was handed a torch to set the pyre aflame.

On the third day, the family returned to "Gather the Flowers." The wood and the body had burned themselves out. All that was left were bones and ashes. These were to be collected in cloth bags and taken to a holy spot on the Ganges River, where they were to be scattered, just as had been done to the remains of all our family members, going back thousands of years. Throughout the funeral, I cried only twice: once when my father released his sobs, and then when I came across one unburned mother-of-pearl button among the ashes.

It is thought by Hindus that after thirteen days the human soul, having fully disentangled itself from the earth, ascends heavenwards to become one with the Universal Soul. Mourning ends. This Thirteenth Day is celebrated with a family feast.

And what a feast it is. On the table are laid out a collection of unusually delicious vegetarian foods, all cooked by the family, all prepared according to rules followed only on such a day, rules that seem impossible to fathom. No turmeric, asafetida, garlic, or onions could be used. In preparing the delicate rice pudding *kheer*, the rice first had to be stir-fried in a teaspoon of clarified butter (ghee). *Urad dal* (a split pea of Indian origin) was required to make an appearance in as many incarnations as possible, in stuffings, dumplings, sweets. . . .

I did not care about the rules. All I knew was that my grandfather's Thirteenth Day feast, as befitted the man we were celebrating, was nothing short of spectacular. Most of our aunts, uncles, and cousins had trooped into the long, river-facing dining room and gathered around the tables. The green pumpkin, cooked with cloves, fennel, and fenugreek, was impossible to ignore. I returned to it again and again, wrapping little morsels in delicate *poori*s (puffed, fried breads) and devouring them in haste. The potatoes, made mainly with ginger, tomatoes, and cumin, were simple yet extraordinary—earthy, gingery, and hot. There were slim stuffed okra, tiny taro patties smothered with ajowan seeds, meltingly soft *urad dal* dumplings in yogurt (*dahi baras*), a salad of grated white radish (*churri*), and assorted desserts, including the rice pudding. I ate and ate until I could eat no more. I then got on my bicycle and rushed to Number 5, where I immediately started a letter to Kamal to give her *our* news.

EPILOGUE

Kamal's Return • A Gift of Coca-Cola •
Sailing to a New Life • Mingling the Flavors
of the Past and the Future

Kamal returned with suitcases full of fashionable gifts for all of us. I received a pair of pedal pushers and a black-and-white-striped T-shirt that practically became my uniform. She also presented me with a light tartan shawl and a sterling silver charm bracelet with the Eiffel Tower dangling from it.

My sister's medical saga, though, was not over. The Indian doctors now discovered that Kamal did not have cancer after all but fibrous dysplasia, a decalcification of the bone that could be cured, could always have been cured, with a simple graft. She went on yet another journey, this time to Bombay, accompanied by my father and Bhaiyyadada. Again we waited by the telephone. The call came. It was too late. The many radiation sessions had completely destroyed her skin and flesh. Part of her leg would have to be amputated. She was only twenty.

I remember being on a bus that day, returning from college, unable to control the sense of devastation. And yet I never heard Kamal complain. Just once I saw her walking along the Number 5 front wall on her crutches, weeping silently into the sweet peas.

Brijdada and his wife, Asha Bhabi (center), with their two sons,
Anuj (far left) and Atul (far right).

I was now seventeen and no longer a child. I went to the Delhi University coffee shop to drink cup after milky cup of sweetened coffee in the company of male friends from the neighboring St. Stephen's College.

One day the largest possible truck had stopped outside the Number 5 gate. The truck had COCA-COLA emblazoned on it. I thought it was there by mistake. I knew Coca-Cola only from *Life* magazine and movies. I went up to the gate and asked the driver if he needed help. Was he at the wrong address? He was at the right address, he said, and looking for me. He said my name.

*Lalit and Madan at their wedding reception, held in
the garden at Number 7.*

Kamal with my father on her wedding day.

*Kamal, garlands of jasmine in her hair,
with Hussain, on her wedding day.*

He said he was carrying a gift for me from the Coca-Cola Company of America. At this he pulled out dozens of crates and carried them to the house.

I was a "student leader" and had been preselected, I was told. I fell for the promotional ruse, throwing party after party to use up my "gift," and, equating Coke with my newfound internationalism, took to swigging it from the bottle. I had yet to see the rest of the world, but, already armed with a pair of pedal pushers, the charm bracelet, and the Coke, I felt that that phase of my life had to be just around the corner.

Within the next few years, my sister Kamal would marry a handsome Gujarati doctor, Hussain, and settle easily into a life of domesticity and children; Lalit would marry her tall Punjabi fiancé, Madan, and move to England, where she would spend her lifetime teaching English; Veena stayed in India and continues to sing its praises; Bhaiyyadada married Maya, a beautiful Bengali educated at Smith College in America, and looks out for his sisters; my eldest brother, Brijdada, whose marriage to Asha, Shibbudada's first wife's niece, was arranged by Shibbudada, would be the only one to carry on the inkpot-and-quill line with all the Kayastha traditions that we had been so steeped in. As for Shibbudada, he would die suddenly of a penicillin allergy the year I left home, leaving my father and brothers to run his business, and leaving his own children so openly angry that they would start a war and hit at our family, the only target left, like battering rams day after day after day. . . .

Of course, I did not know all this at the time. I was busy playing Hamlet in an all-woman version at college, working in more

I appear in The Comedy of Errors *as performed by
St. Stephen's College.*

*A picture from my college's production—with an
all-girl cast—of* The Importance of Being
Earnest. *I played Gwendolyn.*

I graduated from Miranda House,
Delhi, in 1953. My days at drama
school were still to come.

professional theatrical productions of playwrights I was discovering—Jean-Paul Sartre, Jean Cocteau, Christopher Fry, and Tennessee Williams—and also falling in love. Then, armed with a set of drama scholarships to the Royal Academy of Dramatic Art in London, I found myself sailing due west on a Pacific & Orient ocean liner, all alone but all ready for a new life I was breathless to taste.

I knew less than the rudimentaries of cooking then, and found myself writing home to my mother, begging her to teach me, which she did, through airmail letters that arrived regularly in the post. I hardly knew that my old and the new worlds would start to mingle as soon as they touched, and that so much of my past would always remain my present.

The innocent Indian honey of my infancy was now mixed with the pungencies of Indian spices, the sour and bitter, the nutty, and the tinglingly aromatic. Births, deaths, illnesses, caste, and creed had woven their way through the flavors like tenacious creepers, and yet, somewhere in my depths, each bite, each taste of all I had eaten, lay catalogued in some pristine file, ready to be drawn up when the moment was ripe.

FAMILY RECIPES

Family Recipes

LAMB PATTIES *(Shami Kebab)*

SERVES 6–8

My brother Bhaiyyadada was talking to me recently with nostalgic relish about his more youthful hunting days. "There we were in the fields, with quail and partridge darting out from the bushes. After a few hours of that, we would take a break. Out would come the hard-boiled eggs, the pastries from Davicos [our local English tea hall], and the *shami*s. Oh, the *shami*s. They tasted so good."

Our menfolk all loved our homemade *shami kebabs*. When properly prepared, they had the texture of a pâté but the shape of a patty. They had a gently seasoned, melt-in-the-mouth body but a spicy, pungent, crunchy (green chilies, onion, and mint) center. They were served with a spicy cilantro-mint Green Chutney (see page 292) and paper-thin onion rings. The *shami* patties are customarily made with meat that has been cooked with yellow split peas and then ground on a grinding stone to a paste. The stone is essential. No machine is good enough. I have worked out quite another method to get a similar result, mainly because I know my audience and know that few would use the stone. I actually bake my *shami*s and serve them cut into squares.

In the evenings, *shami kebabs* are sometimes served with drinks or as part of a large, diverse meal.

1 pound ground lamb
1 teaspoon salt
1 teaspoon freshly ground black pepper
2 tablespoons finely chopped fresh mint leaves
2 tablespoons finely chopped fresh cilantro

1½ tablespoons peeled and finely grated fresh ginger
1½ teaspoons garam masala (see page 295)
¼ teaspoon cayenne pepper
4 teaspoons plain yogurt
4 teaspoons chickpea flour
2 teaspoons olive or peanut oil

For the Stuffing

2 tablespoons very finely chopped
    onion
1 tablespoon very finely chopped
    fresh mint leaves

2 teaspoons very finely chopped
    fresh, hot green chili (use bird's-
    eye or cayenne-type chilies with
    thin skins)

For the Garnish

A few sprigs of fresh mint
1 medium onion, peeled, cut
    crosswise into paper-thin rings,
    soaked in cold water for at least

    1 hour, then drained and
    thoroughly dried off
Lemon wedges

Combine the lamb, salt, pepper, mint, cilantro, ginger, garam masala, cayenne, and yogurt in a bowl. Mix thoroughly, cover well, and refrigerate for 16–24 hours.

Put the chickpea flour in a small cast-iron frying pan and set it over medium heat. Stir and fry the flour until it is very lightly browned. Remove it from the pan quickly and add it to the meat. Mix it in well.

Preheat the oven to 350°F.

Lightly grease a 7–7½-inch-square nonstick baking pan with a teaspoon of the oil. Form a ball with the meat, then flatten it out slightly. Mix all the ingredients for the stuffing and put the stuffing in the center of the large meat patty. Close in the meat over the stuffing and form a ball again. Flatten the ball. Put the meat in the center of the baking pan and, using slightly wetted hands, spread the meat out to the edges, smoothing and patting as you go. Dribble the remaining teaspoon of oil over the top and spread it out. Bake for 30 minutes, then place under the broiler for about a minute, or until the top browns. Cut into 1½-inch squares and arrange in a single layer on a plate. Garnish with the mint sprigs, onion rings, and lemon wedges.

GROUND LAMB WITH PEAS *(Keema Matar)*

SERVES 4–6

I cannot imagine our picnics or train rides in India without this dish. For my grandchildren, growing up in America, it is an all-time favorite. Sometimes we eat it with *poori*s, the deep-fried puffed breads, as we did so often in India, and sometimes with rice. When cooking for the children, I leave out all the chilies, whether the powdered red kind or the fresh green variety. My parents did the same for us when we were growing up.

I use low-fat yogurt, but you may use whole-milk yogurt if you prefer.

1 cup plain yogurt
½ teaspoon ground turmeric
¾ teaspoon cayenne pepper
1 teaspoon ground cumin
1 tablespoon ground coriander
1¼ teaspoons salt
One 2-inch piece fresh ginger, peeled and grated to a pulp
3 good-sized cloves garlic, peeled and crushed to a pulp
2 pounds ground lamb
4 tablespoons peanut or olive oil
2 sticks cinnamon, about 2 inches each in length

4 whole cardamom pods
2 bay leaves
1 medium onion, peeled and finely chopped
½ cup puréed tomatoes (also labeled strained tomatoes or *passata*)
1½ cups fresh (or frozen and defrosted) peas
3 tablespoons finely chopped fresh cilantro
1–2 finely chopped fresh bird's-eye or cayenne-type green chilies
1 teaspoon garam masala (see page 295)

Put the yogurt in a bowl and whisk lightly until smooth and creamy. Add the turmeric, cayenne, cumin, coriander, salt, ginger, and garlic. Mix until well blended.

Put the lamb into a large bowl. Pour the yogurt mixture over the top and mix (I use my hands) until thoroughly blended. There should not be any pools of yogurt left.

Pour the oil into a large (preferably nonstick) sauté pan and set over medium-high heat. When it is hot, put in the cinnamon, cardamom, and bay leaves. Stir once or twice, and then add the onion. Stir and fry about 5 minutes, or until the onion pieces are reddish brown.

Add all the meat. Stir and cook, breaking up the meat until no lumps and no pinkness are left, about 5 minutes.

Add the tomato purée and stir it in. Bring to a simmer. Cover, turn the heat to medium-low, and cook for 30 minutes, stirring every 6–7 minutes and making sure there is enough liquid so the lamb does not stick to the bottom. Uncover. Most of the liquid should have evaporated by this time. Stir and fry the meat for the next 5 minutes, removing and discarding the cinnamon sticks, cardamom pods, and bay leaves. After 5 minutes, spoon out as much of the fat as you can and discard it. Now put in the peas, cilantro, green chilies (if desired), garam masala, and 6 tablespoons water. Mix, cover, and cook on low heat another 6–7 minutes, or until the peas are tender.

MEATBALL CURRY *(Koftas)*

SERVES 4–6

These were our everyday meatballs, which could be eaten with rice or *phulka*s. We often took them on train journeys and picnics, where we would eat them with *poori*s.

For the Meatballs

1 pound ground lamb (make sure it is not too fatty)

½ medium onion (about 2½ ounces), peeled and finely chopped

One 2-inch piece fresh ginger, peeled and grated

3 cloves garlic, peeled and crushed to a pulp

1 tablespoon ground coriander

1¼ teaspoons ground roasted cumin seeds

½ teaspoon Kashmiri red-chili powder (or cayenne)

¾ teaspoon salt

3 tablespoons chopped fresh cilantro

1 egg, lightly beaten

For the Sauce

One 2-inch piece fresh ginger, peeled and chopped

4–6 cloves garlic, peeled and chopped

2 fresh hot green chilies

1 tablespoon ground coriander

1 teaspoon ground cumin

¼ cup olive or other vegetable oil

2 large black cardamom pods, lightly crushed

1 teaspoon whole cumin seeds

4–6 whole cloves

One 2-inch stick cinnamon

4–5 green cardamom pods

2 medium onions (10 ounces), peeled and finely chopped

4 medium tomatoes, grated on the coarsest part of a grater, or enough to yield 1½ cups (see headnote on page 255)

½ teaspoon Kashmiri red-chili powder (or cayenne)

4 tablespoons plain yogurt

¾ teaspoon salt

Combine all ingredients for the meatballs, mix well, and form 24 meatballs with wetted palms. Arrange the meatballs in a single layer on a plate, cover, and refrigerate for 4–6 hours.

Make the sauce: Put the ginger, garlic, green chilies, ground coriander, and ground cumin, along with 3 tablespoons water, into a blender. Blend until you have a smooth paste.

Pour the oil into a wide, heavy pan or sauté pan, and set over medium-high heat. When it is hot, add the black cardamom, cumin seeds, cloves, cinnamon, and green cardamom. Stir once or twice, and put in the onions. Fry over medium-high heat, stirring for about 8 minutes, or until the onions are reddish brown. Add the ginger paste, turn the heat down a little, and stir for 2 minutes. Add the grated tomatoes and red chili powder. Stir and cook over medium-high heat until the tomatoes are reduced to a thick, dark paste and you begin to see the oil. Turn the heat to medium, and add the yogurt, a tablespoon at a time, until it blends with the sauce. When all the yogurt has been added this way, pour in 2 cups water and the salt. Stir to mix. Slide in the meatballs, making sure they lie in a single layer, and bring to a simmer. Cover and simmer gently for 50–60 minutes, shaking the pan every now and then but never stirring with a spoon.

LAMB WITH SPINACH *(Saag Gosht)*

SERVES 4–6

There are so many good recipes for Lamb with Spinach. If you look through my cookbooks, you are bound to find at least three or four. I have to confess here that I have been trying for years to make a dish that tasted like what my Muslim friends at Queen Mary's Higher Secondary School used to bring in their tiffin-carriers (see pages 175–76). I had little success at it. What was I missing? I so desperately wanted that Muslim taste, not the rich Moghul version of it, but the common-man dish I had eaten under the tall shade trees at my old school.

In 2005, I was in Delhi to write about two famous local restaurants, the Bukhara and Dumpukht, for London's *Financial Times*. I was in their common kitchen—both restaurants are in the Maurya Sheraton Hotel—and the Muslim chefs there were showing me how to prepare some elegant, highly elaborate meat dishes, all worthy of emperors. "But," I asked one of the chefs, Nisar Waris, "how would you cook a *simple saag gosht* in your own home? I am looking for an everyday recipe." To me it is these home dishes that, rather like Italian food at its best, form the heart of our great cuisine. The chef paused in his stirring. Indian chefs are always surprised when you don't show a preference for their grand recipes. He thought for a bit and then went back to stirring as he rattled out a rough recipe, "Put some mustard oil in a pan . . ." Ah, here was a difference already. The oil. My notebook and pencil were already poised. I began writing. I noticed that there were no onions in the recipe, only ginger and garlic. Another difference.

A year passed without my testing the recipe, but when I did, the gratification was instant. Here was the dish that I had been dreaming about for so many decades.

If you do not wish to use the strong-tasting, pungent mustard oil, which I happen to love and which has been used in India since ancient times, try an extra virgin olive oil instead. They have entirely different flavors, but both are intense in their own way.

One 3-inch piece fresh ginger, peeled and finely chopped

6 good-sized cloves garlic, peeled and chopped

½ teaspoon ground turmeric

¾ teaspoon cayenne pepper (use less, if preferred)

1 teaspoon salt

3 tablespoons mustard or extra virgin olive oil

2 pounds boneless lamb from the shoulder, cut into 1½-inch cubes

1 pound spinach, washed and chopped finely (cut stacks of leaves crosswise into fine ribbons first, then lengthwise into small pieces)

6 tablespoons coarsely grated fresh tomato (1 medium tomato) (see headnote on page 255)

1 teaspoon ground cumin

1 teaspoon garam masala (see page 295)

Put the ginger, garlic, and 5 tablespoons water into a blender. Blend until smooth. Add the turmeric, cayenne, and salt. Blend to mix.

Pour the oil into a large, wide, preferably nonstick sauté pan and set over medium heat. When it is hot, put in the meat pieces and stir them around for about 2 minutes. Add the paste from the blender. Continue to stir and cook for 2 minutes. Drop in a handful of spinach and stir it in until it is quite wilted. Add all the spinach this way, a handful at a time. Cover, turn the heat to low, and cook 30 minutes, checking the meat every now and then to make sure there is some liquid in the pan. Remove the cover. Put in the grated tomato and turn the heat up to medium-high. Stir and cook the meat until all the liquid has evaporated and the meat just starts to brown, about 10 minutes. Now add ½ cup water, stir it in, and turn the heat down to low. Cover and cook another 15–25 minutes, or until the meat is tender. There should be a little bit of liquid left in the pan to make a thickish sauce.

Sprinkle the cumin and garam masala over the top and stir them in. Cover and cook on very, very low heat another 5 minutes.

MAYA'S MEAT AND POTATOES *(Aloo Gosht)*

SERVES 4–6

Maya, Bhaiyyadada's wife, is the creator of this recipe. In India, this dish is always made with goat. Pieces with bone from the neck and shoulder and marrow bones (which are smaller than lamb marrow bones) are combined with boneless pieces, such as those taken from muscles.

You could try making this with goat, which is now widely available in ethnic markets. If you can't get it, you can always fall back on either boneless lamb or a combination of some lamb pieces with bone and others without.

Grating tomatoes is not something that was done at home. I remember watching my mother cook in London when she and my father had come to visit my sister Lalit and me. She put whole, chopped tomatoes into the pan for whatever sauce she was making, and then, once the pieces had softened, painstakingly picked off all the skins. It was years later, when I was in the Punjab collecting recipes for a BBC program, that I learned this other, clever trick, which I have used ever since. Tomatoes can be grated on the large, coarse holes of a grater to provide a fresh purée . . . and the skin stays behind. Just hold one side of a tomato against the large holes, push a bit, and start grating. Sometimes the coarse skin needs to be cut off, but I never bother. I just persist. Keep grating until you have most of the tomato skin left in your hand. Flatten your palm, and grate the tomato flesh off the skin.

4 medium waxy potatoes (such as red potatoes), a little less than 1 pound total

Salt

Ground turmeric

One 3-inch piece fresh ginger, peeled and chopped

10–12 medium cloves garlic, peeled and chopped

Olive or other vegetable oil

8 whole cloves

2-inch stick cinnamon

2 large black cardamom pods, lightly crushed

2 teaspoons whole cumin seeds

8 green cardamom pods

2 medium onions (about 10 ounces), peeled and very finely chopped

2 medium tomatoes, grated on the largest holes of the grater (you need about 1 cup)

1½ teaspoons Kashmiri red-chili powder (or ½ teaspoon cayenne plus 1½ teaspoons good sweet red paprika)

2 pounds lamb (or goat), boned or not, cut into cubes of about 1 inch (see headnote)

1½ teaspoons salt, or a bit more to taste

Boil the potatoes in their jackets until tender. Allow them to cool completely, then peel. Cut into halves or quarters, depending on size. You need large, chunky pieces. Rub a little salt and turmeric on them.

Put the ginger, garlic, and ¼ cup water into a blender. Blend until you have a smooth paste.

Pour about 2 tablespoons oil into a medium, well-seasoned frying pan. Add the potatoes, and brown lightly on all sides. Lift carefully out of the oil without breaking them, and set aside.

Pour 5 tablespoons oil into a wide, heavy pan, and set over medium-high heat. When it is hot, add the cloves, cinnamon, black cardamom, cumin seeds, and green cardamom. Stir once, and put in the onions. Stir-fry for 6–8 minutes, or until the onions are golden brown. Add the ginger-garlic paste, and fry for another 2 minutes, turning the heat down slightly. Now put in the tomatoes and the red-chili powder. Stir and cook over medium heat until the tomatoes are reduced to a dark paste and the oil begins to show.

Put in the meat. Stir it around for a minute. Add ¼ cup water, and cover. Cook the meat over medium heat, stirring now and then, until it has browned a bit. Don't let it burn. Add another 1½ cups water and the salt, and bring to a boil. Cover, and let the meat simmer gently on low heat for 60–80 minutes, or until tender (goat takes longer). Add the potatoes, and shake the pan. Cover, and cook over very low heat for 5 minutes.

BIMLA'S CHICKEN CURRY *(Dahi Murgh)*

SERVES 4

This recipe comes from Bimla, who married my cousin Shashi, Saran Bhua's son. The recipe is very like my mother's, only Bimla keeps the sauce thick and clinging to the chicken pieces. It is utterly delicious.

I buy a 3¼-pound organic chicken and get the butcher to skin it and cut it into small serving pieces. Legs should be separated into drumsticks and thighs, and each breast should be cut into two pieces.

Serve with rice or *phulka*s.

3 medium onions, peeled and coarsely chopped

20 medium cloves garlic, peeled and coarsely chopped

One 3-inch piece fresh ginger, peeled and chopped

6 tablespoons olive or other vegetable oil

8 green cardamom pods

Two 2-inch sticks cinnamon

8 whole cloves

14 whole peppercorns

1 teaspoon Kashmiri red-chili powder (or ½ teaspoon cayenne plus ½ teaspoon of a nice sweet red paprika)

1 medium chicken, preferably organic, skinned, cut, and chopped into small serving pieces, net weight about 2 pounds 10 ounces

1½ cups plain whole-milk yogurt

1½ teaspoons salt, or to taste

Put the onions into a blender. Add the garlic and ginger, and blend until you have a smooth paste.

Pour the oil into a large, heavy sauté or frying pan set over medium-high heat. When it is hot, put in the cardamom, cinnamon, cloves, and peppercorns. Ten seconds later, add the onion paste and the red-chili powder. Now stir-fry for about 10 minutes, turning the heat down to medium if necessary, until the paste has turned a rich golden brown. Whenever it seems to stick, sprinkle in a little water and stir it in.

Now add the chicken pieces, a few at a time, and stir them in. Again, sprinkle in some water if the sauce sticks to the bottom. When all the chicken has been added, begin to put in the yogurt, a tablespoon at a time, and stir it in just as you did the water. When the sauce sticks, add yogurt and stir it in. Do this for about 10–12 minutes. When only ½ cup of yogurt is left, put it all in and stir it around. Add the salt as well, and stir to mix. Now cover, turn the heat to low, and cook for 10 minutes, stirring now and then.

Uncover and stir, making sure the sauce is clinging to the chicken.

Chicken Cooked in a Yogurt-Almond Sauce *(Murgh Korma)*

SERVES 4–6

This is one of my favorite dishes when I am entertaining. It is relatively simple to prepare, looks rich but isn't (as I use nonfat yogurt), and tastes heavenly. It is also authentically Moghul/Delhi in style.

The chicken needs to be cut for a curry: First, it should be skinned. Each breast piece should be halved, and legs must be divided into drumsticks and thighs.

One 2½-inch piece fresh ginger, peeled and chopped

4–5 good-sized cloves garlic, peeled and chopped

3 tablespoons blanched, slivered almonds

1½ cups plain yogurt

1½ teaspoons garam masala (see page 295)

1 tablespoon ground coriander

½–1 teaspoon cayenne pepper, to taste

1½ teaspoons salt

5 tablespoons peanut or olive oil

2 medium onions, peeled, cut in half lengthwise, then sliced into fine half-rings

Two 2-inch sticks cinnamon

8 whole cardamom pods

2 bay leaves

3¼ pounds chicken, cut into 8 pieces (see headnote)

2 tablespoons golden raisins (sultanas)

3 tablespoons finely chopped fresh cilantro

Put the ginger, garlic, and ¼ cup water into a blender. Blend until you have a smooth paste. Add the almonds and another 2 tablespoons water. Blend again until you have a smooth paste.

Put the yogurt in a bowl. Whisk it lightly with a fork or whisk until smooth. Add the garam masala, ground coriander, cayenne, and salt. Stir well to mix.

Put the oil into a large, preferably nonstick sauté pan and set it over medium heat. When it is hot, put in the sliced onions. Stir and fry for 10–12 minutes, turning the heat down, if necessary, until the onion slices are reddish brown. Remove the onion slices with a slotted spoon, squeezing out as much of the oil as you can with the back of a second spoon, and leaving that oil behind in the pan. Spread the onion slices over a paper towel–lined plate.

Put the cinnamon, cardamom, and bay leaves into the same pan over medium heat. Stir, once or twice. A minute later, put in the chicken pieces, only as many as the pan can hold easily in a single layer. Brown the chicken pieces lightly on both sides, removing them to a bowl when done. Do all the chicken pieces this way. Add the golden raisins. Stir a few times and then add the paste from the blender. Stir and fry for 2 minutes. Now put in the contents of the bowl with the chicken, including all accumulated juices, the contents of the yogurt bowl, and the fried onions. Stir to mix and bring to a simmer, still on medium heat. Cover, turn the heat to low, and cook gently for 25–30 minutes, stirring gently now and then, until the chicken pieces are tender. Sprinkle with the chopped cilantro and serve.

CLASSIC DUCK CURRY WITH CORIANDER AND CARDAMOM *(Battuck Lajavaab)*

SERVES 4

Here is one of my favorite dishes for small dinner parties. It cooks with relative ease, may be made ahead of time, and is exquisitely delicious. Even though it was made in our family with the mallards that were routinely hunted by the menfolk in the winter months, I make the dish with fresh-killed Peking (Pekin) ducks sold by most butchers and available in most Chinese markets.

Ask the butcher to cut up the duck for you as he might a chicken. Each leg should be divided into drumstick and thigh, and the two breasts should each be halved, creating four breast sections. These are the eight pieces that I serve guests. But I cook the entire duck. The rest of the pieces may be served, family style, more informally. Besides, they add flavor to the sauce. These include the neck, which should be cut into 2-inch lengths, the back, the sternum, the gizzard (not the liver), and the wings. Cut off and discard the wing tip, though. When you bring the cut-up duck home, examine each piece, one by one. Cut off all fat and skin that hangs from the sides or ends, leaving only the skin that sits firmly on top of the meat. You need this to hold the meat together. You should, however, remove all the skin from the neck and any blobs of visible fat.

All Indian spice shops sell cardamom seeds already removed from their shells.

One 4-inch piece fresh ginger, peeled and chopped

6 good-sized cloves garlic, peeled and chopped

4 tablespoons whole coriander seeds

2 teaspoons whole cumin seeds

1 teaspoon cardamom seeds

½ teaspoon whole cloves

One 2-inch stick cinnamon, broken up

1 teaspoon Kashmiri red-chili
powder (or ¾ teaspoon
cayenne pepper)
½ teaspoon ground turmeric
2 tablespoons red wine vinegar
4 tablespoons olive or peanut oil

One 6-pound duck, cut and skinned
partially, as suggested above
2 medium onions, peeled and very
finely chopped
8 tablespoons plain yogurt
1¼ teaspoons salt, or to taste

Put the ginger, garlic, and ¼ cup water into a blender. Blend thoroughly until you have a smooth paste.

Combine the coriander seeds, cumin seeds, cardamom seeds, cloves, and cinnamon in a clean coffee grinder or other spice grinder. Grind as finely as possible. Empty the spice mixture into a small bowl. Add the red-chili powder, turmeric, vinegar, and about 3 tablespoons water to make a thick, dryish paste.

Pour the oil into the largest sauté pan you own, or into a large, deep frying pan, and set over medium heat. When it is hot, put in as many duck pieces as will fit easily, skin side down.

Brown the duck on one side. Turn the pieces over and brown the second side. Remove them to a bowl. Continue to brown all the duck pieces this way.

Put the onion into the same hot oil. Stir and fry until the onion pieces turn reddish. Add the ginger-garlic paste and turn the heat to medium-low. Stir and cook about 2 minutes, then add the spice paste, stirring and cooking over medium-low heat for another minute. Add 1 tablespoon of the yogurt. Stir and cook until it seems to disappear. Add the remaining yogurt in the same way, a tablespoon at a time. Now put in all the browned duck and any juices that may have accumulated in the bowl, the salt, and 2¾ cups water. Stir and bring to a boil. Cover, turn the heat to low, and simmer gently for 1 hour and 15 minutes, or until the duck is tender. Stir gently every 10 minutes or so during the cooking period, turning the duck pieces over now and then.

Lift out the duck pieces and place them in a bowl (or serving bowl, if eating soon). Tilt the cooking pan and spoon off as much of the fat as possible from the sauce. Pour the defatted sauce into a blender and blend it finely. Pour this sauce through a course sieve right over the duck pieces, pressing down on the sieve to extract all the possible juices. The duck may be reheated and served the same day, or it may be refrigerated and served a day or two later.

GRANDMOTHER'S CAULIFLOWER WITH CHEESE (*Cheese Vali Gobi*)

SERVES 4–6

I don't have my grandmother's exact recipe. I never asked her, being too young at the time to know better. But the recipe here is a good approximation (as Jimmy Durante, the American comedian, used to say, "Da nose knows") and utterly delicious.

Do not use jalapeño or serrano chilies for Indian dishes. They have the wrong texture and flavor. Green bird's-eye chilies or any long, slim, thin-skinned variety, such as cayenne, are ideal. If you can't find them, use ½–¾ teaspoon cayenne pepper instead of ¼ teaspoon.

2 tablespoons olive or other vegetable oil

1 teaspoon whole cumin seeds

1½ pounds (8 cups) medium-sized cauliflower florets, cut so each floret has a stem

1¾ cups grated fresh tomatoes (see headnote on page 255)

One 1-inch piece fresh ginger, peeled and grated to a pulp on the finest part of a grater or Microplane

2 fresh hot green chilies, cut into slim rounds

¼ teaspoon cayenne pepper

¼ teaspoon ground turmeric

1 tablespoon ground coriander

¾ teaspoon salt, or to taste
¼ cup chopped fresh cilantro
3 tablespoons heavy cream

¼ cup coarsely grated sharp Cheddar cheese

Preheat the oven to 450°F.

Pour the oil into a large, preferably nonstick sauté pan over medium-high heat. When it is hot, put in the cumin seeds. Let them sizzle for 10 seconds. Add the cauliflower florets, and stir them around for 2 minutes. Add the grated tomatoes, ginger, chilies, cayenne, turmeric, ground coriander, and salt. Stir to mix. Stir and cook for 5–6 minutes, or until the tomatoes are almost absorbed and the cauliflower is almost done. Add the cilantro and mix it in.

Put the contents of the pan into an ovenproof dish about 8 inches square, add the cream, mix, and sprinkle the cheese over the top. Put in the top third of the oven and bake for 10–12 minutes, or until the cheese has melted and developed a few light brown spots. Serve hot.

Everyday Cauliflower *(Roz ki Gobi)*

SERVES 4

This is one of the ways our cauliflower was often cooked at home. I use a 2-pound head of cauliflower that yields about 7 cups of florets. When cutting the florets, make sure that each piece has a head about 1½ inches wide, has a stem, and is about the same in length, or longer, as the width at the top.

6 tablespoons olive or peanut oil
7 cups delicate cauliflower florets
½–¾ teaspoon salt

¼ teaspoon ground turmeric
¼ teaspoon cayenne pepper
1 teaspoon ground coriander

½ teaspoon ground *amchoor* (green mango powder) or 1 tablespoon lemon juice

Generous pinch of ground asafetida

½ teaspoon whole cumin seeds

One 1-inch piece fresh ginger, peeled and cut into very fine julienne

strips (cut into very thin slices first, then stack the slices and cut into fine strips)

2 tablespoons finely chopped fresh cilantro

1 teaspoon finely chopped fresh green chilies (optional)

Pour the oil into a large frying pan and set over medium heat. When it is hot, put in all the cauliflower florets. Stir and fry them until they turn reddish in spots. Remove them with a slotted spoon and spread them out on a platter lined with paper towels.

Turn off the heat under the frying pan and remove all but 1 tablespoon of the oil.

Put the drained florets in a bowl. Sprinkle the salt, turmeric, cayenne, coriander, and *amchoor* over the top. Toss gently to mix. Taste for balance of flavors, making adjustments if needed.

Set the frying pan with its 1 tablespoon of oil over medium heat. When it is hot, put in the asafetida, and a second later the cumin seeds. Let the seeds sizzle for 10 seconds. Now put in all the ginger shreds and stir for 30 seconds. Put in all the cauliflower and stir gently to mix. Add a generous sprinkling of water, cover, and turn the heat down very, very low. Cook for about 1–2 minutes, or until the cauliflower is just done and all the flavors have blended. Sprinkle the cilantro and green chilies, if desired, over the top. Toss and serve.

STUFFED OKRA *(Bhari hui Bhindi)*

SERVES 4–6

We all loved this dish. It was made with young, slim pods, straight out of our garden. Even if you don't grow your own okra, look for small, tender pods. The behemoths that are sold in many groceries, with tough, fibrous skins and overdeveloped seeds, are good for nothing. Just pick the smallest and most delicate pods you can find.

¾ pound whole fresh okra
1 tablespoon ground coriander
1 tablespoon ground cumin
1 tablespoon ground *amchoor* (green mango powder)
¼ teaspoon cayenne pepper
½ teaspoon salt

Freshly ground black pepper, to taste
5 tablespoons olive or other vegetable oil
1 small onion (about 2 ounces), peeled and cut into fine half-rings

Rinse the whole okra quickly, and pat them with paper towels until very dry. (I actually wipe each with a damp cloth, as my mother did. You could also spread the okra out in an airy spot to dry.) Now trim the okra by cutting off the tip and either trimming off the cone-shaped top or peeling it so its shape is preserved.

Mix together in a bowl the coriander, cumin, *amchoor*, cayenne, salt, and black pepper. Make a slit in each okra pod, being sure you stop at least ¼ inch short of the two ends and that you don't go through the whole pod. Stick a thumb into the slit to keep it open, and with the other hand take generous pinches of the seasonings and stuff them in. Stuff all the okra this way.

Use a large frying or sauté pan that can hold all the okra in a single layer (a 10-inch pan is ideal), add the oil, and set it over medium-high heat. Put in the onion, and stir-fry until it just begins to brown. Add all the okra in a single layer, and turn the heat to medium-low. The okra should cook slowly, uncovered. Turn the okra pods gently until all sides are very lightly browned. This should take about 15 minutes. Cover the pan, and cook over very low heat for 5 minutes.

CARROTS WITH FENUGREEK
GREENS *(Gajar Methi)*

SERVES 4

I have always loved this winter specialty. Fenugreek greens, with their small oval leaves and their very earthy aroma, appear in Delhi only in the winter months, so it is then that they are eaten, mixed either with carrots or with potatoes. They can also be used as a stuffing for the fried puffed breads known as *bedvi*s. The greens are never eaten on their own (except by camels in Morocco, I am told!).

Although many Indian grocers in the West carry these greens, they are not universally available. What most Indians do—and this I have learned from the generation of Indians that came west before me—is to use a decent amount of cilantro as a substitute to get the correct texture, then add some crumbled dried fenugreek leaves for their aroma. All Indian grocers carry packages, labeled "dried fenugreek leaves" or "*kasoori methi*." The dried leaves retain their aroma about as well as dried thyme does and are often crumbled and sprinkled over fish that is to be grilled or roasted.

If you can get fresh fenugreek ("fresh *methi*" is what you would ask for), you need to get a rather large bunch, as only the leaves are used, not the stems. These need to be chopped fine, and you should have enough to pack a cup.

2 tablespoons peanut or olive oil

Generous pinch of ground asafetida

¼ teaspoon whole cumin seeds

1 pound carrots, peeled and cut into ⅓-inch dice

Enough very finely chopped fresh cilantro to pack a cup

1 bird's-eye chili, finely chopped, or ⅛ teaspoon cayenne pepper (use more if you like)

3 tablespoons dried fenugreek leaves, well crumbled with stems removed

½ teaspoon salt

Pour the oil into a medium frying pan and set over medium-high heat. When it is hot, put in the asafetida and cumin. Stir once or twice and put in the carrots. Stir once and turn off the heat. Add all the remaining ingredients and 3 tablespoons water. Stir well and bring to a simmer over medium heat. Cover, turn the heat to very low, and simmer very gently for 3–4 minutes, or until the carrots are done, stirring once or twice during this period.

PUMPKIN *(Kaddu)*

SERVES 4–6

This dish appears at most of our family banquets, especially vegetarian ones. It goes particularly well with *bedvi*s and *poori*s.

I find that a 3-pound piece of pumpkin with skin yields the 2 pounds without skin needed for this dish.

¼ cup olive or other vegetable oil
½ teaspoon whole cumin seeds
½ teaspoon whole brown mustard seeds
¼ teaspoon nigella seeds (*kalonji*)
¼ teaspoon whole fennel seeds
⅛ teaspoon whole fenugreek seeds

2–3 dried hot red chilies
About 2 pounds pumpkin, without skin or seeds, cut into 1-inch cubes
¾–1 teaspoon salt
1½ tablespoons light brown sugar

Pour the oil into a large, preferably nonstick pan, and set it over medium-high heat. When it is hot, put in the cumin and mustard seeds. As soon as the mustard seeds begin to pop, a matter of seconds, add the nigella, fennel, fenugreek, and red chilies. Stir once quickly, and put in all the pumpkin. Stir for a minute or two. Cover, turn the heat down to low, and cook for 40–45 minutes, or until just tender, stirring now and then and replacing the cover each time. Uncover, and add the salt and sugar. Stir gently, mashing the pumpkin lightly.

POTATOES WITH TOMATOES *(Bazaar Jaisay Aloo)*

SERVES 4–6

These were our picnic potatoes and the ones we had at special Sunday breakfasts. We ate them with *poori*s or *bedvi*s.

6 medium-sized waxy potatoes, about 1⅓ pounds

3 tablespoons olive or other vegetable oil

Pinch of ground asafetida

1½ teaspoons whole cumin seeds

½ teaspoon whole fennel seeds

¼ teaspoon whole fenugreek seeds

3 whole dried hot red chilies

About 3 medium tomatoes (¾ pound), grated on the largest holes of a grater (see headnote on page 255)

1½ teaspoons very finely grated peeled fresh ginger

1 teaspoon salt, or to taste

Boil the potatoes in their jackets until tender, and allow them to cool. Peel.

Pour the oil into a wide, medium-sized pan, and set it over medium-high heat. When it is hot, put in first the asafetida, then the cumin, and finally the fennel, fenugreek, and chilies together. Two seconds later, add the grated tomatoes and ginger. Stir-fry until the tomatoes turn a deep red and the oil begins to show, turning down the heat as the cooking progresses so nothing burns. Add 1½ cups water.

Now break the potatoes by hand into pieces that are, very roughly, ½-inch cubes. They will be all different shapes, but that is the charm of the dish. Add the potato cubes to the pan together with the salt, then stir and bring to a boil. Cover the pan, turn the heat to low, and cook gently for 12–15 minutes, stirring now and again.

BLACK BEANS COOKED IN A PUNJABI STYLE *(Kali Dal)*

SERVES 6–8

The beans used here are not the Central American black beans but a slightly more viscous, ancient Indian variety known in much of North India as whole *urad dal* with skin (and in the state of Punjab, where this recipe is from, as *sabut ma*). All Indian grocers carry these black-skinned beans. It is important to ask for them by their full name as written in the recipe, as they are available in many forms—whole and skinned, whole and unskinned, skinned and split, unskinned and split, and even as a flour. In a pinch, Mexican black beans (*frijoles negros*) may be used as a substitute; their taste and texture will be slightly different although their general appearance is fairly similar.

I have loved the skinned and split version, known as *urad dal*, since I was very young. When Punjabi refugees opened the restaurant Moti Mahal in Delhi in the late 1940s (see page 191), I fell in love with their three signature dishes never before served in my hometown, tandoori chicken, *naan*, and *kali dal*, and most especially their *kali dal* made with whole, unskinned beans, which I had never eaten before.

It was made, as was everything else in that restaurant, in the clay "tandoor" ovens. When all the daily cooking was done, the ovens were put to sleep for the night with the barest of leftover charcoal embers still ensconced inside. This way the oven stayed warm overnight and did not have to be heated up the next day from scratch. But why waste the embers? It was a tradition to partially bury closed earthen pots full of whole beans and water in the embers so they would cook slowly through the night. The next day, simple seasonings—garlic, ginger, tomatoes, chilies, cream, and butter (the last two being almost staples in the Punjab)—were added to produce the deeply satisfying *kali dal*.

In the villages of the Punjab, *kali dal* is an everyday food, eaten with an enrichment of homemade white butter. Whole-wheat flatbreads and seasonal vegetables are served on the side. You may serve the *dal* with rice as well.

2 cups whole *urad dal* with skin

5 good-sized cloves garlic, peeled and chopped

One 4-inch piece fresh ginger, peeled and chopped

½ teaspoon cayenne pepper (this will make a very mild *dal;* if you prefer it hotter, put in ¾–1 teaspoon)

¼ cup peanut or olive oil

¾ cup puréed tomatoes (also called strained tomatoes or *passata*)

1½ teaspoons salt

6 tablespoons heavy cream

2 tablespoons unsalted butter (optional)

Pick over the beans and wash them in several changes of water.

Drain the beans and soak them in 5 cups water overnight. (Alternatively, put the washed beans and the same amount of water in a pan and bring it to a boil. Boil for 2 minutes. Cover it and turn off the heat. Set aside for 1 hour.)

Drain the beans again. Put the beans in a pan, add 5 cups fresh water, and bring it to a boil. Turn the heat to low (the beans should simmer very gently), cover partially, and cook 1½–2 hours or until the beans are tender. Stir every now and then.

Meanwhile, put the garlic, ginger, cayenne, and ¼ cup water in a blender. Blend until you have a smooth purée. Set a small (6-inch), preferably nonstick frying pan with the oil in it over medium heat. When it is hot, add the paste from the blender. Stir and fry for 3–4 minutes. When the beans are tender, pour this mixture into the pan with the beans. Add the tomato purée, salt, and cream. Stir the beans and bring to a gentle simmer. Cover partially and simmer gently, stirring now and then, for 15 minutes. Stir in the butter, if desired, and serve.

MOONG DAL WITH GREENS *(Alan ka Saag)*

SERVES 4–6

This is an ancient (we think) family recipe made with dried mung beans that have been split, thus qualifying them as a *dal,* but that have not been hulled, so they still have their green skins showing on one side. The addition of greens (spinach and fenugreek leaves) makes this dish exceedingly nutritious, full of protein, fiber, and vitamins. It's generally eaten from a small bowl (*katori*) with *phulka*s and the addition of a little butter and lime juice.

5 tablespoons olive or other vegetable oil

½ teaspoon whole cumin seeds

Generous pinch of ground asafetida

¼ teaspoon whole fenugreek seeds

1 pound trimmed spinach, finely chopped

1 tablespoon well-crumbled (stems removed) dried fenugreek leaves (*kasuri methi*)

1 cup *moong dal* with skin (sold in Indian stores as *chilkevali moong dal*), washed in several changes of water and drained

¼ teaspoon ground turmeric

1½ teaspoons salt, or to taste

1 tablespoon chickpea flour (sometimes sold as gram flour or *besan*), mixed slowly with 5 tablespoons water

2 thin slices peeled fresh ginger, cut into very fine slivers

2 tablespoons very finely slivered peeled shallots or onion

2–4 fresh hot green chilies

Pour 2 tablespoons of the oil into a large heavy-bottomed pot, and set over medium-high heat. When it is hot, put in the cumin seeds. Ten seconds later, add the asafetida and fenugreek seeds. Stir once, and quickly put in the spinach, the crumbled dried fenugreek leaves, the drained *moong dal*, turmeric, and 8 cups water. Stir and bring to a boil.

Watch carefully so that the contents of the pot don't boil over. Cover, leaving the lid very slightly ajar. Turn the heat to low, and cook very gently for 50 minutes, or until the beans are tender. Add the salt, and stir to mix. Stir the chickpea-flour mixture, and add it to the beans. Stir, and cook very gently for another 10 minutes.

Put the remaining 3 tablespoons oil in a small frying pan, and set over medium-high heat. When it is hot, add the ginger, shallot, and whole green chilies. Stir-fry until the shallot turns brown. Now empty the contents of the frying pan into the pot with the beans. Stir to mix.

Chickpea-flour Stew with Dumplings *(Karhi)*

SERVES 6

We always ate this great favorite with plain Basmati rice. At our house, *kofta*s, vegetables, salads, and chutneys were always served on the side.

For this dish it helps if the yogurt is quite sour. If I have old yogurt sitting in the refrigerator, I tend to use that. Otherwise, I leave very fresh yogurt in a warm place overnight and it sours sufficiently.

2 cups plain yogurt
1 cup chickpea flour (sometimes sold as gram flour or *besan*)
2 tablespoons olive or other vegetable oil
½ teaspoon whole cumin seeds
¼ teaspoon whole fennel seeds

¼ teaspoon whole nigella seeds (sold as *kalonji*)
15 fenugreek seeds
2 whole dried hot red chilies
¼ teaspoon ground turmeric
1 teaspoon salt

For the Dumplings

1 cup chickpea flour
¼ teaspoon salt
½ teaspoon baking soda

½ cup plain yogurt
Olive or other vegetable oil for deep-frying

Put the 2 cups yogurt in a large bowl. Beat lightly with a fork or whisk until smooth and creamy. Slowly add 1 quart water, mixing as you go.

Put the first cup of chickpea flour in another large bowl. Very slowly, add the yogurt mixture, a little at a time, mixing as you do so. If lumps form, blend them in as you go along, before adding more liquid. If the final paste is a bit lumpy, just strain it.

Pour 2 tablespoons of oil into a large pan, and set over medium heat. When it is hot, put in the cumin, fennel, nigella, fenugreek seeds, and, last, the whole dried chilies. When the chilies darken—this takes just a few seconds—put in the turmeric and, almost immediately, the chickpea-flour-and-yogurt mixture. Add the salt and bring to a boil. Turn the heat to low, cover partially, and simmer gently for 25 minutes. Turn off the heat.

While the *karhi* is cooking, make the dumplings. Put the chickpea flour for the dumplings into a bowl. Add the salt and the baking soda. Mix. Add the ½ cup yogurt and mix well with a wooden spoon. You should have a thick, droppable paste. If necessary, add another teaspoon of yogurt. Continue to beat the paste with a wooden spoon (or a beater) for about 10 minutes, or until it becomes light and airy.

Pour the oil for deep-frying into a large frying pan to a depth of about ¾ inch. Set the pan over medium heat. When it is hot, pick up a blob of paste about ¾ inch in diameter on the tip of a teaspoon. Release it into the oil with the help of a second teaspoon. Make all the dumplings this way, dropping them into the oil in quick succession. Turn the dumplings around and fry them slowly until they are reddish in color and cooked through—about 6–7 minutes. Remove the dumplings with a slotted spoon, and spread them out on a plate lined with paper towels. Let them cool slightly, and then cover tightly with plastic wrap.

Ten minutes before you sit down to eat, warm up the *karhi* over medium heat, stirring as you go. When it is hot, put in all the dumplings. Cover, and continue to simmer over low heat for 10 minutes.

RICE WITH PEAS *(Tahiri)*

SERVES 6

Tahiri, another dish that came to us from the Muslim traditions of Delhi, is a pilaf made with fresh peas. As peas were available to us only in the cold winter months, this dish, rather like the *risi e bisi* of Venice, is a beloved seasonal delicacy, always made with the finest Basmati rice to complement the sweetest of fresh peas. There are many recipes for this dish, all with the slightest of variations. This particular one is yellow in color as it has some turmeric in it.

I make this *tahiri* with frozen peas since they are available year-round and their quality is good and unvarying.

2 cups Basmati rice
2 tablespoons peanut or olive oil
3 bay leaves
2 whole black cardamom pods (use green cardamom as a substitute)
8 whole peppercorns
½ teaspoon whole cumin seeds

1 medium onion, peeled, cut lengthwise in half and then cut into fine half-rings
1 teaspoon salt, plus a bit more for the peas
½ teaspoon ground turmeric
1 cup (5 ounces) frozen peas

Wash the rice in several changes of water. Drain. Then leave it to soak for 30 minutes in water that covers the rice generously. Drain again, and leave in a strainer set over a bowl.

Put the oil in a heavy, medium pan and set over medium heat. When it is hot, put in the bay leaves, cardamom pods, peppercorns, and cumin seeds. Stir once or twice, and add the onions. Stir and fry until the onion slices turn reddish brown. Now add the drained rice, the teaspoon of salt, and the turmeric. Turn the heat down to medium-low. Stir the rice in very gently, almost folding it in as if it were a soufflé, and fry it for 2 minutes without breaking any of the grains. Now add 2⅔ cups water and bring to a boil. Cover with a tight-fitting lid and turn the heat down to very, very low. Cook very gently for 25 minutes.

Meanwhile, cook the peas according to package instructions and drain. Lift the lid of the rice pan and quickly put the peas in. Cover immediately and let the rice rest for 10 minutes. Use a large slotted spoon to transfer the rice to a serving dish, breaking up all lumps with the back of the spoon and mixing the peas in gently as you go.

PHULKAS

MAKES 12

*Phulka*s were our daily bread. Rather like the chapati for the average North Indian, or the tortilla for the Mexican, the flat-bread served for our everyday Indian meals was the *phulka*. Though it was closely related to the chapati and made of the same finely ground whole-wheat flour, it could be called the chapati's more refined, upper-class cousin. *Phulka*s were smaller, thinner, and more delicate.

As we ate our meals, stacks of at least three or four *phulka*s kept appearing from the kitchen, all hot and puffy. As we neared the conclusion of the meal, someone in charge would declare, "No more *phulka*s!"

Some people like to smear a little butter on their *phulka*s as soon as they are made, but our family generally liked them plain.

Like chapatis, *phulka*s are traditionally made on a *tava,* or slightly concave cast-iron griddle, but any cast-iron pan will do. I have taken to using my old pancake pan, as the size is right and the pan heats up evenly. A *phulka* spends about 40 seconds on the griddle. Then, in India at least, it is put directly on a hot flame for a few seconds to puff up. I find that this function can be mimicked almost perfectly by a microwave oven. A *phulka* demands two things: the dough should be soft so it remains pliable, and it should cook fast or it will turn hard and brittle.

1 cup chapati flour (*ata*), plus more
  for dusting and rolling

Put the cup of flour in a bowl. Now slowly add water, mixing and kneading as you go, until you have a soft, workable dough. You should need less than ½ cup water. Knead the dough for 7–8 minutes, then cover it with plastic wrap or a damp cloth and leave it for 30–60 minutes. The dough may also be refrigerated overnight.

When you are ready to eat, put your cast-iron pan over medium heat and let it sit there for a good 7–8 minutes. Meanwhile, knead your dough again (if it is sticky, flour your hands; if it feels hard, wet your hands) and divide it into twelve balls. Flour your work surface lightly and roll out one ball into a 5¼-inch round, turning it over halfway through the rolling, and dusting with flour when necessary. Remove excess flour by slapping the dough between your hands. Now slap the *phulka* onto the hot griddle for 20 seconds. It should pick up a few brown spots. Turn it over, and let it cook for another 20 seconds. The second side should also pick up brown spots. Now lift it up and put it into the microwave for about 12 seconds on full power. It should puff up. Put the *phulka* between two plates, the second turned over the first, and make the rest of the *phulka*s the same way.

If you don't have a microwave oven, either press down on the *phulka* with a wad of cloth, one section at a time but with speed, to push the air around so it will puff up, or else put it over the medium flame of a burner for a few seconds.

Puffed Spiced Breads with Fenugreek *(Methi Wali Bedvi)*

MAKES 12

In our family, we ate these *bedvi*s with potato curries and pickles for breakfast on Sundays. Usually, one person rolled the breads while another fried them, keeping up a steady rhythm until all the dough had been used up. The breads cook fast, taking less than a minute each, so it is a good idea to have everything ready and then cook them just before you sit down to eat. My daughters used to help me, but now even my grandchildren join in the rolling, almost fighting each other to wield the rolling pin. I still do not allow them to come near the hot oil. They are allowed to watch from a safe distance.

*Bedvi*s are best when they are just fried. If you wish to eat them somewhat later, stack them one on top of the other (they will deflate, but no matter) and keep them well covered. Do not refrigerate them. Serve them at room temperature or wrap them in a bundle of foil and heat in a medium oven for 10 minutes.

2 cups chapati flour (*ata*), or a mixture of 1 cup sifted whole-wheat flour and 1 cup all-purpose, unbleached white flour

½ teaspoon salt

⅓ teaspoon ground coriander

½ teaspoon ground cumin

¼ teaspoon cayenne pepper

2 tablespoons corn, peanut, or olive oil for the dough, plus more for deep-frying and rubbing on the dough

3 tablespoons very finely chopped cilantro

2 tablespoons dried fenugreek leaves (*kasoori methi*), well crumbled, dried stalks removed

Put the flour and salt in a bowl. Dust with the coriander, cumin, and cayenne. Mix well. Dribble in the 2 tablespoons oil and rub into the flour. Add the cilantro and rub it well into the flour, letting it release its moisture during this process. Now add the fenugreek and mix thoroughly. Slowly add enough water, a little at a time, so you can gather all the dough together into a ball. You are aiming for a stiff dough. Knead the dough for 10 minutes until smooth. Form the dough into a ball. Rub the ball with a little oil, then slip it into a ziplock or other plastic bag and leave for 30 minutes.

Pour the oil for deep-frying into a wok or Indian *karhai,* or a frying pan, and set on medium heat. In a wok or *karhai,* the oil should extend over a diameter of at least 6 inches. In a frying pan, you will need at least a 1-inch depth of oil. Allow it time to heat up, about 7–10 minutes. Have a large baking sheet lined with paper towels next to you.

Meanwhile, knead the dough again and divide it into twelve balls. Keep eleven covered. Take the twelfth ball and rub it lightly with oil. Now flatten it into a patty and roll it out into a 5- to 5½-inch round. Lift the round and fearlessly lay it on the surface of the hot oil without allowing it to fold up. It may sink, but should rise to the surface almost immediately. Using the back of a slotted spoon, keep pushing the *bedvi* under the surface of the oil with rapid, light strokes. It will resist and puff up in seconds. Turn it over and count to 2. Now lift the *bedvi* out of the oil and deposit it on top of the paper towels. Make all the *bedvi*s this way.

Yogurt with Tiny Dumplings *(Boondi ka Dahi)*

SERVES 6–8

This yogurt dish was served at all family weddings from a four-bowled serving apparatus with a single handle. The server flew around, doling out the yogurt, tamarind chutney with bananas, and other relishes and pickles. We all loved the yogurt, filled as it was with the tiniest dumplings or *boondi,* which means "droplets."

These days, Indian stores have taken to selling ready-made *boondi,* all fried and ready to go. They come in a bag, just like potato chips. I have tried them, and find that they are generally stale, nothing like what you might make at home.

In India, these dumplings are made by pushing the paste through the holes of a slotted spoon directly into the hot oil. The slotted spoons there have ⅛-inch holes. If you don't have such a spoon, use a colander or anything else with similar-sized holes.

For the Dumplings

4 heaping tablespoons chickpea flour (sometimes sold as gram flour or *besan*)	¼ teaspoon salt
	¼ teaspoon ground cumin
¼ teaspoon baking powder	Any vegetable oil for deep-frying, enough for a depth of 1 inch

For the Yogurt

6 cups plain yogurt	1¼ teaspoons ground roasted cumin seeds (see page 296)
1½ teaspoons salt	
Freshly ground black pepper, to taste	¼ teaspoon cayenne pepper

Place the chickpea flour and baking powder in a bowl. Slowly add water, about ⅓ cup, and mix to a thick, smooth paste, stiff enough to stand in tiny peaks. Use a wooden spoon or your fingers to do this. Add the salt and cumin and mix in. Set aside.

Pour the oil for deep-frying into an 8–10-inch frying pan, and set over medium heat. Have your slotted spoon or colander at hand. Fill a bowl with warm water, and keep this nearby as well. When the oil is hot, put a tablespoon of paste on the slotted spoon or colander, and push it through with the back of a wooden spoon. Little droplets will fall into the oil. Cover the surface of the oil this way. The droplets should cook slowly, turning crisp but staying a golden yellow. They should not turn brown. This will take about 5 minutes. Adjust the heat if necessary. As each batch gets done, remove it with a slotted spoon and drop into the bowl of warm water. Continue until all the paste is used up. Let the dumplings soak in the water for 30 minutes.

Put the yogurt in a bowl and mix well. Then add the salt, pepper, roasted cumin, and cayenne, reserving a little of the cumin and cayenne for final garnishing. Cover, and refrigerate the yogurt until almost ready to serve.

Just before serving, remove a handful of dumplings from the water. Lay your other palm over them and squeeze out excess water. Do not break them. Put them in a serving dish, pour the yogurt over them, and mix gently. Sprinkle a little roasted cumin and cayenne over the top. Serve at room temperature or cold.

As a variation, if you want a slightly sweet-and-sour yogurt, you could add 1 tablespoon sugar and 1 tablespoon golden raisins that have been soaked in boiling water for an hour and then thoroughly drained.

MUNG BEAN FRITTERS IN YOGURT *(Dahi ki Pakori)*

MAKES 36–38 FRITTERS AND SERVES 6–8

These are the split-pea fritters that, along with their siblings, split-pea patties *(dahi baras)*, are always to be found in the baskets of Delhi's snack-food vendors who specialize in yogurt-sauced foods (pages 75–76). Our family has always loved their melt-in-the-mouth, spicy, sweet-and-sour quality.

To make them, you need the fritters themselves and two sauces, one made of yogurt and the other with tamarind. The yogurt sauce is nothing more than beaten-up yogurt with a little salt in it. I find that in this day and age, Delhi's snack shops have started adding sugar to the yogurt, a general trend towards sweetness that I find totally unnecessary and unappealing. The Tamarind Chutney for Snack Foods (see page 290) *is* sweet and sour, as it should be, offering a pleasant contrast. It is used only in small doses and may be made a few days in advance, or just defrosted, if you have frozen it.

In India, the batter for the fritters is made by soaking hulled and split mung beans overnight, grinding them into a batter on a stone, and then whipping up the batter to make it light and airy— all more than I ever wanted to do. I have now worked out a simpler solution. I soak the beans overnight and then just grind them in a food processor (not a blender, which works differently). The food processor grinds the beans to the slightly grainy consistency I want, and, at the same time, fluffs up the batter, saving me from extra work. It is important to start frying the fritters while the batter is still fluffy. For this reason I set the oil to heat before I start grinding the beans.

The hot yellow chili powder is sold by some Indian grocers. If you cannot find it, just leave it out.

For the Fritters

1 cup hulled and split mung beans
   (called *moong dal* in Indian shops)
Peanut or olive oil for deep-frying
   (enough to have 2 inches in the
   center of a wok or Indian
   karhai)
Salt
Generous pinch of ground asafetida

For the Yogurt Sauce

4 cups plain yogurt (you may use
   low-fat yogurt, if you like)
1¾ teaspoons salt, or to taste

For Sprinkling over the Top

¾ teaspoon ground roasted cumin
seeds (see page 296)
¼–½ teaspoon cayenne pepper
¹⁄₁₆ teaspoon yellow chili powder, if
available

2–3 tablespoons finely chopped fresh
cilantro

Put the hulled and split mung beans (*moong dal*) in a bowl. Wash in several changes of water. Drain in a sieve. Put back in the bowl. Add 5 cups fresh water and leave to soak overnight—for 12–13 hours. Drain thoroughly.

Pour the oil for deep-frying into a wok or an Indian *karhai*, or a frying pan. You should have about 2 inches in the center. Set over medium-low heat. It should take about 10 minutes to heat up.

Pour 5 cups hot water into a bowl and add 1 teaspoon salt. Mix it in and keep near the cooking area. Prepare a second bowl of salted hot water exactly the same way.

Put the mung beans into a food processor. Process at medium speed until the beans are reduced to tiny fragments, stopping the machine and turning the batter over with a rubber spatula when needed. Add 4½ tablespoons water and the asafetida. Continue to process for another 5 minutes or so. The batter should be very slightly grainy but lighter in color and fluffy (½ teaspoon batter dropped in water should now float).

Work quickly now. The oil should be hot by this time. Using two regular teaspoons, remove a heaping ¾ teaspoon of batter with one teaspoon and with a second release it into the hot oil. Make about 19 fritters this way. Wait about a minute and then turn them over. Stir and fry them until they are a rich golden color, about 7 minutes. Remove with a slotted spoon and drop them into the bowl of salted hot water. Make a second batch exactly the same way, dropping it into the second bowl of salted hot water.

Each batch should sit in the water bath for 15–20 minutes. Meanwhile, put the yogurt and salt in a large, wide serving bowl and beat lightly with a fork or a whisk until smooth and creamy. Add ¼ cup water and beat again. The yogurt should be of a pouring consistency.

Remove one fritter at a time from the water. Put it into the open palm of one hand and squeeze down very lightly with the open palm of the other. You should squeeze out most of the water without crushing or breaking up the fritter. Put the fritter into the bowl with the yogurt. Remove and squeeze out all the fritters the same way, dropping them gently into the yogurt bowl. (If you do not wish to use all the fritters immediately, squeeze them out anyway and arrange them neatly in several layers in a flat plastic storage container. Cover them with a lid and refrigerate. They may be used within the next few days. Cut down on the yogurt sauce proportionately.) Sprinkle the roasted cumin, cayenne, yellow chili powder, and chopped cilantro over the top. Dribble about 4 tablespoons of the Tamarind Chutney for Snack Foods (page 290) over the top as well—you will now see both the white of the yogurt and the brown of the tamarind chutney. Serve.

Mung Bean Fritters *(Moong Dal ki Pakori)*

MAKES ABOUT 38 FRITTERS

While mung bean fritters may be dunked into a yogurt sauce as dumplings (preceding recipe), they may also be spiced, fried, and served just the way they are, as a snack with Green Chutney (see page 292). We often had them this way at teatime or with drinks and just loved them.

The recipe for the fritter batter is almost exactly the same as that for the dumplings, except for the addition of seasonings.

1 cup hulled and split mung beans (called *moong dal* in Indian shops)

Peanut or olive oil for deep-frying (enough to have 2 inches in the center of a wok or Indian *karhai*)

Generous pinch of ground asafetida

1 teaspoon salt

2 tablespoons finely chopped fresh cilantro

1 teaspoon peeled and very finely grated fresh ginger

1–2 teaspoons very finely chopped fresh hot green chilies (of the bird's-eye or cayenne varieties)

¼ teaspoon baking soda

⅛ teaspoon ground turmeric

Put the hulled and split mung beans (*moong dal*) in a bowl. Wash them in several changes of water. Drain in a sieve. Put the beans back in the bowl. Add 5 cups fresh water and leave them to soak overnight—for 12–13 hours. Drain thoroughly.

Pour the oil for deep-frying into a wok or an Indian *karhai*, or a frying pan. You should have about 2 inches in the center. Set over medium-low heat. It should take about 10 minutes to heat up.

Put the mung beans into a food processor. Process at medium speed until the beans are reduced to tiny fragments, stopping the machine and turning the batter over with a rubber spatula when needed. Add 4½ tablespoons water, the asafetida, and the salt. Continue to process for another 5 minutes or so. Add the cilantro, ginger, green chilies, baking soda, and turmeric. Process for another minute. The batter should be very slightly grainy but lighter in color and fluffy (½ teaspoon batter dropped in water should now float).

Work quickly now. The oil should be hot by this time. Using two regular teaspoons, remove a heaping ¾ teaspoon of batter with one teaspoon and with a second release it into the hot oil. Make about 19 fritters this way. Wait about a minute and then turn them over. Stir and fry them until they are a rich golden color, about 7 minutes. Remove with a slotted spoon and spread them out on a plate lined with paper towels. Make a second batch exactly the same way, again spreading the fritters out on paper towels to drain. Eat while still warm, with Green Chutney (see page 292).

GROUND LAMB SAMOSAS *(Keema Samosa)*

MAKES 24 MEDIUM-SIZED SAMOSAS

Samosas, the deep-fried, cone-shaped, savory pastries that came to India, probably from Iraq, as early as the tenth century A.D. are what we, in our family, ate at more formal teas or as snacks. They were served either with Tamarind Chutney (see page 290), or with the fresh cilantro-mint Green Chutney (see page 292).

In the bazaars of Delhi—indeed, in most of India—samosas are served as snacks throughout the day, almost as sandwiches or hamburgers might be. The bazaar samosas are rarely filled with meat, as were the original tenth-century samosas (or *sambusak*s, as they were then called). Over the centuries, the street filling became a cheaper, spicier mixture of potatoes and peas. The dipping sauce, once mustard, changed into the pungent chutneys of India.

When we wanted potato samosas, they were sent for from the bazaar. The meat samosas, however, were always made at home. We never served them as a first course at dinner, as many restaurants in the West do now, but you may certainly follow their example, if you wish.

For the filling, you will need to make Ground Lamb with Peas (see page 249). Make sure it is nice and spicy. Taste it about 5 minutes before its cooking time is up, and then add either more chopped fresh green chilies or cayenne pepper as desired. Also add enough lemon juice to give it some tartness, about 2 tablespoons, and stir it in, making sure that the lamb has no liquid left by the time it has finished cooking. Let the filling cool off before using it. You will not need it all. What is left can be eaten with rice or *phulka*s for a nice meal.

When forming the cone, make sure that you seal all edges by using water as a glue and then pressing down firmly. There is nothing more annoying than samosas that open up during the frying. If you have trouble forming the triangular samosa, just make the more common turnover (pasty) shape. The advantage here is that you will have to "glue" them down on only one side.

Ghee (clarified butter) is sold by all Indian grocers. If you wish to make your own—after all, you need only 4 tablespoons here—just put about 5 tablespoons sweet butter in a small, heavy pan and set over very, very low heat. Let the butter melt and then bubble very gently until all the milky particles stick to the sides and bottom of the pan and just start to brown. The butter should retain its yellow color. Now strain the clarified butter through a sieve lined with a paper towel. Allow it to cool off before using. You may end up with a little more than you need.

1½ cups unbleached white flour
¼ teaspoon salt
4 tablespoons *ghee*
Ground Lamb with Peas (page 249), prepared to the recipe and allowed to come to room temperature

Olive or peanut oil for deep frying, enough to have at least 2½ inches in the center of a wok or Indian *karhai*

Sift the flour and salt into a bowl. Rub the *ghee* into the flour. Slowly add about 5 tablespoons water. Mix, kneading as you go. Gather the flour into a ball and knead for 2–3 minutes to make a stiff dough. The dough will not necessarily be smooth at this stage. Make a ball and slip it into a plastic bag. Set aside for 30–60 minutes. The dough can also be made a day ahead and refrigerated.

Knead the dough again. It should be smooth now. Roll into a long snake and divide into 12 equal pieces. Roll the pieces into balls. Keep covered.

Put one or two large platters near you that can hold 24 uncooked samosas. Also place a bowl of water and a sharp knife nearby.

Remove one ball and, without using any extra flour, roll it out into a 6-inch round that is a little more oval than circular. Cut the oval crosswise with a sharp knife. Lift up one section. Join half of the cut side to its other half to form a cone with a ¼-inch overlapping "seam." Stick the "seam" together with water, pressing down on it so it will stay together. Hold the cone loosely in one hand, and with the other, fill it with 1 heaping tablespoon of the lamb-and-pea mixture, making sure that you have a clear ¼ inch left at the top. Now put some water along the open top edges and stick them together, pressing them well to close firmly. You may either crimp this top edge or press down on it with a fork as for a pie. Stand the samosa on a plate with its pointed end up. Keep the plate in a cool place. Make all 24 samosas this way.

Pour the oil into a wok or Indian *karhai* and set it over medium-low heat. Let it heat slowly. This can take about 10 minutes. When it is hot, drop in as many samosas as will lie in a single layer. Let them fry, turning them over gently when needed, until they are golden in color, about 7 minutes. Remove with a slotted spoon and spread out on a platter or baking sheet lined with paper towels. Make all the samosas this way.

SAVORY BISCUITS STUDDED WITH CUMIN SEEDS *(A Kind of Mutthri)*

MAKES 24

My grandmother always had an enormous tin of *mutthris*, savory cookies, tucked away in the storeroom next to our kitchen. We ate them with the sweet, hot-and-sour ginger-mango chutney that she also stored close by. It was one of our favorite snack foods to have at teatime.

Over the years I have come up with my own variation of the traditional recipe. Instead of using ajowan seeds, which taste rather like thyme, I use cumin seeds, and I make my *mutthris* much thinner. My grandchildren just love them this way.

1 cup unbleached white flour	2 tablespoons *ghee* (clarified butter),
¼ teaspoon salt	plus a little more for rubbing
¼ teaspoon whole cumin seeds	Olive or peanut oil for deep-frying

Sift the flour and salt into a large bowl. Add the cumin seeds and mix them in. Rub in the *ghee*. Slowly add about 5 tablespoons water, gather the flour together, and make a ball. You are aiming for a stiff dough. Knead very briefly, form into a ball again, and rub it with a little *ghee*. Put the ball in a plastic bag and set it aside for 30 minutes.

Knead the dough again until it is smooth, and divide into 3 parts. Keep two covered while you work with the third. Roll it out as thin as possible, about ⅙ inch thick. Using a biscuit cutter, cut out 3-inch rounds. Prod the cookies with a fork and spread out on a tray. Make all the cookies this way.

Pour about 1 inch oil into a frying pan and set over medium-low heat. Give the oil 7–10 minutes to heat up. When it is hot, put in as many cookies as the pan can hold easily and fry them, turning now and then, until they are golden on both sides. Lift them out with a slotted spoon and let them drain on paper towels. Make all the *mutthri*s this way. When they have drained and cooled thoroughly, store them in a cookie tin or a ziplock plastic bag. They will last at least a week.

TAMARIND CHUTNEY FOR SNACK FOODS

The best version of this chutney is made from tamarind that is sold in the form of a brick. The skin and seeds have already been removed. Make sure that the brick you buy is pliable, as you will need to break off a piece of it. Indian tamarind bricks have a better texture for chutneys than Thai ones.

(This chutney may also be made from a new product now available in Indian shops. It is called Natural Tamarind Concentrate. It is a tamarind paste that comes already sweetened and salted—to a degree. As only 4 tablespoons are required for the Mung Bean Fritters in Yogurt recipe [page 281], you might want to go with this easier, less traditional version. Both recipes follow.)

For the Traditional Recipe

SERVES 4–6

A piece of tamarind the size of a
   large tangerine, from a brick
6 tablespoons sugar, or to taste
¾ teaspoon salt
1½ teaspoons ground roasted cumin
   seeds (see page 296)

¼ teaspoon cayenne pepper
1 teaspoon powdered ginger
1 heaping tablespoon chopped fresh
   mint

Put about ⅔ cup boiling water into a small bowl. Break up the tamarind into small pieces and drop them in. The water should just cover the tamarind. Leave to soak overnight. The next morning, mash the tamarind with your fingers, loosening as much paste into the water as possible.

Set a coarse strainer over a bowl and pour in the tamarind and liquid. Push down with your fingers or with the back of a wooden spoon until you have squeezed out as much tamarind paste as possible. Do not forget to collect the paste that hangs at the bottom of the strainer. Put the fibrous tissues that remain in the sieve back into the now empty soaking bowl. Add another 2 tablespoons of hot water, and mix and mash with your fingers. Push this second lot of tamarind through the strainer as well. This is the basic tamarind paste.

To make the tamarind chutney served with snack foods, add all the remaining ingredients and mix well. The chutney may be thinned out with extra water if it seems too thick. It should have the texture of heavy cream. This chutney will last 7–10 days in the refrigerator. It also freezes beautifully.

For the Newer, Less Traditional Recipe

MAKES ABOUT 4 TABLESPOONS

2 tablespoons Natural Tamarind Concentrate
½ teaspoon ground roasted cumin seeds (see page 296)
Generous pinch of cayenne pepper
⅛ teaspoon powdered ginger
1 teaspoon sugar
2 teaspoons finely chopped fresh mint leaves
Pinch of salt, as needed

Put the tamarind concentrate in a small bowl. Add 2 tablespoons of water and mix. Now add all the remaining ingredients and mix well.

GREEN CHUTNEY *(Hari Chutney)*

This is one of those fresh, vitamin-rich chutneys that was ground in our home on a daily basis and appeared at every lunch and dinner, and even at snack time if it was warranted. It always was, and still is, ground on a grinding stone, rather than in the blenders and food processors that most middle-class homes now have. The reason is simple enough: the basic ingredients—mint, cilantro, and green chilies—need to be ground together with a bare sprinkling of water. Most grinding machines just spin uselessly unless fed a decent dosage of liquid, which makes the chutney too thin and watery. As a result, many of us in the West have begun adding a little yogurt or tomato purée, either to get the right texture or to make our machines spin efficiently.

Green Chutney may be served at all Indian meals. It goes particularly well with kebabs, fritters, and all manner of snack foods.

2 teaspoons lemon or lime juice
¾ cup finely chopped tomato
1 well-packed cup fresh mint leaves, coarsely chopped
1 well-packed cup fresh cilantro leaves, coarsely chopped
5–6 fresh, hot green chilies with their seeds (use either bird's-eye or cayenne-type chilies), chopped
½ teaspoon sugar
⅛–¼ teaspoon salt

Combine all the ingredients except the salt in a blender. Blend until you have a smooth paste, pushing down with a rubber spatula whenever necessary. Add the salt, a little at a time, and blend until you have a balance of flavors you like. You can add more of any of the seasonings, if necessary.

WHITE RADISH RELISH *(Churri)*

SERVES 4–6

Served at *bedvi* and *poori* meals in the inner city of Delhi, and at all our family vegetarian feasts, this relish is very simple to make. All you need is white radish, also known as daikon. The more tender it is, the better. I try to get something with a diameter of less than 1½ inches. Other than that, all you need is a minimum amount of spices and lemon or lime juice.

It's best to keep the radish grated in a bowl until just before you eat. Add the seasonings towards the end, as the radish tends to sweat.

One 5-inch segment white radish, weighing about 5 ounces
½ teaspoon salt

Freshly ground black pepper, to taste
¼–½ teaspoon cayenne pepper
1 tablespoon lemon or lime juice

Peel the radish, and grate it on the coarsest part of the grater. Just before eating, add all the other ingredients and mix well.

LIGHT RICE PUDDING *(Phirni)*

SERVES 4

This simple rice pudding made with ground rice grains is much loved by children and adults. In this recipe I have used rice flour, available at Indian grocers, but at home Basmati rice was ground very coarsely—you could see tiny bits of rice—and then used. If you wish to do that, wash the rice first in several changes of water, drain it, and spread it out to dry in the sun. Then grind it in a clean coffee-grinder.

My mother always set the pudding in shallow individual bowls, *shakoras*, made of rough terra-cotta. We could taste the earth in the pudding. Those days are gone now, even for most of us in Delhi!

This recipe may easily be doubled or tripled.

5 teaspoons rice flour (also called rice powder)
3 tablespoons plus 1 quart milk
⅛ teaspoon cardamom seeds

¼ cup sugar, or to taste
1 tablespoon chopped shelled unsalted pistachios

Put the rice flour in a medium bowl. Slowly add the 3 tablespoons milk, and mix to a smooth paste.

Set the remaining quart of milk to boil in a heavy, smallish pan, over medium-low heat. Crush the cardamom seeds in a mortar and add them, as well as the sugar, to the milk. As soon as the milk begins to boil and rise, remove it from the heat. Stir the rice paste in the bowl once again. Slowly pour the hot milk into the bowl with the rice paste, mixing with a whisk as you do so. Now pour the contents of the bowl back into the pan, place over low heat, and bring to a simmer. Stir frequently with a whisk and simmer very gently for about 15 minutes. Pour into four shallow individual bowls, and allow to cool and set slightly. Sprinkle the pistachios over the top, and refrigerate. Serve cold.

Fresh Limeade *(Neebu ka Sharbat)*

MAKES 1 TALL GLASS

Indian limes are juicy and small. Use whatever limes you can find.

5 tablespoons freshly squeezed lime juice
4 tablespoons superfine sugar

¾ cup water, plain or fizzy
Ice cubes

Mix the lime juice and sugar in a small bowl. Let the sugar dissolve completely. Pour into a tall glass. Pour in the water, either plain or fizzy, and add a few ice cubes. Stir.

GARAM MASALA

MAKES ABOUT 3 TABLESPOONS

An aromatic spice mixture made with the more expensive "warming" spices, this is generally, though not always, used towards the end of a cooking period to add a rich but still delicate whiff of elegance. It may be bought, already prepared, in spice stores, but generally has too many filler spices such as cumin and coriander and not enough of the more expensive cardamom and cinnamon. Indian grocers sell cardamom seeds already removed from their pods. Nutmegs are soft and may be broken by tapping with a hammer. Here is a family recipe:

1 tablespoon cardamom seeds
1 teaspoon whole black peppercorns
1 teaspoon whole black cumin seeds
1 teaspoon whole cloves

About ⅓ of a nutmeg
One 2-inch stick of cinnamon,
    broken up into small pieces

Put all the spices into the container of a spice grinder or clean coffee grinder and grind as finely as possible. Store in a tightly lidded jar, away from sunlight. It will keep for several months.

Ground Roasted Cumin Seeds

MAKES ABOUT 3½ TABLESPOONS

3 tablespoons whole cumin seeds

Put the cumin seeds into a small cast-iron frying pan and set over medium-low heat. Stir and roast the seeds until they give out a sharp, roasted aroma and turn a shade darker. Empty the seeds onto a piece of paper towel to cool off, and then grind well in a clean coffee grinder or other spice grinder.

Acknowledgments

I would like to thank the following for all their help in putting this book together:

Anupjija, Krishna, Inder Bhabi and Ajay, Santoshjiji, Suresh, Madhu, Bimla, Lovy, Shashi, Om, Brijdada, Bhaiyyadada, Maya and Siddhartha, Lalit, Kamal, Ruth Jhabwala, Anita Desai, Amitav Ghosh, and Viru and Juji Dayal.

I would also like to offer thanks to *The New Yorker*, *Gourmet* magazine, the *Financial Times*, and *Ms.* magazine, from which some lines, thoughts, and words have been taken.

ALSO BY MADHUR JAFFREY

*"The final word on the subject . . . perhaps the best
Indian cookbook available in English."*
—*Craig Claiborne*, The New York Times

AN INVITATION TO INDIAN COOKING

*Classic Indian Dishes—
Mostly the Subtle, Spicy Cooking of Delhi*

Written especially for Americans, this book demonstrates
how subtle, varied, exciting, and inexpensive Indian cooking
can be, and how you can easily produce authentic dishes at
home. Included are over two hundred recipes for appetiz-
ers, soups, desserts, and leftovers, all carefully worked out
in American measurements and ingredients for American
kitchens.

Cooking/978-0-394-71191-1

VINTAGE BOOKS
Available at your local bookstore, or visit
www.randomhouse.com

STUFFFED
Adventures of a Restaurant Family
by Patricia Volk

This delicious memoir lets us into Volk's big, crazy, loving, cheerful, infuriating, and wonderful family, where you're never just hungry, you're starving to death, and you're never just full, you're stuffed. Volk's family fed New York City for one hundred years, from 1888 when her great-grandfather introduced pastrami to America until 1988, when her father closed his Garment District restaurant. Writing with great freshness and humor, Patricia Volk will leave you hungering to sit down to dinner with her robust family—both for the spectacle and for the food.

Memoir/978-0-375-72499-2

MY LIFE IN FRANCE
by Julia Child and Alex Prud'Homme

Here is the captivating story of Julia Child's years in France, where she fell in love with French food and found "her true calling." From the moment the ship docked in Le Havre in the fall of 1948 to the first perfectly *soigné* meal that she and her husband, Paul, savored, Julia had an awakening. Soon this tall, outspoken gal from Pasadena, who didn't speak a word of French, was steeped in the language, chatting with purveyors in the local markets, and enrolled in the Cordon Bleu. This memoir reveals the spirit and determination, the sheer love of cooking, and the drive to share that with her fellow Americans that made her the extraordinary success she became.

Memoir/978-0-307-27769-5

INDIA IN MIND
Edited and with an introduction by Pankaj Mishra

This superb anthology gives us some of the best writing about the world's second most populous nation. From Mark Twain's puzzled fascination with Indian castes and customs, to Allen Ginsberg's awe at the country's spiritual and natural splendors, or from J. R. Ackerley's delightful recollections of his visits with an eccentric gay Maharajah, to Gore Vidal's unforgettable scene in his novel *Creation*, in which his character finally meets the Buddha and is bewildered—*India in Mind* reveals a place that evokes reactions ranging from fear and perplexity to astonishment and wonder.

Literature/Travel/978-0-375-72745-0

THE LANGUAGE OF BAKLAVA
by Diana Abu-Jaber

This vibrant, humorous memoir weaves together stories of being raised by a food-obsessed Jordanian father with tales of Lake Ontario shish kabob cookouts and goat stew feasts under Bedouin tents in the desert. These sensuously evoked repasts, complete with recipes, illuminate the two cultures of Diana's childhood—American and Jordanian—while helping to paint a loving and complex portrait of her impractical, displaced immigrant father who, like many an immigrant before him, cooked to remember the place he came from and to pass that connection on to his children. *The Language of Baklava* invites us to sit down at the table with Diana's family, sharing unforgettable meals of grace, difference, faith, love.

Memoir/978-1-4000-7776-2

HEAT
An Amateur's Adventures as Kitchen Slave, Line Cook, Pasta-Maker, and Apprentice to a Dante-Quoting Butcher in Tuscany
by Bill Buford

Buford left his job at *The New Yorker* for a most unlikely destination: the kitchen at Babbo, the revolutionary Italian restaurant created by superstar chef Mario Batali. Finally realizing a long-held desire to experience restaurant cooking, Buford soon finds himself drowning in improperly cubed carrots and scalding pasta water on his quest to learn the tricks of the trade. His love of Italian food then propels him further afield: to Italy, to discover the secrets of pasta-making and, finally, how to properly slaughter a pig. Throughout, Buford details the complex aspects of Italian cooking and its history, creating an engrossing narrative stuffed with insight and humor.

Biography/Cooking/978-1-4000-3447-5

ARE YOU REALLY GOING TO EAT THAT?
Reflections of a Culinary Thrill Seeker
by Robb Walsh

From the top of the Blue Mountains of Jamaica for the perfect cup of coffee to the jungles of Thailand for an encounter with the abominable "stinkfruit," Robb Walsh has traveled the globe, immersing himself in the world's most interesting culinary phenomena. Food is a window on culture, and his essays brim with insights into our world. Whether he's discussing halal organic farming with Muslims, traversing the hills of Trinidad in search of hot-sauce makers, or savoring the art of black Southern cooking with an inmate-chef in a Texas prison, Walsh provides a deeper understanding of food.

Cooking/Essays/978-1-4000-7716-8

FRENCH LESSONS
Adventures with Knife, Fork, and Corkscrew
by Peter Mayle

The French celebrate food and drink, and Mayle shows us just how contagious their enthusiasm can be. We visit the Foire aux Escargots. We attend a truly French marathon, where the beverage of choice is Château Lafite-Rothschild. We search out the most pungent cheese in France and eavesdrop on a heated debate on the perfect way to prepare an omelet. We even attend a Catholic mass in the village of Richerenches, at which thanks are given for the aromatic, mysterious, and breathtakingly expensive black truffle. With Mayle as our inimitably charming guide, we come away with a satisfied smile (if a little hungry).

Travel/Food/978-0-375-70561-8

THE MAN WHO ATE EVERYTHING
by Jeffrey Steingarten

When Jeffrey Steingarten was appointed food critic for *Vogue*, he systematically set out to overcome his distaste for such things as kimchi, lard, Greek cuisine, and blue food. He succeeded at all but the last: Steingarten is "fairly sure that God meant the color blue mainly for food that has gone bad." In this impassioned, mouth-watering, and outrageously funny book, Steingarten devotes the same Zen-like discipline and gluttonous curiosity to practically everything that anyone anywhere has ever called "dinner." Stuffed with offbeat erudition and recipes so good they ought to be illegal, this is a gift for anyone who loves food.

Cooking/Essays/978-0-375-70202-0

BACCHUS AND ME
Adventures in the Wine Cellar
by Jay McInerney

Jay McInerney on wine? Yes, Jay McInerney on wine! The best-selling novelist has turned his command of language and flair for metaphor on the world of wine, providing this sublime collection of untraditional musings on wine and wine culture that is as fit for someone looking for "a nice Chardonnay" as it is for the oenophile. Includes recommendations on the world's most romantic wines and the best wines to pair with a meal.

Wine/978-0-375-71362-0

VINTAGE AND ANCHOR BOOKS
Available at your local bookstore, or visit
www.randomhouse.com